T0360555

THE GLOBAL DEVELOPMENT
OF POLICY REGIMES TO
COMBAT CLIMATE CHANGE

THE TRICONTINENTAL SERIES ON GLOBAL ECONOMIC ISSUES
(ISSN: 2251-2845)

Series Editor: John Whalley *(University of Western Ontario, Canada)*

Published:

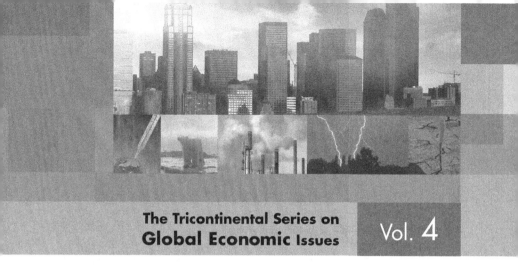

The Tricontinental Series on Global Economic Issues Vol. 4

THE GLOBAL DEVELOPMENT OF POLICY REGIMES TO COMBAT CLIMATE CHANGE

Editors

Nicholas Stern
London School of Economics and Political Science, UK

Alex Bowen
London School of Economics and Political Science, UK

John Whalley
University of Western Ontario, Canada

 **World Scientific**

NEW JERSEY · LONDON · SINGAPORE · BEIJING · SHANGHAI · HONG KONG · TAIPEI · CHENNAI

Published by

World Scientific Publishing Co. Pte. Ltd.

5 Toh Tuck Link, Singapore 596224

USA office: 27 Warren Street, Suite 401-402, Hackensack, NJ 07601

UK office: 57 Shelton Street, Covent Garden, London WC2H 9HE

Library of Congress Cataloging-in-Publication Data
Stern, N. H. (Nicholas Herbert)
  The global development of policy regimes to combat climate change / by Nicholas Stern (London School of Economics, UK), Alex Bowen (London School of Economics, UK), and John Whalley (University of Western Ontario, Canada).
    pages cm. -- (The tricontinental series on global economic issues, ISSN 2251-2845 ; vol. 4)
  Includes bibliographical references and index.
  ISBN 978-9814551847
  1. Climatic changes--Government policy--Case studies. 2. Environmental policy--Case studies.
3. Sustainable development--Case studies. I. Bowen, Alex. II. Whalley, John. III. Title.
  QC903.S832 2014
  363.738'74561--dc23

                                                          2013038486

British Library Cataloguing-in-Publication Data
A catalogue record for this book is available from the British Library.

In-house Editors: Sandhya Venkatesh/Chitralekha Elumalai

Typeset by Stallion Press
Email: enquiries@stallionpress.com

Printed in Singapore

Contents

About the Contributors

Monica Alessi is a Programme Manager and Research Fellow at CEPS since September 2006, in the Climate Change and Energy Policy Unit. She is involved in research on different aspects of EU and international climate change and energy policy, including the EU ETS, the role of cities to address climate change, and the SET-Plan. Other focus of research includes EU water policy. Before CEPS, she worked as a consultant for the International Fund for Agricultural Development (IFAD) on the subject of genetically modified organisms as well as auditing development projects. She graduated with an MPhil in Environmental Policy from the University of Cambridge in the United Kingdom.

Scott Barrett is the Lenfest-Earth Institute Professor of Natural Resource Economics at Columbia University in New York City, where he holds a joint appointment in the School of International and Public Affairs and the Earth Institute. He was previously on the faculties of the Johns Hopkins University School of Advanced International Studies in Washington, DC and the London Business School. He has also been a visiting scholar at Princeton and Yale. His research focuses on institutional remedies to global collective action problems such as disease eradication, high seas overfishing, and, of course, climate change.

Samuela Bassi is a Policy Analyst at the Grantham Research Institute on Climate Change and the Environment at the London School of Economics and Political Science and the Centre for Climate Change Economics and Policy, where she focuses on green growth and climate change policy. Previously, she worked as a Senior Policy Analyst at the Institute for European Environmental Policy, and for an Italian environmental consulting company. She graduated in Economics from University of Trieste, Italy, and holds an MSc in Economics from Birkbeck College, London.

Alex Bowen joined the Grantham Research Institute on Climate Change and the Environment at LSE in 2008 as Principal Research Fellow, after many years at the Bank of England, most recently as Senior Policy Adviser, Monetary Stability. He first became involved in climate change issues when seconded as lead economist to the Stern Review on the Economics of Climate Change. His research interests include the design of public policies for a low-carbon economy and the macroeconomic aspects of climate change policies. He has been a consultant to a wide range of UK government departments and international bodies, including the World Bank and OECD. Dr Bowen has a BA in Economics from Cambridge University and a PhD in Economics from the Massachusetts Institute of Technology, where he studied on a Kennedy Scholarship.

Shurojit Chatterji is an economic theorist at the School of Economics, Singapore Management University. His principal research field is Microeconomic Theory. He has worked on economic dynamics under learning, on strategy proof mechanism design, and more recently on climate change economics.

Christian Egenhofer has more than 25 years of experience on EU policy analysis in the areas of energy, climate, environment, transport, and water. Currently, he is Associate Senior Research Fellow and head of the Energy, Climate and Environment Programme at the Centre for European Policy Studies (CEPS) in Brussels. He is also Visiting Professor at the College of Europe in Bruges (Belgium) and Natolin (Poland), SciencesPo, Paris and Guido Carli LUISS University in Rome.

Sayantan Ghosal is a Professor of Economics at the Adam Smith Business School, University of Glasgow. He was a Professor of Economics at the University of Warwick from October 2004 to March 2013. He was Research Director for the ESRC Centre for Competitive Advantage in the Global Economy (CAGE) from 2010 to 2012 and continues his association with CAGE as a Research Fellow. He obtained his PhD from CORE, Universite Catholique de Louvain. His research is in economic theory and its applications including foundations of general equilibrium; behavioral welfare economics; internal constraints and deprivation traps; financial crisis; endogenous formation of networks and groups; global cooperation and climate change; long-run growth. He has published in a number of peer-reviewed economic journals including the *Journal of Economic Theory, Economic Journal, Journal of Economic History, Journal of International Economics, Games and Economic Behavior, Journal of Public Economics,*

Economic Theory, International Journal of Game Theory, Social Choice and Welfare, and *Journal of Mathematical Economics* and has authored a number of policy reports/briefings and media pieces.

Ruth Kattumuri is Co-Director of the Asia Research Centre and India Observatory at the London School of Economics (LSE). With over 25 years of experience in higher education, research, and policy engagement, she has pioneered several innovative international research and development programs. Her current research and policy publications and engagement pertains to sustainable and inclusive green growth in Asia. Ruth is an Associate with the Grantham Research Institute on Climate Change and the Environment at the LSE and she is also a Cambridge Commonwealth Fellow. Prior to joining the LSE, she was a Professor in Statistics and Computer Science in Chennai, India.

Huishan Lian is working for the International Finance Corporation (IFC) of the World Bank Group. She is An Access to Finance Operations Analyst of the China Energy Efficiency Finance Program (CHUEE). Huishan Lian has been studying and working in the climate change space since 2006 and was a delegate to UNFCCC COP 15 Copenhagen Conference. Apart from the CHUEE Program, she is currently working in the China Emission Trading Program and China Green Building Program in IFC. Prior to IFC, she worked at the Chinese Academy of Social Science (CASS). Huishan holds a Master's degree in International Political Economy from the London School of Economics and Political Science (LSE).

Darshini Ravindranath is currently pursuing her PhD with a focus on the interactions between climate change and land-use change at the Institute for Sustainable Resources at University College London (UCL). She has worked as a Researcher at LSE's Asia Research Centre, on green growth and climate vulnerability and resilience. In the past, she has worked as a consultant with Asian Development Bank (ADB) and UNDP, India. She has also authored several reports for local authorities in the UK while working as a sustainability consultant in London. Darshini holds an MSc in Environment and Development from the LSE and a BA (Hons) in Economics from the University of Manchester.

James Rydge is Dahrendorf Research Fellow at the Grantham Research Institute on Climate Change and the Environment at the London School of Economics and Political Science and the Centre for Climate Change

Economics and Policy. He works closely with Nicholas Stern, collaborating across a wide range of research areas, including on green growth, international agreements, and energy and climate policy in developed and developing countries. James has a PhD in Economics and a Master's in Finance from the University of Sydney. Previously, he worked at the Bank of New York Mellon in London and PricewaterhouseCoopers in Sydney.

Nicholas Stern is IG Patel Professor of Economics and Government at the London School of Economics and Chairman of the Grantham Research Institute on Climate Change and the Environment. He has taught and researched at Oxford, MIT and the Ecole Polytechnique and held chairs at Warwick and the College de France and visiting professorships at the People's University of China and the Indian Statistical Institute. He was Chief Economist of the European Bank for Reconstruction and Development and of the World Bank. Lord Stern was Head of the UK Government Economic Service 2003–2007, and led the Stern Review on the Economics of Climate Change. He was knighted for services to economics in 2004 and made a cross-bench life peer as Baron Stern of Brentford in 2007. He is currently President of the British Academy.

Sean Walsh is an economist and is a Research Associate from the University of Western Ontario who has been studying the course of the climate change negotiations, and how they may impact developing countries in particular, for over 6 years. He has participated in an official UNEP hosted session in Copenhagen.

Mou Wang, Dr in Science, Associate Professor, Research Centre for Urban & Environmental Studies, Chinese Academy of Social Sciences. Received his PhD in 2005, major in Environment and Climate Change Process. Research interests include environment and social dimensions of sustainable development, energy and development, post 2020 climate architecture, and economics of the environment and natural resources, CDM and Programmatic CDM issues.

John Whalley is a Professor of Economics at the University of Western Ontario (Canada) and a Research Associate of the Centre for Competitive Advantage in the Global Economy (CAGE) at the University of Warwick (UK). He has published extensively both on climate change and on other areas of applied economics. He is a Fellow of the Econometric Society and a Fellow of the Royal Society of Canada.

Yamin Zhou, a Postdoctoral Fellow in Institute for Urban and Environmental Studies, Chinese Academy of Social Science (CASS), assistant research fellow in national institute of international strategy, CASS. The main research interests are environmental economics, global governance, sustainable development, and low-carbon development. The published paper is related to how to control non-CO_2 GHG emission in China, green job development in China, and how to address climate change issues. The translated books are about human risk and global governance and energy economics. The author has taken part in several international conferences, such as Doha climate change conference, and annual meeting of international trade and finance association.

About the Editors

Alex Bowen joined the Grantham Research Institute on Climate Change and the Environment at LSE in 2008 as Principal Research Fellow, after many years at the Bank of England, most recently as Senior Policy Adviser, Monetary Stability. He first became involved in climate change issues when seconded as lead economist to the Stern Review on the Economics of Climate Change. His research interests include the design of public policies for a low-carbon economy and the macroeconomic aspects of climate change policies. He has been a consultant to a wide range of UK government departments and international bodies, including the World Bank and OECD. Dr Bowen has a BA in Economics from Cambridge University and a PhD in Economics from the Massachusetts Institute of Technology, where he studied on a Kennedy Scholarship.

Nicholas Stern is IG Patel Professor of Economics and Government at the London School of Economics and Chairman of the Grantham Research Institute on Climate Change and the Environment. He has taught and researched at Oxford, MIT and the Ecole Polytechnique and held chairs at Warwick and the College de France and visiting professorships at the People's University of China and the Indian Statistical Institute. He was Chief Economist of the European Bank for Reconstruction and Development and of the World Bank.

Lord Stern was Head of the UK Government Economic Service 2003–2007, and led the Stern Review on the Economics of Climate Change. He was knighted for services to economics in 2004 and made a cross-bench life peer as Baron Stern of Brentford in 2007. He is currently President of the British Academy.

John Whalley is a Professor of Economics at the University of Western Ontario (Canada) and a Research Associate of the Centre for Competitive Advantage in the Global Economy (CAGE) at the University of Warwick (UK). He has published extensively both on climate change and on other areas of applied economics. He is a Fellow of the Econometric Society and a Fellow of the Royal Society of Canada.

Acknowledgments

The editors would like to acknowledge the support of the Centre for Climate Change Economics and Policy (CCCEP) at the Grantham Research Institute on Climate Change and the Environment, London School of Economics and Political Science, and of the Centre for Competitive Advantage in the Global Economy (CAGE) at the University of Warwick (UK). Both research centres are designated research centres of the UK Economic and Social Research Council, for whose support and funding we are grateful. Financial support was also provided through the China Policy and Research Group (CPRG) at the University of Western Ontario (Canada) for the participation of Chinese researchers in the project. CPRG acknowledges support from the Ontario Research Fund.

Introduction

Alex Bowen and Nicholas Stern
Centre for Climate Change Economics and Policy,
Grantham Research Institute on Climate Change and the Environment,
London School of Economics and Political Science (LSE),
Houghton Street, London WC2A 2AE

and

John Whalley
University of Western Ontario,
The Centre for International Governance Innovation and NBER

1. Background

The importance of the problem of human-induced climate change has become glaringly evident over the past 25 years. Reflecting its global relevance, it has become deeply embedded in the structures of the United Nations (UN) since the late 1980s. The UN involvement started with the Intergovernmental Panel on Climate Change, established in 1988 by two UN bodies, the World Meteorological Organization and the United Nations Environment Programme, to assess "the scientific, technical and socioeconomic information relevant for the understanding of the risk of human-induced climate change," providing a mechanism to filter and distil scientific research findings. These have fed into country negotiations through the UN Framework Convention on Climate Change (UNFCCC) process, inaugurated at the UN Conference on Environment and Development in Rio de Janeiro in 1992. This process works through the "Conferences of the Parties" (or COPs), which provide the focus for substantive negotiations and develop agendas for subsequent meetings. Much has been learnt about the science, ethics and political economy of climate change, and a number of national and international initiatives to reduce greenhouse gas emissions have been launched, stimulated by the UNFCCC discussions, but so far global actions have been modest and not on the scale required to meet global aspirations.

Reminiscent of the negotiating rounds in the General Agreement on Tariffs and Trade (GATT) and later in the World Trade Organization (WTO), COP meetings are intended to discuss matters broadly related to climate change, and from time to time, move forward to substantive treaty-like negotiations.

The first of these occurred in 1997 at the COP 3, when the Kyoto Protocol was negotiated. This divided the world into a group of countries (effectively "developed countries") making commitments to limit emissions in various ways related to a 2012 benchmark, and a larger group of developing countries, which were not subject to any limitations. This was an embodiment of the principle agreed at the birth of the UNFCCC, under which developing countries were to be subject to "common but differentiated responsibilities." Kyoto, however, proved to be weak discipline for a number of reasons. The Senate of the US, the largest emitter at the time, failed to ratify the treaty, so the US did not implement it. Nor did Australia, with one of the highest levels of greenhouse gas emissions per capita on the planet. Mechanisms for assessing compliance were vague, and there was very little by way of effective measures to enforce compliance. More recently, two key countries, Canada and Japan, have withdrawn from the Protocol. It has been left with little force or impact outside Europe, although it may have helped develop monitoring, verification and reporting regimes and stimulated some development of carbon markets. This has inevitably meant that subsequent attempts to conclude a global deal to fight climate change have first had to strengthen the foundations for agreement.

The more recent Bali Road Map process effectively became the second round of global negotiations on climate change policy, initiated by nations' desire to have a global regime in place at the end of the first Kyoto Protocol implementation period in 2012. This began within a COP meeting in Bali in December 2007 (COP 13) that greatly broadened the scope of the UNFCCC discussions to include the four elements of mitigation, adaptation, finance and innovation. The aim was to come to a comprehensive global agreement at COP 15 in Copenhagen in 2009. However, the UNFCCC negotiators were unable to travel quite that far. The Copenhagen Accord, agreed at COP 16 in Cancun, primarily embedded in an international agreement pre-existing unilateral commitments made by parties (although many of those commitments were probably made with an eye on the need to strengthen countries' negotiating positions at the Copenhagen COP). The two substantive innovations, or elements of progress, were the support for the Accord from both the US and the larger developing countries, led by

India and China. The hope was that more substantive commitments were to follow, and many countries have indeed volunteered stronger national action plans to reduce greenhouse gas emissions relative to "business as usual." The Copenhagen–Cancun targets of the USA, China, and the EU look likely to be met. But for progress after 2020, COP 21 is key. This will be in Paris at the end of 2015, preceded by COP 20 in Lima at the end of 2014.

The commitment to the UNFCCC process as a framework for negotiation also remains. COP 17 in Durban in 2011 adopted the "Durban Platform for Enhanced Action," which agreed to "launch a process to develop a protocol, another legal instrument or an agreed outcome with legal force ... applicable to all parties" by 2015, which would enter into force by 2020. COP 17 also recognized the gap between existing pledges and commitments and the 2°C target, the temperature objective agreed by UNFCCC participants. Progress toward a strong deal in 2015 is slow and uncertain, with only very little advance at COP 18 in Doha in 2012 and COP 19 in Warsaw, in late 2013. The UNFCCC executive is planning to table at COP 20 in Lima a draft for agreement in Paris a year later.

This volume contains nine chapters dealing with various aspects of global climate change negotiations, principally under the 1997 UNFCCC, touching on the 1992 Kyoto negotiations and the process of implementation that followed, the later (December 2007) Bali Road Map process culminating in the 2011 Durban COP, and the prospects beyond for whatever may follow.

The chapters develop analysis of the post-Durban outlook in various ways and set out a number of country perspectives, including those of key developing countries, China and India, on the state of play and perspectives on some key negotiation issues. The issue of implementation through enforcement arrangements and the merits of alternative approaches, including multilateralism, are also considered.

It is evident that there is a strong commitment around the world to the established UN institutions and processes within which the search for further agreed actions will occur. The volume does, however, highlight the large gaps that still exist between developed and developing countries, as well as the limited achievements of the Kyoto Protocol, one of the building blocks for future constraints on emissions. The chapters note some of the major problems arising from varying interpretations of the "common but differentiated responsibilities" of developing countries agreed as part of the UNFCCC, as well as of historical responsibility for emissions. When combined with other issues, such as the choice of consumption or production as the basis for mitigation commitments, the appropriate time frame and base date for their measurement and whether level or intensity commitments are to be negotiated, one can see that the challenges that need to be overcome are considerable. Strong political will and civic action are required. It is against this background that the papers in the volume proceed.

2. The Global Perspective

In their broad introductory chapter to the volume, "Global Cooperation and Understanding to Accelerate Climate Action," James Rydge and Samuela Bassi argue that, partly as a result of the global negotiations, public policy on climate change now has a far higher profile than six or seven years ago. However, as was recognized in Durban, even the emissions targets for 2020 leave a major gap between what is planned and what is consistent with a (50–50 chance) 2°C path by 2050. They look more consistent with a distribution of the possible temperature increase centered around 3.5–4°C. The authors suggest that, to be consistent with a 2°C path, global emissions would need to fall by a factor of 2.5 and emissions intensity by a factor of seven or eight: a major global industrial revolution. They suggest that the rate and direction of technical progress are encouraging but must accelerate and that the low-carbon industrial revolution to come will benefit from overlap with waves of technical change in information, communications and technology and biotech. They suggest, there should be a broad approach to encouraging new technology, as it would be a mistake to close off any option. Richer countries need to think through how best to rejuvenate their economies and there is great potential for low-carbon growth that at the same time will help to encourage stronger action in the developing world. They argue that strong action could see an intense period of innovation and discovery across the board, with top-down (collective international action) and bottom-up (national policy) approaches both important to action on the scale required.

3. Country and Regional Perspectives

The volume investigates perspectives on climate change policy prospects from the vantage points of the US, India, China and the EU.

In their chapter, "The US and Action on Climate Change," Samuela Bassi and Alex Bowen note that the US is currently the second biggest emitter of greenhouse gases and one of the highest ranked in terms of per capita emissions. The country will have to cut emissions more sharply than others if a UNFCCC agreement to seek a 2°C ceiling to global warming is to be fulfilled. Fortunately, however, despite non-participation in the execution of Kyoto targets, there are some grounds for limited optimism. At international level, the US is becoming less of an outlier. It had a pivotal role in Copenhagen in helping to shape the Copenhagen Accord. The approach endorsed at Durban and building on Copenhagen, with an increased emphasis on the need for developing countries to participate in emissions control, fits well with the US position. Also, given the weakness of federal policy to reduce emissions, the emissions intensity of the economy has fallen remarkably. New actions are being taken at federal, state and local levels so that, in the words of one academic observer, "the reality surpasses the rhetoric" (Stavins, 2012). They suggest that, domestically, US climate change policies need more coherence and ambition, and are being held back by widespread political opposition. They argue that the introduction of a single carbon price across the American economy would improve the cost effectiveness of climate change mitigation, speed the introduction of clean energy technology, reduce investor risks and create a level playing field across states.

Wang Mou, Lian Huishan and Zhou Yamin, in "Challenges and Reality: China's Dilemma about the Durban Platform Negotiation," note that at the 2011 Durban Conference, the UNFCCC adopted a series of decisions, including a second commitment period for the Kyoto Protocol and a new mandate for the Durban Platform. This outcome could symbolize a significant milestone in the global climate negotiations. But behind this positive progress, divergences of parties on key issues such as the sources and scale of finance mechanisms, technology transfer, emission reduction targets and the legal form of the outcome have not been substantially resolved. In 2012, a complicated negotiation scenario emerged, with three parallel negotiation tracks operating under two UNFCCC mandates. To minimize the deep divide between the North and South on main negotiation issues, key sticking points may be moved to the Durban Platform and negotiated under this new track. The Durban Platform as a new negotiation mandate has taken center stage in the global community. Key negotiation issues such as the principle of "common but differentiated responsibilities," the issue of legal form and the framework, agenda, roadmap and timetable of the Durban Platform remain to be addressed in future negotiations.

They suggest that China may be willing to participate actively and constructively in the Durban platform negotiation, but any expectation that

China will pledge more aggressive emission reduction actions goes against its social and economic development trajectory, which is the dilemma of China's participation in climate negotiations. China as the "factory of the world" is on a fast track of urbanization and industrialization. It shoulders the imperatives to alleviate poverty and narrow domestic regional gaps in living standards. Its coal-based resource endowment and inefficient technologies provide challenges to the curbing of emissions. Decoupling of GHG emissions from social and economic development is a conundrum not just for China but also the world.

Despite these challenges, China agreed to the adoption of the Durban Mandate to initiate negotiations on a post-2020 international climate regime. This regime, they suggest, must be built on the basis of mutual respect and equity in accordance with collective responsibility, and take full account of the right to development of developing countries and their financial and technology constraints in fighting climate change. Unrealistic emission reduction targets and unfair "burden-sharing" mechanisms for developing countries will, they argue, neither facilitate the negotiation nor contribute to international cooperation in addressing climate change. Interestingly, and potentially very significantly, the discussions around the 13th Five-Year Plan, which are gathering pace in 2014, suggest that China may be moving to strengthen its targets. The reasons include increasing recognition of its own vulnerability, of the scale of its own emissions, of the local environmental damage to its cities from air and water pollution and of the potential markets for low-carbon goods services, and technologies.

In their chapter on India, entitled "Sustainable Growth and Climate Change: Evolution of India's Strategies," Ruth Kattumuri and Darshini Ravindranath argue that, with its population of over 1.2 billion and its vulnerability, its history of low per-capita emissions and because of its democratic, cultural, political and scientific strengths, India is a key player in the global climate change debate. They suggest that it has been playing an increasingly constructive role in recent international climate change negotiations. For example, in Cancun, Jairam Ramesh (then India's environment minister and lead negotiator) suggested the idea of "equitable access to sustainable development" as a new interpretation of "common but differentiated responsibilities". India is one of the nations most insistent on equity requiring strong action by and financial support from developed countries as a pre-condition for commitment by developing countries. This language is positive and dynamic, moving away from the language of burden-sharing, which suggests, misleadingly, a zero-sum game. India is progressing in the right direction in its 12th Five-Year Plan objectives for faster, sustainable and more inclusive growth. The country's objectives are achievable but will require faster and stronger action still; efficient implementation strategies; greater co-ordination among states and among sectors; stronger public–private partnerships; and enhanced international collaborations.

Christian Egenhofer in "After Copenhagen and the Economic Crisis: Does the EU Need to Go Back to the Drawing Board?" raises the question, does the European Union need to go back to the drawing board to design its climate change mitigation policy? He sets out the EU's policy approach in the run-up to the Copenhagen Conference of the Parties to the UNFCCC, built on the foundation of the long-term target of keeping the global temperature increase since the pre-industrial era to 2°C or less. The EU had been keen to take on a global leadership role, setting an example by adopting an ambitious set of climate change and energy policies and thus preparing a path towards a global deal. This enthusiasm was bolstered by the desire to tackle problems in the energy sector such as worsening energy security, energy inefficiency, lack of investment in energy systems and volatile but generally rising energy prices. Policy-makers also saw an opportunity to establish a competitive advantage in low-carbon technologies. European policies in the near term were to be driven by the "20-20-20 by 20" targets for emissions reductions, deployment of renewable energy and improvements in energy efficiency by the year 2020. The centerpiece of the policy edifice was the EU Emissions Trading System (EU ETS).

The adoption of a set of EU-wide policy objectives was only made possible by a complex arrangement of burden-sharing based on a mixture of efficiency and equity considerations. Subsequent experience has undermined the edifice. Copenhagen failed to come up with a Kyoto Protocol Mark Two, casting doubt on the EU's attachment to quantitative emissions reduction targets. The global economic downturn, combined with design faults, weakened both EU ETS carbon prices and global carbon market instruments such as the Clean Development Mechanism.

Egenhofer details the evolution of the EU ETS as policy-makers have attempted to correct its design flaws. But he emphasizes the lack of ambition embodied in the EU's 2020 emission reduction targets in the wake of economic crisis, arguing that they are probably inconsistent with the EU's long-term climate goals, the desire to facilitate a strong global deal and the need to generate substantial flows of funds to developing countries through international carbon markets. As a result, Egenhofer concludes post-Durban that the EU needs to consider more radical adjustments, such as raising the 2020 emissions reduction target and, in the EU ETS, introducing stronger market oversight and price stabilization mechanisms. But more fundamentally, the challenge for Europe post-Durban is to reconsider the central role of an emissions trading system in its domestic policies in the absence of a global climate change agreement based on national targets and commitments in a common metric.

4. Issues and Negotiating Approaches

Alex Bowen in "The Scope for 'Green Growth' and a New Technological Revolution" argues that there is much evidence that high-carbon growth will eventually become a contradiction in terms, or, as Stern puts it, "high-carbon growth would kill itself" (Stern, 2010). This paper considers the implications for growth of the findings of the literature on climate-change mitigation costs and then considers the additional elements from the emerging "green growth" literature. The broad conclusion is that well-designed action against climate change could improve well-being for people in the near term as well as over the longer term. A concerted attack on market and policy failures to halt climate change would increase static efficiency and might generate higher growth in the short to medium term as well as the longer term, especially if it stimulated innovation and investment. This perspective, if sufficiently convincing to negotiators, could make reaching an international agreement post-Durban easier, reducing the emphasis on burden-sharing. But the potential size of near-term gains is highly uncertain and it may still make sense to make greater investments now to underpin sustainable development in the future.

Scott Barrett in "Negotiating to Avoid 'Dangerous' Climate Change" is more sceptical about the prospects for progress toward a global deal along Kyoto lines. He notes that, although countries have agreed what they need to do collectively to avoid "dangerous" climate change, they have failed so far to put in place the measures necessary to ensure that their agreed goal will be met. Negotiators need to agree how the goal is to be achieved and how the necessary actions are to be sustained. Compliance is the real problem and will not be solved simply by good negotiating skills. Somehow effective incentives need to be put in place for countries to participate and comply with a global agreement limiting emissions.

Barrett sees the threat as being that the world could pass a threshold beyond which the costs of climate change rise sharply, and irreversibility could, in principle, provide the right sort of incentive. This may be why climate change negotiations have frequently been accompanied by efforts to define such a threshold and persuade people that it is dictated by science. He suggests, however, that unfortunately science is not yet in a position to identify a threshold precisely. While there are undoubtedly threshold effects, scientists have used different metrics to assess them and their estimates using any given metric have differed. The importance of various possible threshold effects depends on the economic and ethical evaluations of their impacts, and these are uncertain too.

Drawing on modeling and results from experiments, Barrett argues that uncertainty about the location of thresholds fatally weakens the threat that Mother Nature will punish free-riding countries. Somehow, he concludes, policy-makers will themselves have to transform the incentives facing nations. He speculates that the strategic application of trade restrictions, or the imposition of technology standards as a condition of market access, could persuade enough countries to reach a tipping point in participation in a global agreement, beyond which it would pay nations to stick to effective emissions-reduction promises.

Chatterji *et al.* discuss the option of relying on unilateral actions rather than negotiated multilateral initiations. In "Unilateral Measures and Emissions Mitigation," they also recognize that the multilateral approach embodied in the Kyoto Protocol has not achieved as much as was hoped. But, unlike Barrett, they look to learning rather than compliance incentives to build up a critical mass of countries willing to make deep reductions in greenhouse gas emissions. Indeed, they assume that enforcement measures designed to make countries go further than the point to which they would unilaterally commit are prohibitively difficult to enact. However, they note the wide range of unilateral measures that have been taken around the world, driven by several factors, such as the search for greater energy security, lower energy costs and other "co-benefits." Some of these measures have been taken at the state level but many at the level of the region, city, firm or even individual.

For groups with a strong collective identity, collective action problems are often easier to solve, as there are effective social sanctions against free-riding, so bottom-up climate change mitigation measures may be easier to initiate, as long as the relevant group has some power of agency in the relevant fields — more likely in more decentralized political systems. However, bottom-up measures can be contagious. They can, for instance, demonstrate low costs of action or actually bring down the costs of action through learning by doing. The authors suggest that the Copenhagen Accord could facilitate log-rolling by pooling information about who is doing what to reduce emissions. They go further and argue that a global treaty would be useful to support a platform for the exchange of information, particularly about the technologies of emission reductions and about measurement, reporting and verification methods. The global intellectual property regime should be amended to facilitate the cross-border transfer of low-carbon innovations. Chatterji *et al.* acknowledge that there remains an issue about how even this modest goal for a global deal could be negotiated and enforced effectively so they, like Barrett, raise the possibility of trade sanctions eventually being used as an enforcement mechanism.

Walsh and Whalley focus on the compliance problems of global climate agreements. In their chapter on "Compliance Mechanisms in Global Climate Regimes: Kyoto and Post-Kyoto," they develop the analysis of compliance mechanisms in global climate change policy regimes. They note the claimed achievements of the Kyoto Protocol, such as the large number of participants, the seeming ambition of the targets for global emissions reductions and the creation of an arbitration and dispute settlement procedure. However, like Barrett, they argue that it set up a global policy regime inadequate to achieve its goals, which in any case were not sufficiently ambitious or long term to match the seriousness of the climate change threat. Walsh and Whalley discuss in detail the methods of enforcement embodied in the Kyoto Protocol. On the one hand, the mechanisms set up to process complaints and arbitrate disputes held up. On the other hand, penalties for non-compliance have been minimal and ineffective, so it is hardly surprising that several countries will miss their Kyoto targets. Canada simply announced that it would withdraw from the Protocol rather than submit to any sanctions for substantially overshooting its emissions reduction objectives. However, the authors see some scope for progress. Negotiators of environmental agreements paid little attention to enforcement issues prior to the Kyoto Protocol (with the notable exception of the Montreal Protocol). Now their importance is more widely appreciated. Lessons may also be taken from the evolution of the world trade policy regime, in which enforcement was tightened up considerably after the Uruguay Round of 1994. There is plenty of scope for using domestic legislation, international contract law, escrow arrangements and international monitoring, as well as the threat of trade sanctions, to strengthen enforcement of climate change agreements, particularly if the latter allow for more piecemeal progress than envisaged by Kyoto

negotiators. One could envisage a two-track process under which each
country chooses either Kyoto-style targets or Copenhagen-Accord-type
unilateral, but public, pledges (assessable according to a common metric).
But the authors emphasize that it would be sensible for objectives,
instruments and enforcement mechanisms to be designed at the same time.

5. The Future

If the results of international climate change negotiation so far have not
been sufficient to put the world on the agreed 2°C emissions trajectory,
it leaves the obvious question of where to go next. Scientists are telling us
that there are risks of rises in global average temperatures to levels not seen
for million of years. Such temperature changes and other related climate
effects, such as reduced agricultural yields, could transform the relationship
between humans and the planet, including where and how they could live.

Key to progress will be resolving fundamental issues that divide the
developed and developing world. The concrete meaning of "common but differentiated responsibilities" is still being debated, although many countries
are now taking action domestically, an encouraging sign of their willingness
to shoulder more responsibility. That sign offers a degree of reassurance
given that, at current growth rates over the next several decades, climate
change negotiation will inevitably come to depend heavily on the attitudes
of China, India and other large emerging-market economies. The role and
implications of historical responsibility are yet to be thrashed out, and many
other issues such as the merits of targets in intensity form rather than levels,
and of targets reflecting emissions associated with consumption rather than
production, also risk complicating negotiations, not least because they
divide large groups of countries from each other. A way forward could be
to develop the concept of Equitable Access to Sustainable Development, as
proposed by India at Cancun.

If international negotiation proves as difficult as these issues (and
past experience) suggest, there nevertheless remain other possibilities for
building up strong action, in turn helping negotiators looking for a global
deal. One is spreading unilateral emissions reductions, as discussed in
papers in the volume. Here there is clear evidence of momentum at national
and sub-national levels in many countries, but the issue remains as to
whether it will be enough. Are such actions window-dressing to satisfy
public opinion, largely small cosmetic commitments, the implementation of
which is delayed, rather than substantive reductions? Another possibility is

for technological progress to bring down emissions intensity rapidly through improvements in energy efficiency, including also moves towards solar, wind and other renewables, and switches away from coal to less emissions-intensive energy sources. The reductions in emissions intensity over the past 30 to 40 years have been remarkable, but for now the reality is that these changes have slowed rather then reversed the growth in emissions.

At the root of the current situation seems to be a high-energy-using, ageing capital stock in developed countries, where major modifications to lifestyle and technological shifts are needed to achieve adequate energy and carbon savings, such changes seem unlikely to be brought about primarily by negotiations between developed and developing countries. Each country, given its endowments and economic opportunities, will have to draw up its own growth strategy for a process of development that overcomes poverty and raises living standards in a sustainable way. Globally, every country is committed to a 2°C target implying very large emissions reductions. Very few have shown both the commitment to emissions reductions on the scale necessary and the recognition of the scale and nature of action necessary to bring them about.

The evolution of the UNFCCC process in 2015 and beyond, and the continuing commitment of UN members to this process, will be a central factor in determining what will happen. And as China and India increase their share of annual global emissions, they will be key to this evolution and to faster progress. Central will be greater political will and leadership across all major countries, backed by civil society. Prime ministers, presidents, and finance ministers must all be involved in the heart of international climate policy-making.

Chapter 1

Global Cooperation and Understanding to Accelerate Climate Action

James Rydge and Samuela Bassi
*Centre for Climate Change Economics and Policy,
Grantham Research Institute on Climate
Change and the Environment, London School of Economics
and Political Science (LSE), Houghton Street
London WC2A 2AE*

International climate change negotiations continue to be slow and problematic, with long-standing differences between rich and developing countries difficult to overcome. Emission reduction pledges put forward at the United Nations Framework Convention on Climate Change (UNFCCC) meeting in Copenhagen in 2009 provided a strong foundation for progress, but a major gap remains between what is planned and emissions reductions consistent with a 2°C path. Despite some advance since COP 15 in Copenhagen, progress remains too slow if the world is to achieve a strong global deal by 2015; all countries need to do more. This chapter reviews recent progress in international climate change negotiations, explores prospects for global emissions to 2030 given current commitments, and discusses how to accelerate action, which will need to be on the scale of a new industrial revolution. There is already much action in the developed and developing world, but stronger policy is needed if we are to act on the scale required. This will involve both bottom-up (national policies) and top-down (collective international action) approaches, which support and encourage each other.

1. Introduction

Public policy on climate change has a far higher profile now than six or seven years ago. However, since the financial and economic crises of the last four to five years, it has moved down the agenda in the rich world, while in several developing countries it has moved up. China's 12th Five-Year Plan, South Korea's, Ethiopia's and Rwanda's low-carbon growth and development plans, and Colombia's Green National Development Plan, are some examples of how the developing world is increasingly integrating environmental responsibility into national policies. In some developed countries, on the other hand, climate change action seems to have lost momentum. The European Union is having great difficulty agreeing measures to strengthen its carbon price, and discussions around a post-2020 climate policy framework are proving very difficult. In other countries, including the US, many are continuing to question the science, calling for weak or delayed action and/or supporting a commitment to a high-carbon growth path fueled by shale gas and oil.

International climate change negotiations continue to be affected by long-standing differences between the rich and developing world, particularly around notions of historic responsibility and equity. These differences have made the negotiation process slow and troublesome and have led to weak outcomes. However, even though the United Nations Framework Convention on Climate Change (UNFCCC) meeting in Copenhagen in 2009 did not produce the strong result many had hoped for, emissions pledges for 2020, embodied in the Copenhagen Accord and confirmed in Cancun in 2010, were an important step forward: they have provided a strong foundation for progress. Nevertheless, these pledges leave a major gap between what is planned and what is consistent with a 2°C path (50-50 chance). There was further progress at the 17th Conference of the Parties (COP 17) in Durban in December 2011 and COP 18 in Doha in late 2012, but the pace of the discussions remains slow.

The world is heading in a difficult and dangerous direction, which is inconsistent with a 2°C path. Continuing on the current path could see temperature rises of around 4–5°C in the early next century. The risk of exceeding thresholds or "tipping points" at these temperatures are high (they are not in the tails of the distribution), with potentially irreversible and unpredictable dynamical interactions, e.g. there is a risk of severely weakening the thermohaline circulation, which could trigger abrupt glacial climate changes (Rahmstorf, 2007).

To be consistent with a 2°C path global emissions must fall from around 50 billion tonnes of CO_2e today to well below 20 billion tonnes in 2050; in other words, by a factor of around 2.5. If world output grows by a factor of 3 over this period, which implies an average world growth rate of around 2.8% per year, then emissions per unit of output would need to fall by a factor of 7 or 8: surely equivalent to a new energy-industrial revolution. All countries and sectors will be involved. As rich countries think through how best to rejuvenate their economies, there is great potential for green growth that, at the same time, will help to promote intensification of action in the developing world. Strong action could see an intense period of discovery,

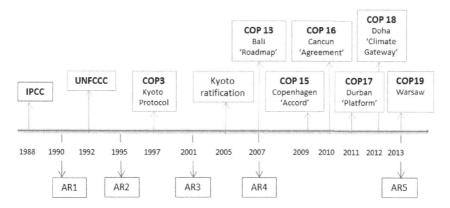

Figure 1. International climate change negotiations: Key dates.

innovation and learning across the board. International discussions and negotiations can help to facilitate and accelerate action and transition to the new low-carbon paths. Both "top-down" and "bottom-up" approaches are important to the making of policy and to action. Together, they foster mutual confidence, which is fundamental to moving forward national action and international agreement.

2. Key Milestones in Climate Change Negotiations

The process of discussion and knowledge building around international action to reduce emissions and adapt to climate change began over two decades ago with the establishment of the Intergovernmental Panel on Climate Change (IPCC). An overview of key milestones and dates is illustrated in Figure 1.

The IPCC was established in 1988 to provide a clear scientific view on the current state of knowledge on climate change and has produced four major assessment reports (ARs), in 1990, 1995, 2001 and 2007, with the fifth expected to be finalized in 2014. The UNFCCC was established at the Rio Earth Summit in 1992 and led, for the first time, to coordinated discussion on changing climate mitigation and adaptation action. The third COP to the UNFCCC was held in Kyoto in 1997 and adopted the "Kyoto Protocol." This agreement set mandatory greenhouse gas emission targets for developed countries during the first commitment period (2008–2012). The Kyoto Protocol was severely weakened by the failure of the US to ratify and its withdrawal in 2001. The agreement finally came into force following

Russian ratification in 2005.[1] Without strong leadership and example from the US, which at the time was the world's key emitter, sentiment on international climate action shifted, and difficulties in international negotiations increased; in particular, this heightened divisions between developed and developing countries.

Despite the US wavering, the pace of global discussion accelerated at COP 13 in Bali, in December 2007, with the adoption of the "Bali Road Map." The Roadmap committed parties to a two-year process to reach global agreement at COP 15 in Copenhagen in 2009 and included the "Bali Action Plan," which set out the process for reaching such an agreement.

COP 15 saw, for the first time, the participation of more than 100 heads of state in the international negotiation process. It was, however, far from the strong and progressive meeting that many had hoped for. Discussion was "cold, chaotic and quarrelsome" (Stern and Rydge, 2012). A number of factors prevented greater progress, including: poor recognition of the total magnitude of the emissions reductions required for a 2°C path; mistrust, misunderstanding and acrimony between countries; and unwieldy and unproductive procedures and organization of the negotiations. Despite these limitations, the meeting produced a document of value, the "Copenhagen Accord," which has proved resilient. The Accord recognized, *inter alia*, the need to limit global temperatures rising to no more than 2°C, the importance of adaptation, the different responsibilities of developed and developing countries, the need for action to reduce emissions from deforestation and degradation (REDD+) and the intention to set up a Green Climate Fund where developed countries would provide US$ 100 billion per annum by 2020 to developing countries for mitigation and adaptation measures. A High-Level Advisory Group was established to study potential sources of revenue and their work was published in 2010 (UN, 2010). In the short term, the Accord referred to the provision of US$ 30 billion of new and additional "Fast-Start Finance" from developed to developing countries for the period 2010–2012. The meeting also led to the submission of emissions plans for 2020 by major emitters, an important step forward. Some countries, like China and the US, presented emission reduction targets for the first time. However, as was generally accepted in Durban, the Copenhagen Accord/Cancun Agreement pledges are not

---

[1]The Kyoto Protocol could only enter into force if ratified by at least 55 nations that, together, accounted for at least 55% of 1990 greenhouse gas emissions.

consistent with a 2°C path, but more likely with a median temperature increase of 3.5–4°C (see Sec. 3).

COP 16 in Cancún in December 2010 confirmed broad acceptance of the principles embodied in the Copenhagen Accord, and led to modest but significant advances across a range of areas. The "Cancún Agreements" confirmed the emissions reduction pledges submitted to the Copenhagen Accord, confirmed the 2°C target, and agreed a review of the adequacy of long-term temperature targets from 2013. The Green Climate Fund was established, and progress was made on a REDD+ framework, new technology mechanisms (including a Technology Executive Committee to identify how to better deploy and diffuse technology in developing countries; and the Climate Technology Centre and Network to build capacity and deploy clean technology and adaptation projects) and a new "Cancún Adaptation Framework" to better plan and implement adaptation projects in developing countries. Developing countries also agreed to produce biennial reports on their greenhouse gas emissions.

At COP 17 in Durban, in December 2011, the parties acknowledged the "emissions gap" between the Copenhagen–Cancun commitments and a 2°C path, although there were no additional emissions reduction commitments. The meeting made progress in other important respects by agreeing to the "Durban Platform for Enhanced Action." Under this agreement, the Kyoto Protocol was extended for a second period — although only the European Union, Norway, Switzerland, Ukraine and Australia will participate. Delegates also agreed to "launch a process to develop a protocol, another legal instrument or an agreed outcome with legal force" by 2015, which would enter into force by 2020 (UNFCCC, 2012). This agreement is "applicable to all parties," which is widely understood to mean that developing as well as developed countries should take on binding commitments in the future (Jacobs, 2012).

The meeting also led to new arrangements for transparency, which aim to increase the accountability of both developed and developing countries on actions to reduce emissions. Furthermore, Durban firmly established a role for market forces and the private sector in the protection of forests, after many years of objections to this from members of the Bolivarian Alliance for the Peoples of Our America (ALBA) countries, including Brazil. The Platform envisaged the possibility of a formal REDD+ market mechanism under the COP, and countries agreed to report their forest reference levels (baseline forest emissions) in order to estimate the benchmarks against which progress will be assessed. More work is now required on how those market mechanisms might work to reduce forest emissions. On financial assistance to developing countries, however, negotiations effectively stalled. Some progress was made toward an agreement on the design of the Green Climate Fund, although not on the source of funding itself. There was disagreement over the share of public and private funding and whether the public funds will be "additional" to existing aid commitments. Moreover, few developed countries have yet said what they will provide in the much shorter term (Jacobs, 2012).

Negotiations at COP 18 in Doha in November–December 2012 had low expectations and achieved only "incremental" progress (WRI, 2012). However, there were important steps forward. First, the rules for a second Kyoto commitment period were agreed; it will run for 8 years from 2013–2020.[2] Second, the separate negotiating tracks for developed (the Kyoto Protocol group) and developing countries (the Long-term Cooperative Action group) were closed, and all countries will now negotiate under the plan for the "Durban Platform" to reach an agreement in 2015. There was also a commitment to submit proposals, by March 2013, on ways to raise emission reduction ambitions, a commitment to review all countries' targets by 2014, a commitment to a heads of state summit in 2014 to drive political momentum, and the launch of a review of the 2°C temperature target. Of significance was a decision to discuss compensation for poor countries for permanent "loss and damage" from climate change impacts. Negotiations on this will continue at the next COP.

There was little or no progress in other important areas, including finance and equity, where resolution is crucial if we are to reach agreement in 2015.[3] In finance, there was no "bridge" or roadmap decided between the "Fast-Start Finance" commitment period 2010–2012 and the US$ 100 billion by 2020. There was also little progress on funding the Green Climate Fund. Negotiations were deferred until COP 19. Developed countries did agree, however, to continue current "fast-start" finance levels, around US$ 10 billion per year, to 2015. The central issue of equity once again raised its head prominently at Doha. Progress on this difficult issue will be central to agreement in 2015. The emissions landscape has changed radically over recent years and the arithmetic is stark — all countries must now be involved in strong action to reduce emissions, even if developed countries reduce their emissions to zero by 2030. Romani *et al.* (2012) discuss ways forward.

---

[2]See http://unfccc.int/kyoto_protocol/doha_amendment/items/7362.php.
[3]There was little progress in MRV and REDD+. See WRI (2012).

COP 19 was held in Warsaw in November 2013. COP 20 will be hosted in Lima in 2014 and COP 21 in Paris the following year. There is much difficult work to be done in the lead-up to COP 21, including on finance and emission reduction plans and commitments. Progress is slow, but acceleration is possible with greater political will from the leaders of the major emitters, including China and the United States.

3. Where Are We Heading?

The world is heading in a difficult and dangerous direction that is completely inconsistent with a 2°C path. Global emissions are now over 50 billion tonnes of carbon-dioxide-equivalent (CO_2e)[4] per year and are likely to keep rising for the next few decades. There are many different ways of looking at where we might be heading, including analysis of the "emissions gap" between Copenhagen Accord pledges and the 2°C target (UNEP, 2010), IEA World Energy Outlook scenarios (IEA, 2012), analysis of China's future emissions (e.g. Chinese Academy of Engineering, 2011; Jiankun, 2012), and forecasts of the world's future reliance on hydrocarbons, which are likely to remain at around 75% to 80% of total energy supply into the 2030s (Romani *et al.*, 2012).[5]

These different perspectives, based on current plans and intentions, arrive at similar conclusions. At best, it appears likely that global emissions will plateau at around 50 billion tonnes of CO_2e for the next two decades, with a strong possibility they may go much higher by the mid-2030s, perhaps to 55–60 billion tonnes per year. If there is no further action to reduce emissions, beyond current policies already in place, we could see emissions of around 65 billion tonnes by the mid-2030s (IEA, WEO, 2012, p. 246). These levels of emissions are completely inconsistent with a 2°C path.

Romani *et al.* (2012) illustrate that emissions in developing countries are likely to rise strongly over the period to 2030 (Figure 2). Developing country emissions could be as high as 37–38 billion tonnes CO_2e in 2030 (around 70% of global CO_2e emissions with perhaps around 55% of world GDP in 2030) and emissions for a 2°C path (50-50 chance) need to be well below 35 billion tonnes CO_2e, probably around 32–33 billion. Strong action on emissions will be required from developing countries, even if rich countries reduce their emissions to zero by 2030 (it is more likely they will reduce emissions to around 11–14 billion tonnes).

---

[4] For an explanation of CO_2e, see: Gohar and Shine (2007).

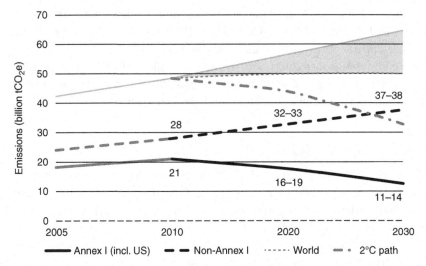

Figure 2. Prospects for global emissions (CO$_2$e) in 2020 and 2030 based on current ambitions, targets and plans.

Source: Romani, Rydge and Stern (2012).

Emissions in the region of 50 to 65 billion tonnes CO$_2$e by the mid-2030s would likely imply concentrations of greenhouse gases in the atmosphere ranging from 650 ppm to 950 ppm at stabilization a century or so from now, consistent with a 50-50 chance of a temperature increases between 3.6°C and 5.3°C (see IEA WEO, 2012, pp. 246–247). The planet has probably not experienced 3°C for over 3 million years, and over 5°C for over 30 million years. This is far outside the range of experience of modern civilizations, with their sedentary agriculture and village settlements, which have been present for the past 8,000 to 9,000 years. Such a scenario would imply the likely lock-in of vast amounts of high-carbon infrastructure, particularly in the rapidly growing developing world, and a much greater need for adaptation on a major scale. Such a scenario may even require us to seriously consider geo-engineering, although recent studies conclude it should be studied much more carefully and should be considered only as part of a wider package of options to address climate change (Royal Society, 2009). At these temperatures, there are also strong possibilities that adaptation will not be possible due to disruptions to climate and local habitats. This would require hundreds of millions of people to move,

---

[5]See, for example, Yergin (2012).

with risks of severe and extended conflicts.[6] Much of the great advances in development, including in health and education, of the last few decades would likely be reversed. The risks are immense.

4. A New Industrial Revolution

Most nations now agree, as expressed in global negotiations (the Cancun Agreement), that limiting the rise in global temperature to 2°C is necessary in the sense that levels above this are (sensibly) regarded as dangerous. A 2°C path is still achievable but the window is fast closing (see IEA WEO, 2012). Figure 3 illustrates global emission paths consistent with this objective. While there are some, albeit limited, options on timing of reductions, global emissions paths that can achieve a 50-50 chance of meeting the 2°C goal would need to peak within 10 years. Starting at the current (2010) level of around 50 billion tonnes of CO_2e, a plausible path should be around 44 billion tonnes of CO_2e in 2020, less than 35 billion tonnes in 2030 and well below 20 billion tonnes in 2050 (see Stern, 2012, *Lionel Robbins Lectures*, Lecture 1).

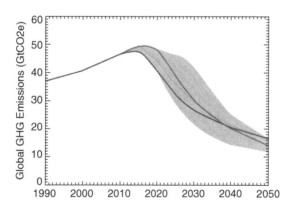

Figure 3.   Paths for global annual emissions that lead to a reasonable chance of a temperature rise of no more than 2°C.

Note: The shaded area represents the range of emissions paths that are consistent with a reasonable (50-50) chance of the 2°C goal and the three lines show specific paths within this range.

Source: Based on Bowen and Ranger (2009).

---

[6]See Box 1–2 and the section on disruptive migration in National Research Council (2013).

This will imply that, in developing countries, emissions will need to be around 25 to 27 billion tonnes in 2030, which is less than their current emissions. In the same year, in developed countries emissions will need to be around 7 to 8 billion tonnes per year, i.e. one-third of their current level.

Given that the world population now is close to 7 billion and is likely to increase up to 9 billion by 2050, this means global emissions per capita should fall from 7 tonnes now to around 4 in 2030 and 2 in 2050. These are essentially a global constraint. If broken, it will be very difficult to catch up later (Stern *et al.*, 2012).

Emissions reductions of this magnitude surely imply change on a scale equivalent to a new energy-industrial revolution. If world output grows by a factor of 3 in the next 40 years, which is equivalent to an average growth rate of 2.8% per year, then emissions per unit of output (GDP) must be cut by a factor of at least 7 or 8 by 2050 (Stern *et al.*, 2012). Change on this scale will require strong action and major investment in all regions of the world and in all economic sectors, leading to a transformation throughout the economy to low-carbon growth. Examples include decarbonization of the power and transport sectors and the recasting of buildings for improved energy efficiency; a new agricultural revolution involving new enhanced yield crop varieties, efficiencies in fertilizer and water use and low-till; a transformation to low-carbon manufacturing with great improvements in materials efficiency; enhanced information and communications technology (ICT) and so on.

The transition to low-carbon growth looks like a far more attractive path than an attempt perpetuate or resuscitate a high-risk, high-carbon growth model. Economic history has much to teach us here. Past periods of economic and social transformation (Figure 4), such as the development of steam engines and railways, or electricity and steel, suggest that major waves of technological innovation are likely to bring two or three decades of dynamic, innovative and creative growth, and large and growing markets for the pioneers (see, for example, Perez, 2002, 2010). The economist Joseph Schumpeter argued that such transitions or economic transformations involve periods of "creative destruction." During these periods, new and innovative firms and progressive ideas displace firms and ideas from the previous period. This process of "creative destruction" generates a dynamic and extended period of innovation, opportunity, employment and economic growth (Stern and Rydge, 2012).

Fostering the new energy-industrial revolution requires good policy for the market failures, such as the greenhouse gas externality, imperfections in

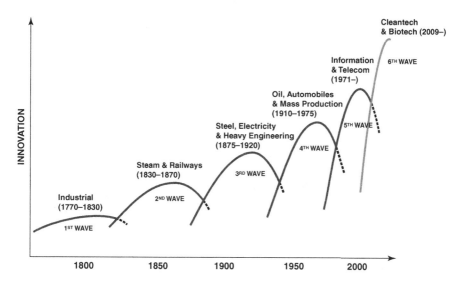

Figure 4. Waves of innovation.

Source: DONG Energy (2009); diagram based on Perez (2002) drawing on report by Merrill Lynch (2008).

risk and capital markets, the public goods nature of research, development and deployment (RD&D) and other market failures related to networks (e.g. electricity grids, public transport) and information (e.g. lack of awareness). See Stern (2012) for details on these market failures and the principles of good public policy. Many countries are at the forefront of the revolution, such as South Korea and China. However, while public policy for the transition is generally in its infancy across the world, technical progress is moving fairly strongly. The new low-carbon, energy-industrial revolution is also overlapping with the ICT and biotech revolution. For example, smart technologies such as smart buildings, smart grids and smart logistics are advancing rapidly and have the potential to cut emissions through the application of advanced ICT.

One area with strong technical progress is renewable energy. There have been great advances in the capital cost of solar photovoltaic (PV): module prices were over US$ 100 per watt (W) in the 1970s, had fallen to around US$ 2/W in 2010, and today are below US$ 1/W (BNEF, 2012a) — see Figure 5. Further falls are expected over the coming years. And discussions with manufacturers indicate that, while opportunities for economies of scale and learning-by-doing are now slowing, there is more scope for technical progress.

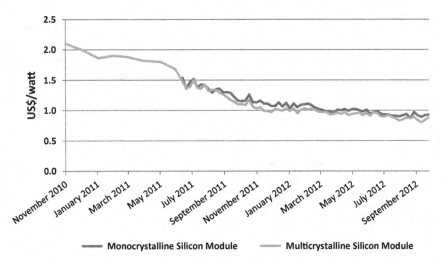

Figure 5. Price for immediate delivery of silicon modules, November 2010–September 2012 (US$/W).
Source: BNEF (2012b).

The cost of solar electricity generation varies depending on a range of factors including location (solar irradiance), shading (cloudiness), financing costs, type of system (residential/commercial/utility), etc. Such is the rapid rate of technical progress that solar PV is forecast to reach grid parity in some countries within the next few years.

In Italy, for example, where levels of solar irradiance and average electricity prices are high, the average costs of electricity generated by large utility scale solar PV are around €0.25/kWh (about US$ 0.35), which is close to grid parity.[7] In Spain, electricity subsidies have a strong market impact, lowering the cost of electricity to around €0.10/kWh (US$ 0.14). Removal of this subsidy would achieve grid parity (EPIA, 2011). In the US, solar PV is at grid parity in California, although only due to the renewable tax credit.

Solar PV is also competitive in developing country markets. In India and Bangladesh, fuel such as Kerosene costs around €0.45/kWh (US$ 0.63). Solar is already at parity in these markets and firms (such as Grameen Shakti) are exploiting this opportunity.

---

[7]In 2011 real prices; conversions calculated using average exchange rate in 2011: €1 = US$ 1.393.

Other renewable technologies are also reaching competitiveness. The capital costs of onshore wind turbines have fallen from €2 million/MW in 1984 (about US\$ 2.9 million/MW) to around €0.88 million/MW (US\$ 1.2 million/MW) in 2011 (BNEF, 2011). There have also been associated falls in operations and maintenance costs. It is estimated that electricity from new onshore wind turbines could be competitive with fossil fuel generation as soon as 2016 (BNEF, 2011). In addition to low-carbon generation technologies at deployment stage, a range of more speculative low-carbon technologies, such as solar paint and nano-batteries, carbon capture and storage (CCS) with storage in cement, or the use of nuclear waste as fuel for new-generation reactors, also hold great promise. Strong support from governments for research and development must be part of their energy policy.

Progress in other sectors, particularly in developing countries, is also encouraging. For example, innovative ideas are emerging to protect forests. Indonesia imposed a two-year moratorium on new logging concessions in selected regions, starting in 2011, with financial support from Norway. In Brazil, deforestation in the Amazon has decreased by nearly 80% over the last 7 years, the result of advanced satellite monitoring and enforcement on the ground.

In agriculture, the concept of Climate Smart Agriculture (CSA) is gaining acceptance and its implementation is accelerating. CSA aims to achieve sustainable increases in productivity and improved resilience, reductions in greenhouse gases and enhanced progress towards national food security and development goals (FAO, 2010). In Niger, for example, crops are protected from drought and erosion through indigenous agro-forestry systems, while China has successfully implemented one of the world's largest erosion control programs, which has returned the devastated Loess Plateau to sustainable agricultural production[8] (World Bank, undated). Tanzania and Ethiopia are leading strong initiatives in the context of a "New Vision for Agriculture," which envisages a 20% increase in crop production, a 20% reduction in emissions and a 20% reduction of poverty, every decade (World Economic Forum, 2012).

Industry also has an important role in stimulating research and innovation on green technology and energy efficiency. DuPont, a multinational science and engineering company, has saved around US\$ 6 billion in energy

---

[8]See http://climatechange.worldbank.org/sites/default/files/documents/CSA_Brochure_web.pdf.

costs over the period 1990 to 2010 through investment in energy efficiency (DuPont, 2011). Waste Management, Inc., a large waste firm in the US, identified a potential of US\$ 9 billion in value from reusable materials it currently sends to landfill (Nidumolu *et al.*, 2009). The Co-operative, a UK retail company, has cut its emissions by 35% and water use by 20% between 2006 and 2011, and is planning further reductions by 2020 (The Co-operative, 2012). The government sector is also involved. For example, the United States Navy is involved in the development and deployment of sustainable biofuels. One of its targets is to sail, by 2016, the "Great Green Fleet," which is a carrier strike group composed of nuclear ships and hybrid electric ships running entirely on biofuel (and aircraft flying on biofuel). The Navy has also conducted a successful trial of sustainable biofuels with Maersk, the private shipping firm (Maersk, 2011).

5. Action in the Developed and Developing World

Stronger and more rapid action across developing and developed countries is possible, but it will require more collaboration and coordination. Developing countries appear to be increasingly aware of the dangers and opportunities from climate change. Not only do they see the dangers of inaction and recognize the importance of responsible behavior, but they also see the attractiveness of the alternative low-carbon path and the potential of new markets. For example, one of the key objectives of China's 12th Five-Year Plan (2011–2015) is to move to a low-carbon and less-polluting economy (Stern, 2011). Specific targets include a commitment to improve energy efficiency of 16% and reduce emissions per unit of GDP of 17% over the period of the plan. China also recently announced an increase in its installed solar capacity target, from 15 to 21 gigawatts by 2015 (The Climate Group, 2012) and it has launched the first of seven regional emissions trading pilot schemes. Other developing countries are also moving. For instance, India has a voluntary target of reducing emission intensity by 20–25% by 2020 and is expected to develop a low-carbon growth strategy as part of its forthcoming 12th Five-Year Plan. Korea adopted a National Strategy and Five-Year Plan for Green Growth, with a budget of US\$ 83.6 billion, around 2% of its GDP. This included the "Green New Deal," which was part of a wider economic stimulus package in response to the global financial crisis that started in 2008. Between 2009 and 2012, a total of US\$ 30.7 billion (around 80% of the package) was allocated across a range of low-carbon initiatives, including renewable energy, energy efficiency, transport and water and waste management. Furthermore, over 50 developing countries have submitted nationally appropriate mitigation actions (NAMAs) to the UNFCCC, which detail a variety of voluntary actions at national level to reduce greenhouse gas emissions.

In the developed world, in contrast, action to manage climate change has moved down the agenda, with some countries witnessing increased calls for delay in action and further questioning of the science. There are many reasons for the decrease in the pace of action on climate change. For example, a hostile US Senate has prevented President Obama's administration from implementing its climate change policy agenda, although there may be more scope for progress in Obama's second term; deep and prolonged economic crises have led to harsh austerity and cuts to low-carbon subsidies; the continued shift in the structure of the world economy, including the rise of China, has caused some to call for a renewed commitment to high-carbon growth. Other factors which have contributed to slowing down the pace of action include: the perceived weakness of COP 15 in Copenhagen, where international negotiations lost momentum; the increasing attacks on the science from within the media and lobbying groups (e.g. following the "Climate-gate"); a widespread failure to understand the scale of risk; ideological attacks on regulation of greenhouse gases that allege "distortion of markets"; and a general failure to understand the Pigou–Meade theory on market failure.

Nevertheless, there has been some significant action across developed countries. Positive examples can be found at the national and state level, including the strengthening of vehicle fuel efficiency standards in the US; the cap-and-trade programmes in California and in the north-eastern states (the Regional Greenhouse Gases Initiative, RGGI); the UK Fourth Carbon Budget; and the impressive growth rates of renewable energy investment in several developed countries, despite the economic slow-down. Cities are also playing a role, for example, through the "Covenant of Mayors" — where around 3,500 signatory EU cities and towns are committed to reducing CO_2 emissions by more than 20% by 2020 compared to 1990 levels. In 2009, the city of New York reduced its emissions by 13% below 2005 levels (surpassing the US average reduction of about 10%) with a target for a 30% reduction by 2030 (The City of New York, 2011). In Germany, Munich is planning to become the first large city in the world to use electricity entirely generated by renewable sources by 2025 (SWM, 2011). Virtuous initiatives are also initiated at firm level — such as the cases of DuPont, the Co-operative, Maersk and Waste Management Inc., discussed above.

These examples are encouraging and demonstrate that action on climate change is widespread and is far from stalling. But much more needs to be done. To be anywhere close to a 2°C path, average emissions per capita will have to decrease from 7 tonnes of CO_2e in 2010 to 6 tonnes in 2020, 4 in 2030 and 2 in 2050. For comparison, in the US, Canada and Australia, current emission levels are between 16 and 19 tonnes of CO_2e per capita per year, Europe and Japan 7–10, China around 7, India almost 2 and much of the Sub-Saharan Africa below 1 (PBL/JRC, 2012). This is a story of strong inequality in current emissions, and even stronger inequality in the history of emissions, with the rich countries responsible for more than 60% of current concentrations of greenhouse gases in the atmosphere.

Developing countries are key to a response on the scale required. By 2050, eight billion out of a world population of nine billion will live in what is currently termed the developing world. Countries with strong emissions growth such as China and India are central to action and will need to limit and reverse emissions growth within the next 10 to 20 years. On current projections, China could account for around 45–50% of global emissions by 2030, with just 20% of the global population (Stern, 2011). Developing countries will require global cooperation to achieve action on this scale; they are unlikely to be able or willing to achieve these ambitious reductions without substantial corresponding action in developed countries and without assistance to shift to a low-carbon growth path, including the transfer of technology and financial support (Stern, 2009b).

6. Bottom-Up and Top-Down Approaches

Arguments that the UNFCCC "top-down" approach is impossible and that individual countries' initiatives, i.e. a "bottom-up" approach, will be enough, have gained traction since COP 15 in Copenhagen. To argue for "bottom-up" without "top-down" is to misunderstand the economics, science and politics. Policy at the national or country level or "bottom-up" policy, and collective action at the international level or "top-down," such as an international agreement of some form, will be necessary. "Bottom-up" and "top-down" are complementary; they support and reinforce each other and can bring countries closer together and spur greater action.

"Bottom-up" is important. If a country sees others moving now to adopt low-carbon policies, and there is a possibility of international agreement in the future, it may see its own actions as part of a bigger picture, with potential new growth markets for the ideas and technologies of those who move early. It will also set a strong example for others to follow and build trust, e.g. those who lead with "bottom-up" action will likely demonstrate to other countries the attractiveness of the low-carbon path. If countries wait and see what others will do it will lead to a very slow pace of action and it will perpetuate the culture of mistrust between developing and developed nations that has continued for many years.

However, despite problems of mistrust of where others are going, many countries argue that it is important to do the responsible thing irrespective of what others are doing. This has been argued powerfully, for example, by Mauritius, which is surely very small in the global emissions picture. The former Prime Minister of Ethiopia, Zeles Zenawi, during the UNFCCC Durban negotiations in 2011, claimed that "it is not equity or justice to foul the planet because others have done so in the past"(Stern, 2012).

From the "top-down" perspective, what happens internationally depends strongly on "bottom-up" action. The greater the example from "bottom-up" action, the more willing countries will be to agree international action on the scale required. For example, China's confidence, having completed work on its 12th Five-Year Plan, in its ability to achieve and probably exceed the emission intensity targets therein, arguably increased its willingness to engage in the COP 17 negotiations in Cancún in 2011. The greater the local, state and national commitment to action, the easier it will be to progress international agreement, which can, in turn, further stimulate a strengthening of the national willingness and determination to act (Stern and Rydge, 2012).

"Top-down" and "bottom-up" approaches therefore are complementary and support each other. There is no artificial horse race between the two. A policy of no commitment until a comprehensive international agreement is reached will likely see no action at all. It therefore makes sense to drop the arguments about "national versus international," and rather focus on how to get national and international initiatives to support each other in a way that allows effective action on the scale and timing required (Stern and Rydge, 2012).

It has also been argued (Stern and Rydge, 2012) that an overly rigid and formal emphasis on "legally binding" agreements may be counterproductive. The key for greater progress is confidence on where others are going and the setting of strong example that will demonstrate the attractiveness of the new low-carbon growth path. Nations such as China and Korea, states such as California and cities such as New York, are setting strong examples that others are watching very closely. The new growth markets that these countries, states and cities are creating are already delivering substantial economic benefits. The power of the example, economics and competition are likely to be stronger drivers of change than legally binding agreements that are difficult to enforce.

7. Conclusion

The central message from the science is strong and clear: continuing on a business-as-usual path involves significant risks of temperature rises not seen on the planet for tens of millions of years, way outside the experience of modern *Homo sapiens*. These temperatures risk significant changes in local and global climate, with the potential for widespread dislocation and severe conflict. The international community has been slow to acknowledge and act on the scale necessary to reduce these risks; since the start of climate change negotiations in 1992 global emissions have more than doubled. The scientific evidence grows ever stronger, and calls from scientists for urgent action to reduce emissions are growing increasingly loud.

Recent international negotiations, such as the UNFCCC meeting in Copenhagen in 2009, have made some progress, but much less than was hoped and much less than the science tells us is required. As was recognized in Durban, the Copenhagen/Cancun COPs pledged commitments leave a major gap between where we are heading as a world and what is consistent with a 2°C path.

While there are many encouraging examples from around the world at local, city, state and national level, more needs to be done, in both developed and developing countries, if global emissions are to fall from around 50 billion tonnes of CO_2e today to well below 20 billion tonnes in 2050. If the world economy grows by a factor of around 3 by 2050, a 2°C path implies that emissions per unit of output would need to fall by a factor of 7 or 8. Change on this scale is surely equivalent to a new energy-industrial revolution.

The scenario of countries willingness to sign up to stronger emissions reduction commitments seems weak given the current economic climate, but this may change over the coming years in the lead up to 2015, when the world has committed to reach global agreement once again. Only modest progress was made at the COP in Doha in 2012 and in Warsaw in 2013 and there is much more work to be done in the next few years if the world is to avoid another weak outcome in 2015. Countries are working to meet their 2020 goals (the reduction in emissions from the recession has helped), and there is evidence of policy action across countries, including in developed countries. However, politicians continue to be divided and the public has lost the sense of urgency which was present in 2009 at Copenhagen. There is an urgent need to regain the interest and concern of the public and create political will for action on the scale required.

Acceleration of the new energy-industrial revolution will help to build political will and push forward international agreement. The pace of action is already encouraging, but much more can be done. To accelerate the transition to low-carbon growth governments can, for example, implement a range of bottom-up actions, including clear and credible policy, to tackle existing market failures, which would include targeted support for low-carbon innovation and deployment. The central policy response is a price on carbon. While it is unlikely that a global price on carbon will be achieved in the foreseeable future due to institutional and political constraints, many countries, through national and regional initiatives, are implementing carbon pricing and/or incorporating estimates of the social cost of carbon in their decision-making. Furthermore, while still in their infancy, many low-carbon technology markets have great growth potential. Indeed many are currently growing at rates far higher than traditional industry, and countries such as China, the US and others are in a race to become market leaders. As competition increases, technologies develop, costs fall and jobs and profits grow in these new low-carbon industries, and as the science becomes stronger and more worrying, we may see public and political will for greater action build and objections and division recede.

If vested interests continue to obfuscate and political vacillation lingers over the coming decade, with the outcome that bottom-up policy action is weak and the new energy-industrial revolution is slow, then a global agreement that commits to action on the scale required is unlikely to be found. This would likely see concentrations of greenhouse gases grow strongly over the coming decades and lead to a greater need for adaptation. However, suggestions that we should simply adapt are unwise. The scale of the risks are so immense that adaptation may prove extremely difficult and costly or not possible at all.

International negotiations and country action is heading in the right direction, but more needs to be done at all levels. Countries, states, sectors, cities, firms and individuals will all act differently according to their circumstances and abilities, but now is the time for strong leadership to accelerate action where it is possible to do so. Strong example will demonstrate that action on emissions is consistent with both short-run objectives and long-run low-carbon structural change, laying out the low-carbon paths for others to follow. Such a commitment and action across society would collectively work to achieve, and exceed, our global emissions objectives and help to achieve a more ambitious global agreement.

References

Bloomberg New Energy Finance (BNEF) (2011). Onshore Wind Energy to Reach Parity with Fossil-Fuel Electricity by 2016. [Press release], 10 November. Available at: https://bnef.com/PressReleases/view/172. Accessed 27 January 2014.

Bloomberg New Energy Finance (BNEF) (2012a). Re-considering the Economics of Photovoltaic Power. [pdf] Bloomberg White Paper. London: BNEF. Available at: https://www.bnef.com/InsightDownload/7178/pdf. Accessed 27 January 2014.

Bloomberg New Energy Finance (BNEF) (2012b). *Solar Spot Price Index*, 2012. BNEF.

Bowen, A. & Ranger, N. (2009). Mitigating Climate Change through Reductions in Greenhouse Gas Emissions: The Science and Economics of Future Paths for Global Annual Emissions. Policy Brief, December. London: Centre for Climate Change Economics and Policy, and Grantham Research Institute on Climate Change and the Environment. Available at: http://www.lse.ac.uk/GranthamInstitute/publications/Policy/docs/PBMitigatingBowenRanger Dec09.pdf. Accessed 27 January 2014.

Chinese Academy of Engineering (2011). *Study on China's Medium and Long Term Energy Strategy.* Beijing: China Science Press.

City of New York (2011). PlaNYC. New York: The City of New York. Available at: http://nytelecom.vo.llnwd.net/o15/agencies/planyc2030/pdf/planyc_2011_planyc_full_report.pdf. Accessed 27 January 2014.

DONG Energy (2009). Rethinking Energy. Ascent Business Leadership Forum 2009, Presentation, 22 October.

DuPont (2011). 2011 Sustainability Progress Report. Wilmington: DuPont.

European Photovoltaic Industry Association (EPIA) (2011). Solar Photovoltaics Competing in the Energy Sector — On the road to competitiveness. Brussels: EPIA. Available at: http://www.epia.org/index.php?eID=tx_nawsecuredl& u=0&file=/uploads/tx_epiapublications/Competing_Full_MR.pdf&t=1390 915764&hash=c83d95eb017376de863eadbe9007d5c3960a5a2e. Accessed 27 January 2014.

Food and Agriculture Organization of the United Nations (FAO) (2010). 'Climate-Smart' Agriculture — Policies, Practices and Financing for Food Security, Adaptation and Mitigation. Rome: FAO. Available at: http://www.fao.org/docrep/013/i1881e/i1881e00.pdf. Accessed 27 January 2014.

Gohar L.K. & Shine K.P. (2007). Equivalent CO_2 and its use in understanding the climate effects of increased greenhouse gas concentrations, *Weather*, **62**(11), 307–311.

International Energy Agency (IEA) (2012). *World Energy Outlook 2012.* Paris: IEA/OECD.

Jacobs, M. (2012). What is the State of International Climate Talks? [online] In *Guardian*'s 'Ultimate climate change FAQ.' Available at: http://www. theguardian.com/environment/2012/sep/17/internattional-climate-talks-faq. Accessed 27 January 2014.

Jiankun, H. (2012). China's strategy for energy development and climate change mitigation, *Energy Policy*, **51**, 7–13.

Maersk (2011). Fill it up with Algae [online.] Available at: http://www.maersk. com/aboutus/news/pages/20111213-131258.aspx. Accessed 27 January 2014.

Merrill Lynch (2008). The Sixth Revolution: The Coming of Cleantech Clean Technology, Industry Overview. Available at: http://www.forseo.eu/filead min/media/forseo/docs/Merril_Lynch_The_Sixth_Revolution.pdf. Accessed 27 January 2014.

National Research Council (2013). *Climate and Social Stress: Implications for Security Analysis*, J. D. Steinbruner, P. C. Stern, and J. L. Husbands (eds.), Washington, DC: The National Academies Press.

Nidumolu, R., Prahalad, C.K. & Rangaswami, M.R. (2009). Why sustainability is now the key driver of innovation, *Harvard Business Review*, September **87**(9), 56–64.

Perez, C. (2002). *Technological Revolutions and Financial Capital: The Dynamics of Bubbles and Golden Ages*. UK: Edward Elgar.

Perez, C. (2010). Full Globalisation as a Positive-Sum Game: Green Demand as an Answer to the Financial Crisis. Available at: http://www.lse. ac.uk/newsAndMedia/videoAndAudio/channels/publicLecturesAndEvents/ player.aspx?id=659. Accessed 27 January 2014.

Rahmstorf, S. (2007). Glacial climates — Thermohaline circulation. In *Encyclopedia of Quaternary Science*, S.A. Elias (ed.), Oxford: Elsevier, pp. 739–750.

Romani, M., Rydge, J. & Stern N. (2012). Recklessly Slow or a Rapid Transition to a Low-Carbon Economy? Time to Decide, Centre for Climate Change Economics and Policy and Grantham Research Institute on Climate Change and the Environment, Policy Paper, December.

Royal Society (2009). Geoengineering the climate: Science, governance and uncertainty, September. Policy document 10/09. London: The Royal Society.

Stadtwerke München (SWM) (2011). The SWM Renewable Energies Expansion Campaign. Available at: http://www.swm.de/dms/swm/dokumente/ english/renewable-energies-expansion-campaign.pdf. Accessed 27 January 2014.

Stern, N. (2009a). *A Blueprint for a Safer Planet*. London: The Bodley Head.

Stern, N. (2009b). Key Elements of a Global Deal on Climate Change. London: LSE. Available at: http://www.cccep.ac.uk/Publications/Other/Global-Deal-Climate-Change.pdf. Accessed 8 November 2013.

Stern, N. (2011). Raising consumption, maintaining growth and reducing emissions: The objectives and challenges of China's radical change in strategy and its implications for the world economy. *World Economics*, **12**, 13–34.

Stern, N. (2012). How We Can Respond and Prosper. Lionel Robbins Memorial Lectures 2012 — Lecture 2. Available at: http://www.lse.ac.uk/public

Events/pdf/20120222%20Lord%20Stern%202.pdf. Accessed 27 January 2014.

Stern, N. & Rydge, J. (2012). The new energy-industrial revolution and international agreement on climate change. *Economics of Energy and Environmental Policy*, **1**(1), 1–19.

Stern, N., Kattumuri, R. & Rydge, J. (2012). *Low-Carbon Growth and Development*. Oxford Companion to Economics in India, New Delhi: Oxford University Press.

The Climate Group (2012). Solar Boom Triggers China to Increase 2015 Targets by 40%. Available at: http://www.lse.ac.uk/publicEvents/pdf/20120222%20Lord%20Stern%202.pdf. Accessed 27 January 2014.

The Co-operative (2012). Setting New Sights Our Ethical Plan 2012-14 (and beyond...). Available at: http://www.co-operative.coop/corporate/csr/our_ethical_plan_2012-2014.pdf. Accessed 27 January 2014.

United Nations Climate Change Secretariat (2012a). Bonn UN Climate Change meeting delivers progress on key issues. [Press release]. Available at: http://www.un.org/wcm/webdav/site/climatechange/shared/Documents/20120525_press%20release_SB6_close.pdf. Accessed 8 November 2013.

United Nations Climate Change Secretariat (2012b). Bangkok climate talks make concrete progress on key issues ahead of Doha. [Press release]. Available at: http://unfccc.int/files/press/press_releases_advisories/application/pdf/20120905_pr_awg-bkk_close.pdf. Accessed 8 November 2013.

United Nations Environment Programme (UNEP) (2010). *Bridging the Emissions Gap — Are the Copenhagen Accord Pledges Sufficient to Limit Global Warming to 2°C or 1.5°C? A Preliminary Assessment*. Nairobi: UNEP. Available at: https://unfccc.int/files/press/press_releases_advisories/application/pdf/20120525_pr_sb6_close.pdf. Accessed 27 January 2014.

United Nations Framework Convention on Climate Change (2012). *Decision 1/CP.17 Establishment of an Ad Hoc Working Group on the Durban Platform for Enhanced Action*. FCCC/CP/2011/9/Add.1. New York: UN. Available at: https://unfccc.int/files/press/press_releases_advisories/application/pdf/20120905_pr_awg-bkk_close.pdf. Accessed 27 January 2014.

World Economic Forum (2012). *Putting the New Vision for Agriculture into Action: A Transformation is Happening*. Geneva: World Economic Forum. Available at: http://www3.weforum.org/docs/WEF_FB_NewVisionAgriculture_HappeningTransformation_Report_2012.pdf. Accessed 27 January 2014.

World Resource Institute (WRI) (2012). *Progress Made at Bangkok Climate Negotiations, But Is It Enough?* WRI Insights. Available at: http://www.wri.org/blog/progress-made-bangkok-climate-negotiations-it-enough. Accessed 27 January 2014.

Yergin, D. (2012). *The Quest: Energy Security and the Remaking of the Modern World*. London: Penguin Books.

Chapter 2

The US and Action on Climate Change

Samuela Bassi and Alex Bowen
Centre for Climate Change Economics and Policy,
Grantham Research Institute on Climate Change and the Environment,
London School of Economics and Political Science (LSE),
Houghton Street, London WC2A 2AE

The US is currently the second biggest emitter of greenhouse gases in the world and one of the highest ranked countries in terms of per capita emissions. Along with other major economies, it will have to cut emissions much more sharply if the UN Framework Convention on Climate Change (UNFCCC) agreement to seek a 2°C ceiling to global warming is to be fulfilled. Fortunately, there are some grounds for guarded optimism. Despite the weakness of federal policy on climate change, the emissions intensity of the economy has fallen remarkably. New actions are being taken at federal, state and local levels so that, in the words of one eminent academic observer, "the reality surpasses the rhetoric" (Stavins, 2012). At the international level, the US is becoming less of an outlier. It had a pivotal role in helping to shape the Copenhagen Accord in 2009. The approach endorsed at Durban two years later increased emphasis on the need for developing countries to participate in emissions control, fitting well with the US position that large emerging-market economies, as well as developed countries, must take action. However, the distributional consequences across countries of action to stop climate change could still undermine the chances of a global agreement. Domestically, climate change policies need more coherence and ambition, but are being held back by widespread political opposition. The introduction of a single carbon price across the US economy would improve the cost-effectiveness of climate change mitigation, speed the introduction of clean energy technology, reduce investor risks and create a level playing field across states.

1. Introduction

Greenhouse gas emissions in the US are among the highest in the world, in both total and per capita terms, reflecting the country's size, wealth and pattern of energy use. Its emissions increased by more than 8% between 1990 and 2011 — an increase that, had it ratified the Kyoto Protocol, would have put the country far behind its estimated target of a 7% reduction. Despite its significant contribution to global emissions, the US has been reluctant so far to be bound by internationally agreed climate change objectives, and is unlikely to commit to quantitative emissions targets in the future, at least unless China and other major emerging-market economies commit to quantitative targets at the same time (Aldy and Stavins, 2009). Domestic political rhetoric on climate change has also become increasingly partisan, and key national policies, such as mandatory domestic emission reduction targets and cap-and-trade systems have so far won insufficient support to be introduced.

So is the outlook for the US' action against climate change bleak? This chapter argues that such pessimism is unwarranted. The emission intensity of production fell from 613 to 419 tonnes per million US$ of Gross Domestic Product (GDP) between 1990 and 2009, faster than in many other advanced industrial countries. New actions are being taken at federal, state and local levels so that, in the words of one eminent academic observer, "the reality surpasses the rhetoric" (Stavins, 2012). Nevertheless, more rapid cuts in emissions are necessary in both the US and the rest of the world if the aspiration of members of the United Nations to keep the rise in global temperature to 2°C is to be met.

This chapter reviews the most recent trends in the US greenhouse gas emissions, provides an overview of the country's contribution in international climate change negotiations and discusses the wide range of federal, state and local policies designed to help tackle anthropogenic climate change. An optimistic reading of domestic measures and the United Nations' framework for global action agreed in Durban in 2011 suggests that the US and other major emitters may begin to build a consensus on how to move forward. In the context of the United Nations Framework Convention on Climate Change (UNFCCC), the achievement in reducing the two streams of negotiations (the Kyoto Protocol group and the Long-term Cooperative Action group) down to a single track (the Working Group on Enhanced Action under the Durban Platform) reached in Doha can enable a level playing field for all countries to agree a new global climate treaty by 2015. At national level, while the issue of climate change was kept relatively quiet during the election campaign in 2012, its importance was re-emphasized during President Obama's State of the Union address in February 2013. Notably, the President announced that, should no bipartisan agreement be reached by the Congress on a market-based cap-and-trade approach, he will use regulations to make progress. It remains to be seen whether the divided US Congress and the national public opinion will support this process and what size of emissions cuts it will achieve.

2. Recent Trends in Greenhouse Gas Emissions in the US

Yearly greenhouse gas emissions in the US peaked in 2007, when they reached about 7.26 billion tonnes of carbon dioxide equivalent (CO_2e).[1] They have since decreased somewhat (Figure 1), and in 2011, emissions were about 6.70 billion tonnes of CO_2e (EPA, 2013). A particularly steep decline was recorded in 2009, as the economic recession intensified. An increase in economic output and warmer summer conditions led greenhouse gas emissions to rise again by more than 3% in 2010 (EPA, 2012a). However, in 2011 these fell by 2.4% (EPA, 2013) thanks to a decrease in the carbon intensity of the power sector (related to a gradual switch from coal to natural gas and an increase in renewables uptake), a decrease in transport-related consumption (due to higher fuel prices and stricter fuel efficiency regulations) and relatively mild winter conditions.

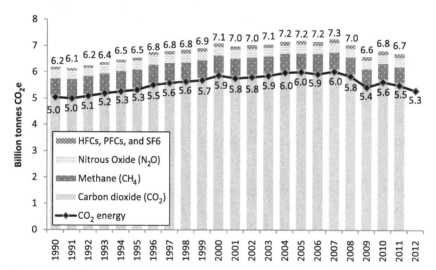

Figure 1. US greenhouse gas emissions by gas, 1990–2012 (billion tonnes CO_2e).
Source: Based on EPA (2013); except CO_2 energy data from EIA (2013).

---

[1]CO_2e is a unit used to compare the emissions from various greenhouse gases. It is derived by multiplying the quantity (e.g. tonnes) of a gas by its associated global warming potential (GWP), which is a measure of how much a given mass of a chemical contributes to global warming over a given time period compared with the same mass of CO_2 (whose GWP is set at 1). Methane for instance has a GWP of 25 over a period of 100 years (IPCC, 2007), so 1 tonne of methane corresponds to 25 tonnes of CO_2e.

Data for 2012 are available only for CO_2 emissions from energy consumption. CO_2 is the largest contributor to the country's greenhouse gas emissions and has been responsible for most of the changes in emissions between 1990 and 2011; and as energy consumption is by far the main contributor of CO_2 emissions, the data is a good approximation of the trend of greenhouse gas emissions. In 2012 CO_2 emissions were about 5.28 billion tonnes (EIA, 2013). They fell by almost 4% since 2011, and were about 12% lower than their 2005 level.

The changes in total CO_2 emissions relative to 1990 in the US and other countries are shown in Figure 2. In 2011, the US was the second largest emitter of CO_2,[2] after China. Its emissions per capita were 17.3 tonnes, one of the top 10 highest levels in the world, and the second highest among large industrialized countries after Australia (PBL/JRC, 2012) (Table 1).

The gradual increase of domestic emissions in the past 20 years was partly due to significant population growth. The country's population increased by almost 25% between 1990 and 2011 (World Bank, 2013a), a much higher rise than that experienced by other large industrial countries

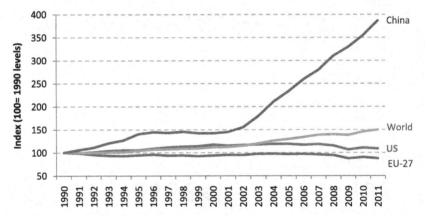

Figure 2. Change in total CO_2 emissions in the US, China, European Union (EU-27) and the world.

Source: PBL/JRC (2012).

---

[2]Estimates include CO_2 emissions from fossil fuel combustion, fugitive emissions from fuels, cement production and other carbonate uses, feedstock and other non-energy uses of fuels (such as for the production of ammonia and other chemicals), waste incineration and fossil-fuel fires. They do not include CO_2 from forest fires related to deforestation/logging and peat fires and subsequent post-burn emissions from decay of remaining above-ground biomass and from drained peat soils (PBL/JRC, 2012).

Table 1. Top 10 major emitters: Total and per capita emissions, 2011.

Rank	Total CO_2 emissions (billion tonnes)		CO_2 emissions per capita (tonne/capita)[3]	
1	China	9.70	Netherlands Antilles	34.04
2	US	5.42	Trinidad and Tobago	33.25
3	EU-27	3.79	Qatar	30.97
4	India	1.97	Kuwait	29.11
5	Russian Federation	1.83	Brunei Darussalam	22.84
6	Japan	1.24	United Arab Emirates	20.87
7	Germany	0.81	Bahrain	20.68
8	South Korea	0.61	Luxembourg	19.24
9	Canada	0.56	Australia	19.00
10	Indonesia	0.49	US	17.30

Source: Based on PBL/JRC (2013).

(except Australia). As a result, emissions per capita in the US have decreased by 14% between 2005 and 2011 (PBL/JRC, 2012), a faster pace than the European Union's (12%) and Japan's (6%).

Furthermore, the large share of global CO_2 emissions for which the US is responsible — 16% in 2011 (PBL/JRC, 2012) — is broadly commensurate with its share of economic output, the largest in the world — about 19% in 2011 (World Bank, 2013b) (Figure 3). Between 1990 and 2011 its GDP[4] increased on average by 2.5% per year, slightly above the OECD average (2.2%; World Bank, 2013c). The emission intensity of its economy decreased significantly, from 613 tonnes per million US$ of GDP[5] in 1990 to 419 tonnes per million US$ in 2009 (the latest data available). Its 2009 emission intensity was slightly below the world average (498 tonnes CO_2 per million US$) and substantially below China's (930 tonnes CO_2 per million US$), although still about a third higher than EU levels (265 tonnes CO_2 per million US$; World Bank 2013d).

---

[3]This selection focuses on main emitters, therefore excluding small countries. Note that, according to the latest data available from the World Bank (2012a), in 2008 the following countries had higher emissions per capita (from fossil fuel and cement production) than the top five emitters listed in Table 1: Qatar (49 tonnes/capita), Trinidad and Tobago (37 tonnes/capita), Kuwait (30 tonnes/capita), Brunei Darussalam (28 tonnes/capita), United Arab Emirates (25 tonnes/capita), Aruba (22 tonnes/capita), Luxembourg (21 tonnes/capita) and Bahrain (21 tonnes/capita).

[4]In Purchasing Power Parity (PPP) at constant 2005 international $.

[5]As above.

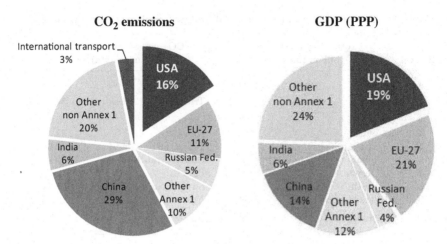

Figure 3. Relative share of GDP (in Purchasing Power Parity, PPP) and CO2 emissions of Annex 1 and non-Annex 1 countries, 2011.

Source: GDP based on World Bank (2013b) data; CO2 emissions based on PBL/JRC (2012).

The trends in CO_2 emissions relative to population and GDP growth in the US and other major emitters are shown in Figure 4.

The main source of CO_2 emissions in the US is electricity generation, which in 2011 accounted for almost 41% of CO_2 emissions from fossil fuel combustion (33% of total greenhouses gas emissions) (EPA, 2013). This is broadly in line with the world average share of CO_2 emissions from the electricity sector, which was about 43% in 2010[6] (IEA, 2012a). Emissions from the power sector increased by 18% since 1990, as demand grew and fossil fuels remained the dominant source for generation (EPA, 2013). But emissions decreased after 2007, largely thanks to a shift in the energy mix. While coal is still the single most important fuel for electricity generation in the US, its contribution to power generation dropped from about 50% in 2009 to less than 40% at the end of 2011 (EIA, 2012a), yet still above the OECD average share of electricity generated from coal, which stood at 34.2% in the same year (IEA, 2012b, p. 18). The fall was due to a combination of mild weather and the increasing price competitiveness of gas relative to coal, following the success of shale gas

---

[6]Coal and peat were responsible for around 13,066 million tonnes of CO_2 worldwide in 2010. In the same year, total CO_2 emission from fuel combustion were 30,276 million tonnes.

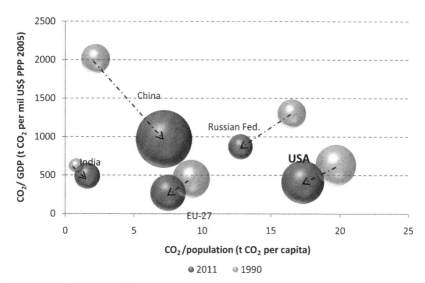

Figure 4.   Trends in CO₂ emissions intensity for the top five emitters, 1990–2011.

Note: Size of circle represents total CO$_2$ emissions from the country in that year.
Source: Based on PBL/JRC (2012).

development. In 2011, the consumption of coal and oil for electricity generation decreased by 5.7% and 19.9%, respectively, compared to the previous year, while the use of natural gas for electricity generation increased by 2.5% (EPA, 2013).

The transport sector is the second major contributor to CO$_2$ emissions and has been the fastest-growing source of emissions since 1990. It accounted for 33% of CO$_2$ emissions from fossil fuel combustion in 2011 (27% of total greenhouse gas emissions) rising by 17% since 1990 (EPA, 2013). This was well above the world average contribution of the transport sector to global CO$_2$ emissions (22% in 2010[7]; IEA, 2012a,b). The US has the highest level of passenger travel per capita in the world (more than 25,000 km per person per year), partly due to its large size and low population density, partly because of low fuel prices, that have contributed to the use of larger vehicles than in Europe (IEA, 2012a). Transport emissions, however, declined since 2008, thanks to new vehicle efficiency improvements, higher oil prices and the economic downturn (EPA, 2013).

---

[7]Transport was responsible for around 6,756 million tonnes of CO$_2$ worldwide in 2010. In the same year, total CO$_2$ emission from fuel combustion were 30,276 million tonnes.

The industrial sector was responsible for 15% of CO_2 emissions from fossil fuel combustion in 2011 (20% of total greenhouse gas emissions); its contribution has steadily declined since 1990, because of structural changes in the economy towards services, fuel switching and efficiency improvements (EPA, 2013).

Greenhouse gas emissions from the residential and commercial end-use sectors instead have increased by around 8% since 1990, due to increasing use of electricity for lighting, heating, air conditioning and operating appliances. Together they account for around 10% of CO_2 emissions from fossil fuels (11% of total greenhouse gases) (EPA, 2013).

An overview of the contribution of the different economic sectors to CO_2 emissions from fossil fuels across time is shown in Figure 5.

The US also consumes a large amount of imported goods, thereby affecting the generation of emissions in other countries. Besides the emissions generated within the country boundaries, it is therefore worth considering the impact that domestic consumption has on greenhouse gas emissions at global level — i.e. the country's "carbon footprint." Estimates by Peters *et al.* (2011) indicate that, in 2008, goods and services consumed in the US accounted for more than 6 billion tonnes of CO_2, which is about 20 tonnes per capita — as shown in Figure 6. This is the highest level of emissions associated to consumption in the world — about one-fifth of the global total. Data also reveal that consumption-based emissions have

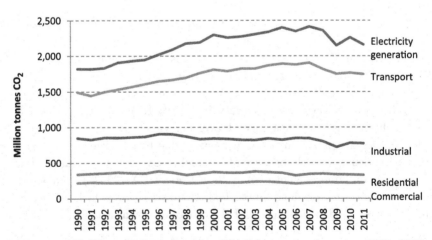

Figure 5.   US CO_2 emissions from fossil fuels by economic sector, 1990–2011.
Source: Based on EPA (2012a, 2013).

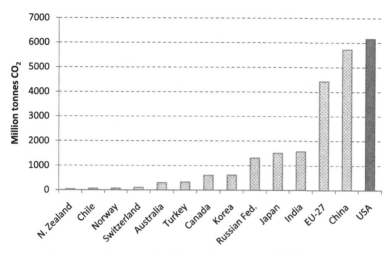

Figure 6. Consumption-based CO_2 emissions in OECD and other major emitting countries, 2008.

Source: Based on Peters *et al.* (2011).

increased by about 25% between 1990 and 2008, which is more than the increase in production-related (i.e. territorial-based) emissions.

3. US Role in Global Climate Change Negotiations

When environmental issues emerged on the international agenda in the late 1960s, and until the 1980s, the US was one of the strongest supporters of international environmental treaties and agreements (Sands, 1994). In the past two decades, however, its engagement with international environmental policy has lessened. Since 1989, the government has ratified only two important international environmental agreements,[8] while the European Union has ratified 12 (Kelemen and Vogel, 2009).

A similar detachment is evident with respect to international negotiations about climate change. As a member of the UNFCCC, the US participates in the periodic Conference of the Parties (COP) meetings, and submits regular reports on its emissions. It is, however, the only advanced industrial country that declined to ratify the Kyoto Protocol's

---

[8]The 1994 Convention to Combat Desertification and the 1994 International Tropical Timber Agreement.

first commitment period (Australia also initially refused, but eventually ratified it in 2007).[9] The US showed rare bipartisan agreement in opposing the Protocol when the Senate unanimously passed the Byrd–Hagel resolution in July 1997. This stated that the Senate would not ratify any international treaty imposing mandatory emissions reduction targets unless this also mandated "new specific scheduled commitments to limit or reduce greenhouse gas emission for Developing Country Parties within the same compliance period" in case it "would result in serious harm to the economy of the United States".[10] The resolution was motivated in large part by senators' objections that the executive branch of government had ignored the constitutional requirement that the Senate advise the executive and consent to the US adherence to international treaties. Even supporters of aggressive action against climate change supported the resolution (see Ellerman, 2013). After a period of ambiguity about the US' position (a period which Ellerman regards as broadly constructive in allowing the Europe Union to take over an international leadership role), President George W. Bush rejected the Kyoto Protocol in March 2001.

Formal opposition to any treaty that did not include binding commitments by developing countries has presented a big obstacle in subsequent negotiations, given the adoption of the so-called Berlin Mandate at the first COP to the UNFCCC in 1995, one year after the UNFCCC itself came into force. This interpreted the "common but differentiated responsibilities" recognized in the Convention to mean that only "developed country Parties" (also known as Annex I countries) were to take on emission-reduction responsibilities, an interpretation that US senators found unacceptable.

The Bush administration instead championed the role of research and development (R&D) and sought to substitute for UN-based partnerships international platforms of its own creation, such as the six-nation "Asia-Pacific Partnership on Clean Development",[11] aiming to foster voluntary goals. Despite these efforts, at COP 13 in Bali the US was "isolated as never before" (Christoff, 2008).

In 2009, the country appeared to change course under the Obama administration. At the international level, the government started to seek

---

[9]Canada withdrew from the Protocol in December 2011.
[10]Senate Report 105-54, p. 24. See http://www.gpo.gov/fdsys/pkg/BILLS-105sres98rs/pdf/BILLS-105sres98rs.pdf.
[11]The other members are Australia, Canada, China, India, Japan and South Korea.

comprehensive agreements involving all countries, although mostly relying on market mechanisms, existing global financial institutions, low-carbon technology R&D and a global "climate technology hub" for exchange of information on clean technologies (Dimitrov, 2010, p. 803), rather than on mandatory targets. Domestically, President Obama announced for the first time the intention to reduce emissions by 17% by 2020 and 83% by 2050 compared with 2005 levels, with interim targets of a 30% cut by 2025 and a 42% cut by 2030 (the same targets as in the Waxman–Markey Congressional proposals).

Using a 1990 baseline — consistent with Kyoto and other national targets — the US pledge, however, translates into a less impressive emission cut of around 3% by 2020 (Table 2). The difference in baseline, however, becomes less significant with more distant targets. By 2050, its commitment would be an emissions reduction of about 80% compared with 1990 levels, close to the EU long-term commitment to reduce emissions by 80% to 95% compared with 1990 levels by 2050 (European Commission, 2011, p. 3), and even more ambitious considering the higher GDP and population growth in the country.

The US had a pivotal role in the preparation of the Copenhagen Accord at the COP 15 in December 2009, together with Brazil, China, India and South Africa. The Accord was criticized for its lack of ambition and for the "undemocratic" procedures with which it was created — having been drafted by a small sub-set of countries — and was simply "noted" (rather than "adopted") by the UNFCCC because of objections from another small set of countries. Nevertheless, the document proved "resilient and of real value" (Stern and Rydge, 2012) in subsequent negotiations. Its principles

Table 2. The US announced commitment on greenhouse gas reduction: 2005 and 1990 baselines (million tonnes CO_2e).

Year	1990	2005	2010	2020	2025	2030	2050
GHG emissions (historical & future*)	6,175	7,204	6,822	5,979*	5,043*	4,178*	1,225*
Announced target (vs. 2005)				17%	30%	42%	83%
Estimated target (vs. 1990)				3%	18%	32%	80%

*Future target emissions estimated on the basis of the announced commitments.
Source: Past emissions based on EPA (2012a).

were broadly endorsed in the 2010 Cancún Agreement adopted at COP 16, and in the 2011 Durban Platform adopted at COP 17.

Whether by 2015 developed and developing countries will reach an agreement that will bring all under the same legal regime by 2020, as agreed in Durban, is unknown. Nevertheless, the outlook post-Doha offers an important opportunity for the US to help shape a new international agreement, especially now that some of the factors preventing its earlier engagement are changing. First, the Copenhagen Accord and the Cancún Agreements began the process of blurring the Annex I/non-Annex-I distinction, which should help the US move beyond the impasse illustrated by the Byrd–Hagel resolution. Second, in the course of the Copenhagen negotiations, the country was successful in removing the reference to "legally binding" outcomes. Although this excision risks weakening the negotiations' ambitions, it may enable future ratification by the US and other countries historically opposed to targets mandated by an international agreement (as opposed to domestically set targets or other objectives enshrined in domestic legislation). As Aldy and Stavins (2012) remark:

> We ought not to overestimate the importance of a nonbinding agreement to reach a future agreement, especially as some developing countries have considered stepping back from this agreement. Nonetheless, this is a significant departure from the past. It is of vast potential importance, but only 'potential,' because just as the Kyoto Protocol's targets and timetables fulfilled the Berlin Mandate's promise, future COPs must deliver on the [Durban Platform for Enhanced Action] with a new post-Kyoto agreement by 2015.

4. Key National Climate Change Policies and Their Development

Although in the past two decades the US has often shown a lack of appetite for, if not overt opposition to, climate change regulations, some important progress has been achieved in domestic policy, both at the federal and state level. An overview of key initiatives, as listed in Box 1, is presented. A brief description of each policy is included in Annex 1.

4.1. *Initiatives at federal level*

Climate change policy at the beginning of the first term of President Obama's administration, in 2009, was characterized by a renewed interest in market-based instruments to achieve domestic emission reductions. Several bills, however, were tabled without success. Most notably, the cap-and-trade

Box 1: Key climate change-related initiatives in the US.

Framework legislation:

o 1970: Clean Air Act
o 1975: Energy Policy and Conservation Act
o 1975: Corporate Average Fuel Economy (CAFE)
o 1992: Energy Policy Act
o 2005: Energy Policy Act
o 2007: Energy Independence and Security Act

Standards:

o 2005: Clean Air Interstate Rule
o 2010: The Light-Duty Vehicle Rule (Tailpipe Rule)
o 2010: Tailoring Rule
o 2011: Heavy-Duty Vehicles Standards
o 2011: Cross-State Air Pollution Rule (Transport Rule)
o 2011: Mercury and Air Toxic Standards
o 2012: New Source Performance Standards
o 2012 and 2013: (Proposed) Carbon Pollution Standard for New Power Plants

Monitoring and reporting:

o 2009: GHG Reporting Rule

Court cases:

o 2007: Massachusetts v. EPA
o 2009: Endangerment finding & Cause or Contribute finding
o 2011: American Electric Power v. Connecticut
o 2012: Coalition for Responsible Regulation v. EPA

Funding:

o 2009: American Recovery and Reinvestment Act (Stimulus Package)

State/regional initiatives:

o 1997 (onward): Renewable Portfolio Standard (RPS)
o 2006: California's cap-and-trade system (AB32)
o 2007: Western Climate Initiative
o 2008: Regional Greenhouse Gas Initiative (RGGI)
o 2010: California Low Carbon Fuel Standard

system proposed under the 2009 Waxman–Markey bill, although approved by the House of Representatives, failed to progress in the Senate.

Despite the inability of the Congress to adopt climate change legislation, command-and-control-type measures were developed by the US Environmental Protection Agency (EPA), using its existing authority under the Clean Air Act. The Act, a landmark piece of legislation originally enacted in 1963, defines the EPA's responsibilities for improving air quality and the stratospheric ozone layer, but had never been used before to regulate greenhouse gas emissions. EPA's legal power to regulate emissions at the federal level was indeed questioned, but eventually formalized, in a number of court cases.

Notably, a lawsuit launched in 2007 by a coalition of states, cities and environmental groups, led by the Commonwealth of Massachusetts, challenged the then Bush administration's refusal to regulate greenhouse gases from motor vehicles under the Clean Air Act. The court ruled in favor of Massachusetts and required the EPA to provide evidence about whether carbon emissions constitute human endangerment. Such evidence was subsequently provided by EPA in 2009, in the so called "endangerment finding." Furthermore, in the "cause or contribute finding," the EPA provided formal evidence of the direct link between vehicle emissions and the dangers posed by greenhouse gases, sanctioning the legitimacy of the Clean Air Act to regulate the matter.

The Supreme Court confronted climate change issues again in the case of American Electric Power v. Connecticut,[12] where a coalition of states sued five electric power producers to cap and reduce their carbon emissions. The Court held that it is the EPA's responsibility, rather than the courts, to oversee and enforce climate change regulations, effectively shaping the path of future climate change litigation. The EPA's endangerment finding and its emission-related rules have so far been upheld in the face of legal challenges.

As a result of the Massachusetts v. EPA case and the publication of the endangerment finding, in 2010, the EPA was able to introduce the Light-Duty Vehicle Rule (or "Tailpipe Rule").[13] The rule set greenhouse-gas emission standards and raised corporate average fuel-economy (CAFE) standards for cars and light trucks produced from 2012. New, more stringent standards have been recently introduced for model years 2017 to 2025, aiming to raise the fleet average performance to 54.5 miles per gallon

---

[12]582 F.3d 309 (2d Cir 2009).
[13]75 FR 25324.

(23.4 km/liter) by 2025 (the standard was 27.5 miles per gallon as late as 2010). Differentiated greenhouse gas and fuel standards for heavy-duty vehicles were also introduced for the first time in 2011 and entered into force in 2014.

With the introduction of these greenhouse gas emission standards for mobile sources, CO_2 became automatically a pollutant regulated under the Clean Air Act. The EPA was therefore required to promulgate regulations also for new and existing stationary sources. As a result, "Best Available Control Technology" (BACT) standards for new major stationary sources of emissions were put in place in 2011 (Townshend *et al.*, 2011). Through its so-called "Tailoring Rule," the EPA set emission thresholds above which greenhouse gas permits were required for new and existing industrial facilities, and required site-specific reviews of pollution control technologies. In 2012, the EPA proposed a rule on a Carbon Pollution Standard for New Power Plants under the Clean Air Act. The rule was challenged in court and subject to a wide public consultation. As a result, a revised proposal was put forward in 2013. If implemented, new large gas-fired power plants would need to meet a limit of 1,000 lbs (454 kg) of CO_2 per megawatt-hour (MWh), equivalent to the emissions performance of a typical new combined cycle gas plant. Emissions from smaller gas-fired plants and from coal-fired plants would be subject to slightly higher, yet stringent limits of 1,100 lbs (499 kg) of CO_2 per MWh. This would imply that, new coal-fired electricity generation will effectively be prohibited (unless endowed with CO_2 abating technologies). Standards for existing power plants have not yet been devised, although potential emission reductions could be significant (Bianco and Litz, 2010). Emission guidelines are expected to be released in 2014.[14] In 2010, the EPA also announced the intention to regulate greenhouse gas emissions from new and modified refineries, as well as guidelines for existing refineries, but as yet no proposal has been tabled (Damassa *et al.*, 2012).[15]

The EPA also passed a number of regulations on other air pollutants with potential co-benefits in terms of greenhouse gas emissions reductions from power plants. Among these, mercury and air toxic standards from coal- and oil-fired power plants greater than 25 megawatt (MW) were introduced in 2011 and will take effect from 2015. In 2012, the EPA also introduced "New Source Performance Standards"[16] for limiting volatile

---

[14]See http://yosemite.epa.gov/opa/admpress.nsf/0/da9640577ceacd9f85257beb006cb2b 6!OpenDocument.
[15]*Ibid.*
[16]77 FR 22392.

organic compound (VOC) and sulfur dioxide (SO_2) emissions from the oil and natural gas sector, including the first federal air standards for wells that are hydraulically fractured (EPA, 2012d).

Emissions of SO_2 and nitrogen oxides (NO_x) from fossil-fuel power plants are also regulated through a cap-and-trade system under the 2005 Clean Air Interstate Rule. A proposal to replace the old regulation with a new system under the 2011 Cross-State Air Pollution Rule was struck down in 2012 by a sentence of the US Court of Appeal,[17] and the Clear Air Interstate Rule re-established until new legislation is issued.

Furthermore, energy efficiency for buildings and appliances is supported through a range of building and equipment standards, which have been developed since the 1970s and are currently coordinated under the Building Regulatory Program.

Besides regulatory measures, the US government has also implemented climate change policy through public subsidies. The American Recovery and Reinvestment Act of 2009 — the US' fiscal stimulus package enacted in response to the recent recession — allocated about US\$ 840 billion though tax cuts and public spending to provide a response to the economic crisis (US Congress, 2009), including about US\$ 80 billion for renewables and energy-efficiency measures (Stavins, 2012). In addition, loan-guarantee programmes have been granted to nuclear power. A conditional commitment loan of US\$ 8.33 billion was offered in 2010 for the construction of two nuclear reactors, the first to be built in the US in the 21st century (Damassa, 2012).

Support for climate change–related research, development and deployment (RD&D) has been a particularly prominent instrument of policy in the past two decades. Examples include the "Advanced Energy Initiative" and the "Climate Change Technology Program" for low-carbon energy sources and climate-related technology (IEA, 2007). Considering that RD&D expenditure across all fields has always been relatively high in the US, compared with other countries, specific support to climate change research has been relatively low. Between 2004 and 2008 this has been about 8.5% of the total RD&D budget — one of the lowest ratios among OECD countries (Figure 7). Nevertheless, the amount of expenditures, both as a share of GDP and in absolute terms, is relatively high. In 2009, about 0.07% of GDP[18] was allocated to RD&D on climate change

---

[17]See http://www.cadc.uscourts.gov/internet/opinions.nsf/19346B280C78405C85257A 61004DC0E5/\$file/11-1302-1390314.pdf.
[18]2009 US GDP was \$13.863 trillion in nominal current values (OECD http://stats.oecd. org/#).

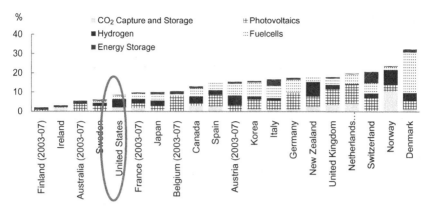

Figure 7. Government RD&D expenditures on selected climate change mitigation technologies, 2004–2008 (percentage of yearly average RD&D budget).

Note: OECD countries with RD&D budget higher than US$ 10 million.
Source: OECD (2010).

mitigation technologies, including energy efficiency, carbon capture and storage, renewables, fuel cells and electricity storage. This is among the largest shares in OECD countries, together with that of Japan (0.08%) and Canada (0.07%). By comparison, EU expenditures in the same year were about 0.02%. In absolute terms, the US public support to climate change–related RD&D amounted to almost $10 billion in 2009. The second and third largest investors, Japan and the EU, spent far less — $4 billion and $3 billion, respectively (IEA, 2011). Such spending is also likely to have generated benefits beyond the borders, due to spill-over effects.

4.2. Initiatives at regional, state and local levels

In addition to the introduction of climate change policies at the federal level, a number of initiatives have also emerged at the regional, state and local levels. Climate leadership at state level in the late 1990s and early 2000s was largely confined to California, New York and a few other early adopters. By 2007–2008, the majority of the 50 states, including some of the most conservative administrations, had begun to implement some form of climate policy (Chatrchyan and Doughman, 2008). Rabe (2006) observes that the increasingly active involvement of states in climate change policy "must be seen as not merely an extension of existing authority but rather a new movement of sorts driven by a set of factors distinct to the issue of climate change," including concerns over local environmental impacts (e.g. due to sea level rise in coastal areas), interest in seizing economic development opportunities from "green" initiatives (e.g. from domestic renewable energy sources) and increasingly forceful advocacy by state-based environmental and energy organizations.

Several states have also set domestic targets for renewable electricity through Renewable Portfolio Standards (RPS). These require electricity producers to supply a certain minimum share of their electricity from designated renewable resources. Currently, 30 states and the District of Columbia have enforceable RPS or other mandated renewable-capacity policies. In addition, seven states have voluntary goals for renewable generation. State RPSs vary widely in terms of programme structure, enforcement mechanisms, size and application. Some have higher ambitions, such as California with its 33% target by 2020, or Hawaii's 40% target by 2030, while others only set minimum capacity targets, such as Iowa's aim to reach 105 MW of renewable energy installed (which has already been exceeded). Most states have targets around 15–20% of total electricity production from renewable or low-carbon sources by 2020, comparable to European Union objectives.

The state of California also enforces its own low-carbon fuel standards, aiming to reduce the carbon intensity of motor-vehicle gasoline and diesel fuels sold within the state by 10% by 2020 through the increased sale of alternative low-carbon fuels (such as biofuels). However, in 2011, a California district court ruled that the fuel standards violate interstate commerce laws, as they discriminate against out-of-state fuel production, which has greater life-cycle emissions due to the greater distance of shipment to California. The future of the programme is uncertain (EIA, 2012b).

Some states have also implemented their own emission cap-and-trade schemes. The pioneer was California, which in 2006 passed the Assembly Bill 32 (the Global Warming Solution Act, or AB32) setting greenhouse gas reduction goals for 2020 and including a cap-and-trade programme. Electric power plants and large industrial facilities are required to comply from 2013, while suppliers of transportation fuels and of natural gas will have to comply by 2015. California is also a member of the Western Climate Initiative, an inter-state programme set up in 2007 involving the Canadian provinces of British Columbia, Manitoba, Ontario and Quebec. The initiative sets a regional goal to reduce emissions to 15% below 2005 levels by 2020

(WCI, 2012) and provides recommendations for a regional cap-and-trade programme. However, some uncertainty remains over the implementation and design of the programme (EIA, 2012b).

Other states are engaged in a cap-and-trade system through the Regional Greenhouse Gas Initiative (RGGI), which currently involves nine[19] north-eastern states and targets fossil-fuel power plants with a capacity of at least 25 MW. Emission permit auctioning began in September 2008. At the end of the first three-year period, total emissions were well below the programme's cap, because of the lower price of natural gas (which caused significant shifts from coal-generation to gas-generation capacity), the economic downturn and mild summers and winters. Allowances have therefore sold at the floor price of US\$ 1.89 because of the lack of a binding constraint. Several states have decided to retire their excess allowances permanently, which will result in the removal of 67 million tonnes of CO_2 (EIA, 2012b). Measures have been announced to tighten the cap from 2014. The possibility of linking the programme to California's and Quebec's carbon markets after the end of the second compliance period (in December 2014) is under consideration.

In some cases, greenhouse gas emission targets have also been adopted at the city level. These vary widely in ambition, baseline and time scale, from relatively modest reductions of 20–25% compared with 2005–2007 levels by 2020 (as in Atlanta, Denver and Miami) to ambitious long-term commitments, such as Seattle's 100% emission reduction target compared with 1990 by 2050 (Figure 8).

5. Lessons from the US Climate Change Policy and the Way Forward

The US legislative efforts to reduce domestic greenhouse gas emissions through a cap-and-trade system held out some hope of bipartisan consensus, given that forms of emission trading have been enacted in the past by Republican administrations, as in the case of SO_2 emissions and the leaded gasoline phase-out. But the debate about environmental policy has become so polarized that even the market mechanism of cap-and-trade has come to be demonized in conservative quarters, an irony noted by Schmalensee

---

[19]Connecticut, Delaware, Maine, Maryland, Massachusetts, New Hampshire, New York, Rhode Island and Vermont currently participate. Pennsylvania, Québec, New Brunswick and Ontario act as observers. New Jersey used to participate but withdrew in 2011.

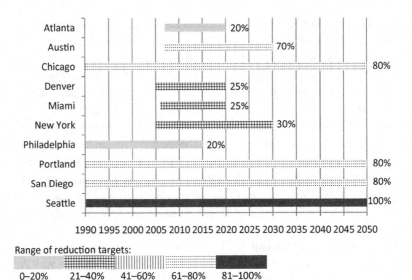

Figure 8. City-wide emissions reductions targets (% planned reduction).
Source: Based on Carbon Disclosure Project (2012).[20]

and Stavins (2012). Hence command-and-control approaches have come to appear to be the only politically feasible instruments for climate change policy at federal level, despite their probably higher costs, with the Clean Air Act assuming a central role in the development of regulations reducing greenhouse gas emissions (Burtraw, 2011).

Meanwhile, legal action has also affected climate change policy developments. The role of the courts in influencing policy in the US is unusual, as citizens are authorized to sue the federal government should it fail to meet its obligations, including those stated in environmental regulations. Environmental law and policy are thus characterized by much higher involvement of the courts than in other countries (Harrison, 2010, p. 77). Some of these lawsuits have been crucial in the development of climate change regulation. But others, like the Eme Homer City Generation vs. EPA case (requiring yet one more revision of the legislation on air pollution), have slowed action. Public-nuisance litigation is likely to continue, with

---

[20]Data for Denver, San Francisco and New Orleans based on responses to a "CDP Cities Information Request." Available on CDP website https://www.cdproject.net/en-US/Results/Pages/responses.aspx.

lawsuits being filed across the country in pursuit of injunctive relief and/or damages. The pace, the promise and the problems of this approach remain uncertain (Stavins, 2010).

Where federal policy has failed to act, some states and local administrations have been front-runners, inspiring policies in other states and eventually at the federal level, as in the case of California's vehicles standards. Others have been successful in coordinating efforts through regional initiatives, such as the RGGI cap-and-trade system, but at the price of a lack of ambition about the extent of emissions reductions. Other programmes, such as Renewable Portfolio Standards, shared some common elements across states, but also displayed major differences in targets and timescale.

The coexistence of state and federal policies raises questions about their interactions (Goulder and Stavins, 2011). State efforts may fail to reduce greenhouse emissions at the national level, simply displacing emissions to elsewhere in the nation. They are likely to result in lower cost-effectiveness compared with coordinated, consistent federal measures. For example, state legislation setting vehicle CO_2 emission and gasoline standards significantly more stringent than the national ones can lead to relocation of economic activity, high carbon leakage and the impairment of firms' competitiveness. State initiatives, however, can also create pressure for more stringent federal policy and serve as laboratories for experimenting with innovative policy approaches, as in the case of regional cap-and-trade systems. Subnational efforts are likely to remain critical in the absence of progress in federal climate change policy (Goulder and Stavins, 2011).

Overall, climate change policy in the US has made important progress. Nevertheless, existing climate and energy regulations lack a common vision and are not fully consistent with stated government ambitions. Analysis by the World Resources Institute indicates that, even if existing federal and state regulatory tools are strongly enforced, greenhouse gas emissions reductions may fall short of President Obama's Copenhagen pledge to reduce emissions 17% below 2005 levels by 2020 (Bianco and Litz, 2010). Estimates by the US Energy Information Administration (2012c) projected only a 9% reduction in energy-related CO_2 emissions by 2020, and expected emissions to rise back to current levels by 2040. Furthermore, some of the existing policies appear to be neither cost-effective nor fully successful in their objectives. For example, analysis of the CAFE policy to reduce vehicle emissions suggests that fuel standards are more expensive than a gasoline tax (Austin and Dinan, 2005) and that they may not reduce fleet greenhouse gas emissions significantly in the absence of complementary measures (Bastani et al., 2012).

Technology innovation subsidies have usually been politically more palatable in the US, although the availability of additional funding for RD&D depends on how fast the country recovers from the economic crisis and the pressure to reduce the federal deficit. Technology alone, however, is very unlikely to produce effective climate change mitigation, for instance because of "rebound effects" (Sorrell, 2007). These arise, for example, where improvements in energy efficiency reduce the cost of a technology, which then prompts higher use of energy-using services (for example, heat or transport), so that the energy saving from the innovation is offset by increased energy consumption.

As noted by Stavins (2010), the increased sensitivity to energy-related issues generated by the Gulf oil spill, combined with the lack of appetite for addressing climate change explicitly, increases the likelihood of so-called "energy-only" legislation. Additional policies and better coordinated state and federal approaches are needed if the US government intends to meet its climate change objectives and, ultimately, a level of emission reductions consistent with the UNFCCC objective of a 2°C ceiling for global warming. This is even more urgent since, as noted by the United Nation Environment Programme (2012), the estimated emissions gap in 2020 for a "likely" chance to staying below the 2°C target is large, and more ambitious national pledges and internationally-coordinated approaches are needed to succeed.

Most economists and policy analysts in the US tend to favor carbon pricing (see for example Nordhaus, 2005, 2007; Metcalf, 2009; Bowen, 2011). This is likely to be the least costly approach in the short term (given heterogeneous abatement costs) as well as in the long term, providing an effective incentive for low-carbon technological change.

However, carbon pricing, either in the form of cap-and-trade or carbon taxes, faces enormous political barriers. A recent public opinion survey (Leiserowitz et al., 2012) shows that, while a large majority of Americans (77% of respondents) believe global warming should be a "very high" (18%), "high" (25%) or "medium" priority (34%) for the president and the Congress, more than half (54%) of respondents would oppose a carbon tax on companies that produce or import fossil fuels, while only 39% would support it. There is also a stark difference between political affiliations, with 53% of Democrats respondents supporting the tax, against only 22% of Republicans.

Any bill introducing a new tax, explicit or implicit, including new energy or carbon taxes, risks encountering broad hostility in the Congress. The Clinton administration's attempt to introduce an energy tax[21] in 1993 that "would have taxed virtually all forms of fossil fuel energy in the United States" (Fisher, 2004) encountered opposition from both major political parties. Cap-and-trade systems have historically enjoyed a somewhat broader consensus. Their popularity, however, appears to have faded recently, and the schemes have sometimes been dismissed as "cap-and-tax." Stavins (2010) notes that what has frequently been interpreted as hostility in the Senate to cap-and-trade is actually broader hostility to the very notion of carbon pricing or even to any climate change policy.

6. Conclusions

Given its economic and population growth, and the reticence about adopting economy-wide climate change policy at the federal level, the US emissions performance has been surprisingly good, especially in the past five years. Nevertheless, the country remains one of the world largest emitters.

At the international level, the US is becoming less of an outlier. It had a pivotal role at COP 15, by helping to shape the Copenhagen Accord and carrying forward a constructive bilateral dialogue with China. It also announced, for the first time, domestic emission reduction targets for 2020 and 2050. COP 17 built on those foundations with the potentially path-breaking Durban Platform for Enhanced Action. In future negotiations, the Nationally Appropriate Mitigation Actions (NAMAs) approach (envisaging voluntary mitigation actions by developing countries, with or without international financial support), and the increased emphasis on the need for developing countries to participate in emissions control, appear to fit well with the US's historical positions. The Durban Platform also allows for a range of options for the legal forms of a future agreement, spanning from "a Protocol, another legal instrument or an agreed outcome with legal force applicable to all Parties" (UNFCCC, 2012). This could, in principle, accommodate the US' preference for — in the words of its special envoy on climate change Todd Stern (2012) — "a more flexible approach that starts with nationally derived policies," which would include

---

[21] A tax levied on the heat content of fuels, measured in British Thermal Units (BTU) — i.e. a BTU tax.

the possibility to act through domestic legislation alone. However, the final format of the agreement, as well as distributional implications of climate change impacts and mitigation across countries, could still undermine consensus.

Despite the US apparent lack of domestic political support for strengthening national climate change policy, and its past reluctance to sign legally binding international commitments, several climate change policies have been implemented at both federal and local level. At the federal level, action has relied on the legal framework governing the EPA and on subsidies to low-carbon and energy RD&D. A few of the gaps in federal climate change policies have been addressed, to varying extent, by state legislation. In some cases, local initiatives have in turn inspired federal measures. Nevertheless, large disparities among state approaches (e.g. on renewable targets) may have led to higher costs and obstacles to the growth of low-carbon businesses and the spread of green technologies.

Recently, climate change policy regained attention in President Obama's inauguration speech in January 2013. That could portend bolder climate change policies in the second term of the Obama administration, but bipartisan agreement will still be needed to pass major pieces of climate legislation, especially in the House of Representatives, where Republicans hold the majority. This may prove to be daunting, as the debate over climate change has become increasingly politicized in the past decade. Notably, in the 2012 Republican National Convention, the party's nominee Mitt Romney claimed "President Obama promised to begin to slow the rise of the oceans and to heal the planet. My promise is to help you and your family".[22] While the victory of the Democratic Party suggests that climate policy will remain part of the government agenda, uncertainty remains on the extent and form of future federal initiatives.

More effective mitigation measures need to be devised and adopted if the US is serious about reaching its recently formulated domestic targets. The measures so far implemented at federal and state level, however significant, are not always coherent and cost-effective, as they have not been designed as part of a single vision. Vehicle CAFE standards are a case in point. Overall, climate change policy would benefit from more coherence and will need to increase its ambition in order to reach the desired outcome. IEA (2007) noted that a closer co-ordination between federal and

---

[22] See http://blogs.wsj.com/washwire/2012/08/30/excerpts-of-romneys-speech-to-the-gop-convention/.

state governments, as well as between executive and legislative branches of the federal government, could help ensure that energy policy challenges are tackled in a more consistent manner. Sub-national efforts will remain critical in the absence of progress in federal policy. But the introduction of a single carbon price across the American economy would be more effective, speeding the more rapid introduction of clean energy technology projects, reducing investor risks and creating a level playing field across states.

Annex 1

Key Federal Initiatives (in chronological order):

1970: Clean Air Act (CAA).[23] The Act defines the US Environmental Protection Agency (EPA)'s responsibilities for protecting and improving air quality and the stratospheric ozone layer at federal level. The law underwent major changes though the Clean Air Act Amendments of 1990,[24] which addressed, in particular, legislation on acid rain, urban air pollution and toxic air emissions, as well as permitting and enforcement programmes. Several minor changes have also been introduced since.

1970s (onward): Building Regulatory Program (BRP). The program resides within the Building Technologies Program (BTP) of the Office of Energy Efficiency and Renewable Energy of the Department of Energy. It combines three existing programs: the Appliance and Equipment Efficiency Standards Program (standards having being developed since 1975 in the Energy Policy and Conservation Act — see below), ENERGY STAR (launched in 1992) and the Building Energy Codes Program (codes being developed since 1976). The first two aim to develop and update equipment standards and test procedures. The latter supports the upgrading of model building energy codes, which set minimum requirements for energy-efficient design and construction for new and renovated buildings (DOE, 2010).

1975: Energy Policy and Conservation Act.[25] Beside extending oil price controls and authorizing the creation of a strategic petroleum reserve, the Act established for the first time mandating "Corporate Average Fuel Economy" (CAFE) standards for passenger cars (see below). The Act also

---

[23]Public Law 91-604.
[24]Public Law 101-549.
[25]Public Law 94-163.

established minimum standards of energy efficiency for major appliances, such as refrigerators, air conditioning systems and television sets (see above). Major amendments to the Act were introduced by the National Appliance Energy Conservation Act of 1987 and the Energy Policy Act of 1992.

1975: Corporate Average Fuel Economy (CAFE).[26] The standards were introduced under the Energy Policy and Conservation Act in 1975 (see above), revised in 2006 and further modified in the Energy Independence and Security Act of 2007 (see below). Their purpose is to reduce energy consumption by increasing the fuel economy of cars and light trucks sold in the US. The programme is administered by the National Highway Traffic Safety Administration (NHTSA), which sets the fuel economy standards, while the Environmental Protection Agency (EPA) calculates the average fuel economy for each manufacturer. The standards apply to passenger cars or light trucks with a gross vehicle weight rating (GVWR) of 8,500 lbs (3,856 kg) or less, and are based on the average mileage travelled by a vehicle per gallon of gasoline.

1992: Energy Policy Act.[27] The Act sets goals and mandates and amends utility laws to increase clean energy use and improve overall energy efficiency in the US. The Act, *inter alia*, directs the federal government to decrease energy consumption in federal buildings and to integrate the use of alternative fuel vehicles in federal and state fleets; authorizes tax incentives and marketing strategies for renewable energy technologies; establishes an energy-efficiency programme, including incentives for energy conservation in buildings and efficiency standards for appliances; and details clean energy incentives, research and development strategies, conservation goals and responsible management practices. Several requirements have been updated or superseded by the Energy Policy Act of 2005 and the Energy Independence and Security Act of 2007 (see below).

2005: Energy Policy Act.[28] The Act aims to promote "dependable, affordable and environmentally sound production and distribution of energy." It includes, *inter alia*, about US$ 8 billion tax credits for renewables and nuclear power and for energy efficiency, loan guarantees for "innovative technologies" that avoid greenhouse gases, support to investment in "clean

---

[26]Title 49 US Code, Chapter 329.
[27]Public Law 102-486.
[28]Public Law 109-58.

coal" initiatives, a renewable fuel standards setting biofuel minimum targets and other measures supporting low carbon energy sources. The Act also updates some of the energy-efficiency standards for appliances set in the 1975 Energy Policy and Conservation Act (see above) (US Government, 2005).

2005: Clean Air Interstate Rule. The rule aims to reduce sulfur dioxide (SO_2) and nitrogen oxides (NO_x) emissions from power plants by 70% in 27 states and the District of Columbia. States must achieve the required emission reductions using one of two compliance options: (1) requiring power plants to participate in an interstate cap-and-trade system, or (2) meeting an individual state emissions budget through measures of the state's choosing.[29] The regulation was meant to be replaced by the 2011 Cross-State Air Pollution Rule (see below), but this was sent back for revision by a sentence of the Court of Appeal. In the interim, the Clean Air Interstate Rule still applies.

2007: Energy Independence and Security Act.[30] The Act aims to improve vehicle fuel economy and reduce the US dependence on oil. It makes a number of important changes to the 1975 Energy Policy and Conservation Act (see above). Notably, it includes an increase of about 40% in the CAFE standards for cars and light-duty trucks, requiring automakers to boost fleet-wide gas mileage to 35 miles per gallon (15.3 km/l) by the year 2020 (see also "Light Duty Vehicle Rule") and, since 2010, it includes for the first time, fuel standards for medium- and heavy-duty commercial vehicles. The Act also establishes new energy-efficiency appliance standards and updates some of the existing ones. Among the most important revisions, new measures concerning lighting energy efficiency will effectively phase out incandescent light bulbs by 2020.

2007: Massachusetts v. EPA.[31] In this Supreme Court case, Massachusetts and eleven other states, along with several local governments and non-governmental organizations, sued EPA for not regulating the emissions of CO_2 and other greenhouse gases from the transportation sector under the Clean Air Act. The court ruled in favor of Massachusetts and required EPA to provide evidence on whether carbon emissions constitute human endangerment.

---

[29]See http://www.epa.gov/cair/index.html#older.
[30]Public Law 110-140.
[31]549 U.S. 497 (2007).

2009: Greenhouse Gas Reporting Rule.[32] The rule requires large emission sources and suppliers to report their greenhouse gas data and other relevant information. The purpose of the rule is to collect accurate and timely greenhouse gas data to inform future policy decisions. The Greenhouse Gas Reporting Program database was published for the first time in January 2012 (EPA, 2012b).

2009: Endangerment Finding and Cause or Contribute Finding. Following the Court's request for evidence in "Massachusetts v. EPA" (see above), EPA signed two findings regarding greenhouse gases under section 202(a) of the Clean Air Act:

— The *Endangerment Finding*, providing evidence on how the current and projected atmospheric concentrations of six greenhouse gases (CO_2, CH_4, N_2O, HFCs, PFCs and SF_6) threaten the public health and welfare; and
— The *Cause or Contribute Finding*, establishing that the combined emissions of such greenhouse gases from new motor vehicles and new motor vehicle engines contribute to the greenhouse gas pollution which threatens public health and welfare.

These findings did not impose any requirements on industry or other entities, but they were a prerequisite to finalizing greenhouse gas standards for light-duty vehicles.

2009: American Recovery and Reinvestment Act (Stimulus Package).[33] The Act (US Congress, 2009) was intended to respond to the economic crisis by providing tax cuts and funding to different sectors of the economy. The original estimated expenditure of US$ 787 billion was increased to US$ 840 billion in 2011. The package includes about US$ 80 billion for renewables and energy-efficiency measures.

2010: The Light Duty Vehicle Rule (Tailpipe Rule).[34] It is a joint rule between EPA and the Department of Transportation's National Highway Traffic Safety Administration (NHTSA) that implements the "Twenty in Ten Initiative," establishing a national programme of harmonized regulations on light-duty vehicles and encompasses both greenhouse gas emissions standards and CAFE (fuel economy) standards. These apply to

---

[32]74 FR 56260.
[33]Public Law 111-5.
[34]75 FR 25324.

new passenger cars, light-duty trucks and medium-duty passenger vehicles, starting with model year 2012. Greenhouse gas standards, defined under the Clean Air Act, are projected to result in fleet average emissions of $250\,g\ CO_2$ per mile (about $155.3\,g\ CO_2$ per km)[35] for model year 2016. The new CAFE standards, regulated under the Energy Independence and Security Act (see above), envisage a fleet average of 35.5 miles per gallon $(15.3\,km/l)$ by 2020. Stricter standards for model years 2017–2025 are under development. These are expected to raise the fleet average to 54.5 miles per gallon $(23.4\,km/l)$ by 2025.

2010: Tailoring Rule. EPA set greenhouse gas emission thresholds to define when greenhouse gas permits are required for new and existing industrial facilities under the New Source Review/Prevention of Significant Deterioration (PSD) and Title V (Operating Permit) of the Clean Air Act. Site-specific review of pollution control technology is required for permits to be issued. The EPA decided to phase-in the applicability of these programmes. In the first step, starting in January 2011, permits are required only for major greenhouse gas sources which are already subject to a permit regime for non-greenhouse gas pollutants. In the second step, from July 2011, permits are required also for the major sources of greenhouse gases[36] that have not been previously covered by the Clean Air Act for other pollutants. Step three starts from July 2013 and extends the requirements to more greenhouse gas sources.

2011: Heavy-Duty Vehicles Standards. While regulations on heavy-duty vehicles emissions, like PM and NO_x, has been in place since the 1980s, this is the first time standards are set on fuel consumption and CO_2. The regulation applies to three categories of heavy-duty vehicles, namely combination tractors, heavy-duty pickup trucks and vans and vocational vehicles. Fuel consumption standards, regulated under the 2007 Energy Independence and Security Act (see above), will be voluntary in model years 2014 and 2015, becoming mandatory with model year 2016. Greenhouse gas emission standards, regulated under the Clean Air Act, will begin with model year 2014. By 2017, these are expected to range from 66 to $120\,g$ CO_2 per tonne of freight per mile (41–$75\,g\ CO_2/tonne/km$) for combination

---

[35]By comparison, the European Union's CO_2 emission targets for passenger cars are $130\,g/CO_2$ by 2012 and $95\,g\ CO_2/km$ by 2020 (Regulation 443/2009).

[36]A "major stationary source" is any source that emits at least 100 or 250 tonnes per year (depending on the source type) of any pollutant subject to regulation under the CAA.

tractors, and from 222 to 373 g CO_2 per tonne of freight per mile (138–232 g CO_2/tonne/km) for vocational vehicles, while for heavy-duty pickup trucks and vans, they will vary according to a range of vehicle characteristics ("work factors").

2011: American Electric Power v. Connecticut.[37] The case stemmed from a coalition of state attorneys general who sued five electric power producers to cap and reduce their carbon emissions, but ultimately the final sentence concerned whether climate change regulations can be decided through the US court system. The Court held that EPA (and the equivalent agencies at the state and local level), rather than the Court, is responsible for overseeing and enforcing any regulations or changes to the regulations regarding climate change. This effectively shaped the path of future climate-change litigation.

2011: Cross-State Air Pollution Rule (or "Transport Rule"). The legislation regulates emissions of SO_2 and NO_x from fossil-fuel power plants greater than 25 MW. Although not directly targeted at CO_2, the rule can have an impact on the design and performance of fossil fuel power plants, indirectly affecting their greenhouse gas emissions. The rule replaces the Clean Air Interstate Rule and interstate emission cap-and-trade programmes for SO_2 and NO_x. It consists of four separate cap-and-trade programmes: two for SO_2 emission (covering 16 and 7 states respectively), one for annual NO_x emissions (covering all the states involved in SO_2 trading) and one on seasonal NO_x (covering 25 states in total). Three cap-and-trade programmes were scheduled to start in 2012, but the Court of Appeal delayed implementation because of legal challenges raised by several power companies and states. In August 2012, the court sent the rule back for revision, on the grounds that the agency overstepped its legal authority and issued standards that were too strict,[38] and reinstated the Clean Air Interstate Rule until a viable new regulation is issued.

2011: Mercury and Air Toxic Standards. These standards, required under the Clean Air Act Amendments, apply to mercury (Hg) and hazardous acid gases, metals and organics from coal and oil-fired power plants with nameplate capacities greater than 25 MW. The standards take

---

[37]582 F.3d 309 (2d Cir 2009).
[38]The court's ruling can be seen at: http://www.cadc.uscourts.gov/internet/opinions. nsf/19346B280C78405C85257A61004DC0E5/$file/11-1302-1390314.pdf.

effect in 2015. Like the Cross-State Air Pollution Rule, the standards may have an indirect effect on plants' performance and greenhouse gas emissions.

2012: Coalition for Responsible Regulation v. EPA.[39] Several states and industry groups challenged the EPA's endangerment finding and greenhouse gas rules, including the Tailpipe Rule and the Tailoring Rule. The US Court of Appeals for the District of Columbia, however, dismissed the petitions, upholding EPA's endangerment finding and its rules setting limits on greenhouse gas emissions from mobile and stationary sources.

2012: New Source Performance Standards.[40] These standards aim to reduce harmful air pollution from the oil and natural gas industry. The final rules are the result of the review of four air regulations required by the Clean Air Act: a new source performance standard for VOCs; a new source performance standard for SO_2; an air toxics standard for major sources of oil and natural gas production; and an air toxics standard for major sources of natural gas transmission and storage. The rules include the first federal air standards for natural gas wells that are hydraulically fractured (e.g. for shale gas and shale oil production). Emission reduction would be accomplished primarily through the capture of natural gas that currently escapes to the air from oil and gas wells. This is expected to reduce methane emissions by 19–33 Mt CO_2e annually (EPA, 2012c).

2012: (Proposed) Carbon Pollution Standard for New Power Plants. A proposed rule under the Clean Air Act would, for the first time, set national limits on the amount of carbon pollution that new power plants will be allowed to emit. Under the proposed standard, all new power plants would need to match the greenhouse gas emissions performance currently achieved by highly efficient natural gas combined cycle (NGCC) power plants, i.e. 1,000 lbs (around 500 kg) of CO_2 per MWh. Power plants using carbon capture and storage (CCS) would have the option to use a 30-year average of CO_2 emissions to meet the proposed standard (EPA, 2012d). Following extensive public consultation, this draft rule was replaced by a new proposal in 2013. This set separate standards for natural gas-fired turbines and coal-fired units. For the former, limits were still set at 1,000 lbs of CO_2 per MWh, while for the latter they were slightly raised to 1,100 lbs (around 500 kg) of CO_2 per MWh.

---

[39] No. 09-1322 (D.C. Cir. June 26, 2012).
[40] See http://www.gpo.gov/fdsys/pkg/FR-2012-08-16/pdf/2012-16806.pdf.

Key State and Regional Initiatives (In Chronological Order):

1997 (onward): Renewable Portfolio Standards. Renewable portfolio standards (RPS), or renewable electricity standards (RES), require or encourage electricity producers within a given jurisdiction to supply a certain minimum share of their electricity from designated renewable resources. Under such standards, each state determines its own levels of renewable generation, eligible technologies and noncompliance penalties. As of September 2012, 30 States and the District of Columbia had enforceable RPS or other mandated renewable capacity policies. In addition, seven

Table 3. Renewable Portfolio Standards in the 30 States with current mandates.

State	Target	Year
Arizona	15% electricity	2025
California	33% electricity	2020
Colorado	20% electricity	2015
	30% electricity	2020
Connecticut	27% electricity	2020
Delaware	25% electricity	2025
Hawaii	40% electricity	2030
Illinois	25% electricity	2025
Iowa	105 MW	No date (already met)
Kansas	20% installed capacity	2020
Maine	10% electricity	2017
Maryland	20% electricity	2022
Massachusetts	15% electricity	2020
Michigan	15% electricity	2015
Minnesota	25–30% electricity	2020
Missouri	15% electricity	2021
Montana	15% electricity	2015
Nevada	25% electricity	2025
New Hampshire	23.8% electricity	2025
New Jersey	22.50% electricity	2021
New Mexico	20% electricity	2020
New York	30% electricity	2015
North Carolina	12.5% electricity	2021
Ohio	25% electricity	2025
Oregon	25% electricity (5–10% for small utilities)	2025
Pennsylvania	18% electricity	2020
Rhode Island	16% electricity	2019
Texas	5,880 MW	2015
Washington	15% electricity (largest utilities only)	2020
West Virginia	25% electricity	2025
Wisconsin	10% electricity	2015

Source: Based on EIA (2012b).

States had voluntary goals for renewable generation. State RSPs vary widely in terms of programme structure, enforcement mechanisms, size and application. Most states have targets of 15–20% of total electricity production from renewable or low-carbon sources by 2020. Some states, such as California, have targets as high as 33%. A common feature is a renewable electricity credit (REC) trading system structured to minimize the costs of compliance (Table 3).

2006: California's Cap-and-Trade System (AB32). California Assembly Bill 32 (AB32), also known as the Global Warming Solution Act, sets California's greenhouse gas reduction goals for 2020 and establishes a multi-year programme to reduce emissions. The Act set up a cap-and-trade programme in January 2012, with enforceable compliance obligations beginning in 2013. The cap is to decline linearly to 85% of the 2013 level by 2020. All electric power plants and large industrial facilities are required to comply from 2013, while suppliers of transportation fuel and of natural gas will have to comply by 2015. Emissions resulting from electricity generated outside California but consumed in the state are also subject to the cap. About half of the emission allowances is distributed through auctions, 7% goes into a cost containment reserve (intended to be called on if allowance process rise above a set amount) and the rest are grandfathered (EIA, 2012b).

2007: Western Climate Initiative: The aim of the programme is to reduce greenhouse gas emissions to 15% below 2005 emission levels by 2020 in the region under the scheme (WCI, 2012). It also provides design recommendations for a regional cap-and-trade programme. The programme initially involved six US states and four Canadian provinces, but a number of participants withdrew in 2010. As of 2013, only California and the Canadian provinces of British Columbia, Manitoba, Ontario and Quebec remained members. Some uncertainty remains over the implementation and design of the final programme (EIA, 2012b).

2008: Regional Greenhouse Gas Initiative (RGGI). A regional initiative to reduce greenhouse gas emissions through a cap-and-trade system, it currently involves nine[41] north-eastern states and targets fossil fuel power plants with 25 MW or greater generating capacity. Emission

---

[41]Connecticut, Delaware, Maine, Maryland, Massachusetts, New Hampshire, New York, Rhode Island, and Vermont currently participate. Pennsylvania, Québec, New Brunswick, and Ontario act as observers. New Jersey formerly participated, but withdrew in 2011.

permit auctioning began in September 2008, with the first three-year compliance period starting in 2009. Revenues are used to promote energy conservation and renewable energy, although as of 2010, three states had used some of the money to balance their overall budget. As a result of the economic downturn, at the end of the first three-year period, total emissions were well below the program's cap of 188 million tonnes and allowances have sold at the floor price of US$ 1.89 because of an excess of available allowances. Several states have decided to retire their excess allowances permanently, equivalent to the removal of 67 tonnes of CO_2 (EIA, 2012b). The possibility of linking the programme to California and Quebec's carbon market after the end of the second compliance period, in December 2014, is under consideration.

2010: California Low Carbon Fuel Standard. The legislation is designed to reduce the carbon intensity of motor gasoline and diesel fuels sold in California by 10% between 2012 and 2020 through the increased sale of alternative low-carbon fuels. Each low-carbon fuel's carbon intensity is measured through life-cycle analyses and measured in grams of CO_2 equivalent emissions per megajoule. In 2011, a California's district court ruled in favor of several trade groups claiming the fuel standards violate the US interstate commerce clause by seeking to regulate farming and ethanol production practices in other states. The future of the programme is uncertain (EIA, 2012b).

Acknowledgments

The authors are grateful for the comments on an earlier draft from Professor Rob Stavins and other participants at the March 2012 CAGE-CCCEP workshop on "The Global Development Post-Durban of Policy Regimes to Combat Climate Change", but remain responsible for all errors and omissions.

References

Aldy, J.E. & Stavins, R.N. (eds.) (2009). *Post-Kyoto International Climate Policy: Summary for Policymakers.* Cambridge: Cambridge University Press.

Aldy, J.E. & Stavins, R.N. (2012). Climate negotiators create an opportunity for scholars, *Science*, **337**, 1043–1044.

Austin, D. & Dinan, T. (2005). Clearing the air: The costs and consequences of higher CAFE standards and increased gasoline taxes. *Journal of Environmental Economics and Management*, **50**, 562–582.

Bastani, P., Heywood, J.B. & Hope, C. (2012). U.S. CAFE Standards — Potential for meeting light-duty vehicle fuel economy targets, 2016–2025. Boston: MIT. Available at: http://web.mit.edu/sloan-auto-lab/research/beforeh2/files/CAFE_2012.pdf. Accessed 27 January 2014.

Bianco, N.M. & Litz, F.T. (2010). Reducing Greenhouse Gas Emissions in the United States Using Existing Federal Authorities and State Action. Washington: WRI. Available at: http://www.wri.org/publication/reducing-greenhouse-gas-emissions-united-states-using-existing-federal-authorities-and. Accessed 27 January 2014.

Bowen, A. (2011). Policy Brief: The case for Carbon Pricing. London: Grantham Research Institute for Climate Change and the Environment and Centre for Climate Change Economics and Policy, London School of Economics and Political Science. Available at: http://www.lse.ac.uk/GranthamInstitute/publications/Policy/docs/PB_case-carbon-pricing_Bowen.pdf. Accessed 27 January 2014.

Burtraw, D. (2011). United States Climate Change Policy Efforts. CEPS Policy Briefs No. 255. Brussels: CEPS. Available at: http://www.ceps.eu/book/us-climate-change-policy-efforts.

Carbon Disclosure Project (2012). Measurement for Management — CDP Cities 2012 Global Report. London: CDP. Available at: https://www.cdp.net/cdpresults/cdp-cities-2012-global-report.pdf. Accessed 27 January 2014.

Chatrchyan, A.M. & Doughman, P.M. (2008). Climate Policy in the US: State and Regional Leadership. In Compston, H. and Bailey, I. (eds.), *Turning Down the Heat: The Politics of Climate Policy in Affluent Democracies.* Basingstoke: Palgrave. pp. 241–260.

Christoff, P. (2008). The Bali roadmap: Climate change, COP 13 and beyond. *Environmental Politics,* **17**, 466–472.

Damassa, T., Bianco, N., Fransen, T. & Hatch, J. (2012). *GHG Mitigation in the United States: An Overview of the Current Policy Landscape,* Working Paper, Washington DC: WRI. Available at: http://www.wri.org/publication/greenhouse-gas-mitigation-united-states. Accessed 27 January 2014.

Department of Energy (DOE) (2010). Building Regulatory Programs Multi-Year Program Plan. Washington DC: DOE. Available at: http://apps1.eere.energy.gov/buildings/publications/pdfs/corporate/regulatory_programs_mypp.pdf. Accessed 27 January 2014.

Dimitrov, R.S. (2010). Inside UN climate change negotiations: The Copenhagen Conference. *Review of Policy Research,* **27**(6), 795–821.

Ellerman, D. (2013). *The Shifting Locus of Global Climate Policy Leadership,* Transworld Working Paper 16, March.

Energy Information Administration (EIA) (2012a). Coal's Share of Total U.S. Electricity Generation Falls Below 40% in November and December. Available at: http://www.eia.gov/todayinenergy/detail.cfm?id=5331. Accessed 11 September 2012.

Energy Information Administration (EIA) (2012b). Annual Energy Outlook 2012 — with projections to 2035. Washington DC: EIA. Available at: http://www.eia.gov/forecasts/aeo/pdf/0383%282012%29.pdf.

Energy Information Administration (EIA) (2012c). Annual Energy Outlook 2013 — Early Release Overview. Washington DC: EIA. Available at: http://www.eia.gov/forecasts/aeo/er/pdf/0383er%282013%29.pdf.

Energy Information Administration (EIA) (2013). Monthly Energy Review April 2013. Washington DC: EIA. Available at: http://www.eia.gov/totalenergy/data/monthly/archive/00351304.pdf. Accessed 27 January 2014.

Environmental Protection Agency (EPA) (2012a). Inventory of United States Greenhouse Gas Emissions and Sinks: 1990–2010. Washington DC: EPA. Available at: http://www.epa.gov/climatechange/Downloads/ghgemissions/US-GHG-Inventory-2012-Main-Text.pdf. Accessed 27 January 2014.

Environmental Protection Agency (EPA) (2012b). Greenhouse Gas Reporting Program. Available at: http://www.epa.gov/ghgreporting/. Accessed 27 January 2014.

Environmental Protection Agency (EPA) (2012c). Overview of Final Amendments to Air Regulations for the Oil And Natural Gas Industry — Fact sheet. Washington DC: EPA. Available at: http://www.epa.gov/airquality/oilandgas/pdfs/20120417fs.pdf. Accessed 27 January 2014.

Environmental Protection Agency (EPA) (2012d). Standards of Performance for Greenhouse Gas Emissions for New Stationary Sources; Electric Utility Generating Units; Proposed Rule. Available at: http://www.regulations.gov/#!documentDetail;D=EPA-HQ-OAR-2011-0660-0001. Accessed 27 January 2014.

Environmental Protection Agency (EPA) (2013). Inventory of United States Greenhouse Gas Emissions and Sinks: 1990–2011. Washington DC: EPA. Available at: http://www.epa.gov/climatechange/Downloads/ghgemissions/US-GHG-Inventory-2013-Main-Text.pdf. Accessed 27 January 2014.

European Commission (2011). A Roadmap for Moving to a Competitive Low Carbon Economy in 2050. Brussels, 8 March. COM (2011) 112 final. Brussels: European Commission. Available at: http://eur-lex.europa.eu/LexUriServ/LexUriServ.do?uri=COM:2011:0112:FIN:EN:PDF. Accessed 27 January 2014.

Fisher, D.R. (2004). *National Governance and the Global Climate Change Regime*. Lanham, MD: Rowman and Littlefield Publishers.

Goulder, L.H. & Stavins, R.N. (2011). Challenges from State-federal interactions in United States Climate Change Policy. *American Economic review: Paper & Proceedings*, **101**(3), 253–257.

Harrison, K. (2010). The US as Outlier: Economic and Institutional Challenges to United States Climate Policy. In K. Harrison and L.M. Sundstrom (eds.), *Global Commons, Domestic Decisions: The Comparative Politics of Climate Change*. Cambridge, MA: MIT Press, pp. 67–104.

International Energy Agency (IEA) (2007). *Energy Policies of IEA Countries. The United States — 2007 review*. Paris: EIA. Available at: http://www.iea.org/publications/freepublications/publication/name,3728,en.html. Accessed 27 January 2014.

International Energy Agency (IEA) (2011). Energy Technology RD&D 2011 edition.

International Energy Agency (IEA) (2012a). CO_2 Emissions from Fuel Combustion 2012. Paris: EIA.

International Energy Agency (IEA) (2012b). Coal Medium-Term Market Report 2012. Paris: EIA.

IPCC (2007). Contribution of Working Group I to the Fourth Assessment Report of the Intergovernmental Panel on Climate Change. S. Solomon, D. Qin, M. Manning, Z. Chen, M. Marquis, K.B. Averyt, M. Tignor and H.L. Miller (eds.), Cambridge, United Kingdom and New York, NY, US: Cambridge University Press. Available at: http://www.ipcc.ch/publications_and_data/ar4/wg1/en/contents.html. Accessed 27 January 2014.

Kelemen, R.D. & Vogel, D. (2009). Trading places: The role of the US and the European Union in international environmental politics. *Comparative Political Studies*, **43**(4), 427–456. Available at: http://cps.sagepub.com/content/43/4/427.short. Accessed 27 January 2014.

Leiserowitz, A., Maibach, E., Roser-Renouf, C., Feinberg, G. & Howe, P. (2012). Public Support for Climate and Energy Policies in September 2012. Yale University and George Mason University. New Haven, CT: Yale Project on Climate Change Communication. Available at: http://environment.yale.edu/climate-communication/article/Policy-Support-September-2012. Accessed 27 January 2014.

Metcalf, G.E. (2009). Designing a carbon tax to reduce U.S. greenhouse gas emissions. *Review of Environmental Economics and Policy*, **3**(1), 63–83.

Netherlands Environmental Assessment Agency (PBL) & European Commission Joint Research Centre (JRC) (2012). Trends in Global CO_2 Emissions — 2012 Report. The Hague: PBL. Available at: http://edgar.jrc.ec.europa.eu/CO2REPORT2012.pdf. Accessed 27 January 2014.

Netherlands Environmental Assessment Agency (PBL) & European Commission Joint Research Centre (JRC) (2013). *EDGAR — Emissions Database for Global Atmospheric Research*. Available at: http://edgar.jrc.ec.europa.eu/index.php. Accessed 27 January 2014.

Nordhaus, W.D. (2005). After Kyoto: Alternative mechanisms to control global warming. *American Economic Review*, **96**(2), 31–34.

Nordhaus, W.D. (2007). To tax or not to tax: Alternative approaches to slowing global warming. *Review of Environmental Economics and Policy*, **1**(1), 26–44.

Organisation for Economic Co-operation and Development (OECD) (2010). Measuring Innovation: A New Perspective. Available at: http://www.oecd.org/site/innovationstrategy/measuringinnovationanewperspective-onlineversion.htm. Accessed 27 January 2014.

Peters G.P., Minx, J.C., Weber C.L. & Edenhofer, O. (2011). Growth in emission transfers via international trade from 1990 to 2008. *PNAS*, **108**(21), 8903–8908.

Rabe, B. (2006). Second generation climate policies in the US: proliferation, diffusion, and regionalization. *Issues in Governance Studies*, 6. Available at: http://www.brookings.edu/research/papers/2006/08/energy-rabe. Accessed 27 January 2014.

Sands, P. (1994). The 'greening' of international law. *Indiana Journal of Global Legal Studies*, **1**, 293.

Schmalensee, R. & Stavins, R. (2012). *The SO_2 Allowance Trading System: The Ironic History of a Grand Policy Experiment*, NBER Working Paper 18306, August.

Sorrell, S. (2007). The Rebound Effect: An Assessment of the Evidence for Economy-Wide Energy Savings from Improved Energy Efficiency. London: UKERC. Available at: http://www.ukerc.ac.uk/Downloads/PDF/07/0710 ReboundEffect/0710ReboundEffectReport.pdf. Accessed 27 January 2014.

Stavins, R.N. (2010). The Real Option for United States Climate Policy. Available at: http://www.robertstavinsblog.org/2010/06/23/the-real-options-for-u-s-climate-policy/.

Stavins, R.N. (2012). United States perspectives on Global Climate Change Policy Regimes. Presentation at the *Workshop on the Global Development Post-Durban of Policy Regimes to Combat Climate Change*, Centre for Competitive Advantage in the Global Economy, 13 March.

Stern, N. & Rydge, J. (2012). The new energy-industrial revolution and international agreement on climate change. *Economics of Energy and Environmental Policy*, **1**(1), 1–19.

Stern, T. (2012). Remarks at Dartmouth College. Available at: http://www.state.gov/e/oes/rls/remarks/2012/196004.htm. Accessed 27 January 2014.

Townshend, T., Fankhauser, S., Matthews, A., Feger, C., Liu, J. & Narciso, T. (2011). *Globe Climate Legislation Study*. London: Globe.

United Nations Environment Programme (UNEP) (2012). The Emissions Gap Report 2012. Nairobi: UNEP. Available at: http://www.unep.org/publications/ ebooks/emissionsgap2012/. Accessed 27 January 2014.

United Nations Framework Convention on Climate Change (UNFCCC) (2012). Report of the Conference of the Parties on its seventeenth session. Addendum Part Two: Action taken by the Conference of the Parties at its seventeenth session. FCCC/CP/2011/9/Add.1. Bonn: UNFCCC. Available at: http:// unfccc.int/resource/docs/2011/cop17/eng/09a01.pdf. Accessed 27 January 2014.

US Government (2005). Energy Policy Act of 2005. Available at: http://www.gpo.gov/fdsys/pkg/BILLS-109hr6enr/pdf/BILLS-109hr6enr.pdf.

US Congress (2009). American Recovery and Reinvestment Act of 2009. Available at: http://www.gpo.gov/fdsys/pkg/PLAW-109publ58/html/PLAW-109 publ58.htm. Accessed 27 January 2014.

Western Climate Initiative (WCI) (2012). Programme Design. Available at: http://www.westernclimateinitiative.org/designing-the-program. Accessed 26 July 2012.

World Bank (2012a). CO_2 emissions (metric tons per capita). Washington: World Bank. Available at: http://data.worldbank.org/indicator/EN.ATM. CO2E.PC. Accessed 27 January 2014.

World Bank (2013a). Population, total. Washington: World Bank. Accessed 29 April 2013. Available at: http://data.worldbank.org/indicator/SP.POP. TOTL. Accessed 27 January 2014.

World Bank (2013b). GDP ranking, PPP based. Washington: World Bank. Available at: http://data.worldbank.org/data-catalog/GDP-PPP-based-table. Accessed 27 January 2014.

World Bank (2013c). GDP, PPP (constant 2005 international $). Washington: World Bank. Available at: http://data.worldbank.org/indicator/NY.GDP. MKTP.PP.KD. Accessed 27 January 2014.

World Bank (2013d). CO_2 emissions (kg per 2005 PPP $ of GDP). Washington: World Bank. Available at: http://data.worldbank.org/indicator/EN. ATM.CO2E.PP.GD. Accessed 27 January 2014.

Chapter 3

Challenges and Reality: China's Dilemma on Durban Platform Negotiation

Mou Wang

Institute for Urban and Environmental Studies,
Chinese Academy of Social Sciences, Beijing, 100732, China
Research Centre for Sustainable Development,
Chinese Academy of Social Sciences, Beijing, 100732, China

Huishan Lian

International Finance Cooperation (IFC), Beijing, 100004, China

and

Yamin Zhou

Institute for Urban and Environmental Studies,
Chinese Academy of Social Sciences, Beijing, 100732, China
Research Centre for Sustainable Development,
Chinese Academy of Social Sciences, Beijing, 100732, China

At the 2011 Durban Conference, the United Nations Framework Convention on Climate Change (UNFCCC) adopted a series of decisions, including the second commitment period of the Kyoto Protocol and a new mandate for the Durban Platform. This outcome symbolized a significant milestone in the global climate negotiations. Behind this positive progress, divergences of parties on key issues such as the sources and scale of finance mechanisms, technology transfer, emission reduction targets and the legal form of the outcome have not been substantially resolved. In 2012, a complicated negotiation scenario was revealed, with three parallel negotiation tracks operating under two UNFCCC mandates. To minimize the deep divide between the North and South on main negotiation issues, key sticking points may be moved to the Durban Platform and negotiated under this new track.

The Durban Platform as a new negotiation mandate has taken center stage in the global community. Key negotiation issues such as the principle of "Common but differentiated Responsibility," the issue of legal form and the framework, agenda, roadmap and timetable of the Durban Platform remain to be addressed in future negotiations.

China is willing to participate actively and constructively in the Durban platform negotiation, but the expectation that China will pledge more aggressive emission reduction actions goes against the social and economic development trajectory of China, which is the dilemma of China about participation in climate negotiations. China as the "factory of the world" is on the fast track of urbanization and industrialization. It shoulders the imperatives to alleviate poverty and narrow the domestic regional gap. Its coal-based resource endowment and inefficient technologies provoke challenges to the curbing of emissions. Decoupling of greenhouse gas (GHG) emissions with social economic development is a conundrum not just for China but also the world.

Despite these challenges, China agreed the adoption of the Durban Mandate to initiate negotiations for the post-2020 international climate regime. This regime must be built on the basis of mutual respect and equity in accordance with respective responsibility and take full account of the right to development of developing countries and their financial and technology constraints in fighting climate change. Unrealistic emission reduction targets and unfair burden-sharing mechanisms for developing countries will neither facilitate the negotiation nor contribute to international cooperation in addressing climate change.

1. How to Interpret the Durban Outcome

1.1. *The North and South achieved a balanced outcome of the Durban Conference*

At the conference, the developed and developing countries made an important compromise about the second period of the Kyoto Protocol and the mandate to start the Durban Platform negotiation. Developing countries highlighted the successful extension of the second period of Kyoto protocol, while developed countries emphasized a single climate framework covering all parties. Both developing and developed countries had more or less achieved their negotiation targets. To this extent, the Durban Conference seemed to live up to the expectations of the international community.

1.2. *Key sticking points remain unresolved*

These may be moved to the Durban Platform and negotiated under this new track. One of reasons for the success of the Durban Conference was that it set up a new negotiating structure and approved a new negotiating mandate. This outcome, to some extent, buffered the tension among Parties on key negotiation sticking points. Parties have divided positions on these key issues but may prefer to negotiate these issues under the new mandate rather than trade off their interests in exchange for compromises. Key negotiation issues, such as the global emission peak, medium- and long-term emission targets in line with the 2°C limit and the legal form of the

AWG-LCA (Ad Hoc Working Group on Long-term Cooperative Action under UNFCCC) outcomes, are major disagreements among Parties, which have little room for compromises. The settlement of these obstacles may either be a weak outcome under the Bali Roadmap Mandate or a refit into the Durban Platform. The later will allow these key sticking points to continue to be negotiated under the new mandate.

1.3. No substantial progress on emission reduction targets, finance mechanisms and technology transfer

Although the European Union agreed to continue the implementation of the second period of Kyoto Protocol in Durban, they were very conservative on their target for emission reductions. The EU's current 20% GHG emission reduction target (with respect to 1990 levels) falls short of the once mentioned 30% reduction target. Other developed countries had no intention of raising the emission reduction targets they had proposed in the Copenhagen Agreement either; their goals were either conservative or designed to use a large share of international offsets such as CERs (Certified Emission Reduction). Developed countries need to improve further the scale and quality of their emission reduction targets as there was no substantial progress made in Durban on this issue. Regarding the issues of finance support and technology transfer, except for some consensus reached on a cooperation framework and mechanism, the Durban conference has made almost no breakthroughs on topics about which developing countries have concerns. Deep concerns of developing countries, such as those about financing sources, scale and verification criteria for finance support and technology transfer, were not addressed in Durban.

1.4. Durban was a milestone in the process of climate negotiation, but hardly was a success

At the Durban Conference, a mandate for Parties to the UNFCCC to negotiate the Durban Platform by 2015 was adopted. It started the process of wrapping up the negotiation mandate of the Bali Action Plan, which has no doubt symbolized a significant development in international climate change negotiation. This outcome provided a platform for future negotiation but, due to its failure to settle key negotiation blockages, it was far less than a success.

2. The Durban Platform and the Post-2012 International Climate Negotiation

2.1. *Three parallel negotiation tracks under two UNFCCC mandates*

In 2012, a complicated negotiation scenario was revealed, with three parallel processes operating under two UNFCCC mandates: the AWG-KP (Ad Hoc Working Group on Further Commitments for Annex I Parties under the Kyoto Protocol) and the AWG-LCA under Bali Road Map mandate; and the ADP (Ad Hoc Working Group on Durban Platform) under Durban mandate. As the new mandate for post-2020 international climate negotiation was adopted and the second commitment period for the Kyoto Protocol was agreed, EU and other developed countries are likely to shift their focus for negotiation to the Durban Platform, and the expectations of the international community about LCA may center around the construction of a new international climate framework after 2020.

2.2. *Divergence of interests between the North and South hampers breakthrough on key negotiation issues*

The EU, US and other developed countries have divergent positions on the legal form of any future climate regime, but they stand on the same ground in advocating a universal emission reduction framework that covers all Parties. Under the current international political economy, it is unlikely for the North to initiate more aggressive emission reduction targets under AWG-KP and AWG-LCA. They have shown more interest in the negotiation of AWG-DP, which may exert more pressure on developing countries to cut GHG emissions. For the South, their interest to accelerate the negation under Durban Platform is slim. They stress more on the ratification of the second commitment period of Kyoto Protocol and the mobilization of 2012–2020 financial and technical support. The divergence of interests between the North and South indicates difficulties in making substantial progress on key negotiation issues. One of the potential compromises is to move these issues to the Durban Platform and negotiate them under the new track. Under this scenario, Parties outside the second commitment period of KP might propose loose emission reduction targets or actions based on respective capabilities. And in terms of financial and technical support, the Platform might establish frameworks to speed up actual implementation while skirting procedural difficulties.

3. Key Issues in the Durban Platform Negotiation

3.1. *"Common but differentiated responsibilities" in the future international regime*

Success in reaching any effective international agreement requires that it is based on widely agreed principles. The Durban Platform is a mandate adopted under the UNFCCC. The guiding frameworks for the mandate should comply with the principles embodied in the Convention. Currently, there is a divergence of opinion among Parties on the understanding and interpretation of the "common but differentiated responsibilities (CBDR)" principle. There is a consensus among developing countries that the Kyoto Protocol demonstrates the principle of CBDR. Based on differentiating responsibilities and capacities, the Kyoto Protocol stipulates asymmetric priorities and commitments for developed and developing countries. Countries listed in Annex I have quantified emission-reduction obligations and responsibilities to provide financial assistance and technical support to developing countries for their effort to mitigate and adapt to climate change. And for developing countries, because of their underdeveloped economic and social conditions, their top priority is to alleviate poverty and sustain economic growth. They are expected to take emission reduction actions based on their respective capacities. Developed countries such as the EU have argued that, as the global economy is leaping forward, the CBDR principle should be interpreted dynamically. Some of the interpretations are in fact denials of CBDR, while some of them actually call for a bigger burden of emission cuts to fall on developing countries. At this stage, there remains a vast conceptual gap among Parties on the understanding of CBDR. How to define CBDR and how to guild the negotiation process under this principle is a key question to Durban Platform negotiation.

3.2. *The issue of legal form*

In recent years, the issue of the legal form for a future climate agreement has taken center stage within the global community. Prior to the Durban Conference, the discussion of the issue of legal form mainly focused on the legitimacy of LCA outcomes, while during the negation process of Durban Platform, Parties were divided over the form of legal outcome. EU and AOSIS (Alliance of Small Island States) reiterated their position on the need for a new universal and legally binding agreement, although China and India disagreed about determining the form of the outcome before Parties have agreed upon the substance of any future agreement. They stressed that due to the uncertainty of social and economic development after 2020, it is premature to decide now the legal form of the post-2020 climate regime. The deep divide over the form of the legal outcome of Durban Platform will keep challenging future negotiations and intensive debate will continue on this front.

3.3. *The framework and agenda of the Durban Platform*

Questions such as how to construct the framework of the Durban Platform and whether it should be based on the groundwork of the Kyoto Protocol and LCA or should be started from scratch remain to be answered in the future negotiations. The agenda of the Durban Platform is expected to address concerns of all Parties, but there are debates on whether the inclusion of previous sticking issues on the new platform can facilitate the process of negotiation. Considering developing countries' concerns about the uncertainty of future social and economic development, it is not difficult to foresee their conservative and cautious attitude toward setting the framework and agenda for the Durban Platform.

3.4. *The roadmap and timetable of the Durban Platform*

Under the new mandate, the Parties initiated the Durban Platform to agree on a new climate treaty by 2015. This is a very demanding timetable. The slow progress in agreeing the emission targets, global emission peak, financial and technical support, in addition, the stalemate of US climate legislation are challenges to conclude a new climate agreement before 2015.

4. China's Dilemma about Taking Part in Negotiations

China is willing to participate actively and constructively in the Durban platform negotiation, but the expectation that China will pledge more aggressive emission reduction actions goes against the social and economic development trajectory of China, which is the dilemma faced by China with respect to participation in climate negotiations. China's total amount of emissions is increasing considerably with its rapid development. The control of carbon emissions and the reduction of energy use became important in order to address climate change, as well as to guarantee China's energy security. Therefore, China is willing to reduce energy consumption voluntarily even without constraints imposed by international agreement.

China has basically achieved its goal of energy intensity reduction by 20% and has reduced carbon emissions by 1.46 billion tonnes through the 11th Five-Year Plan (China Climate Change Info-Net, 2006). China has proactively and constructively participated in international climate negotiations. However, due to inability to predict the future and the challenges of current social and economic problems, China cannot go beyond reality to pursuit unrealistic targets. The challenges include the following.

4.1. Low level of social and economic development

China is currently at a relatively low level of economic development. In 2010, the per capita Gross Domestic Product (GDP) of China was about US\$ 4,283 (International Monetary Fund, 2010) (based on exchange rates of the same year, the same below), only about one-third of the world's average. A remarkable disparity in economic development exists among different regions across China. The income disparity between rural and urban residents was also great. In 2011, the per capita disposable income of urban residents was US\$ 3,461 while that of rural residents was only US\$ 1,107, equivalent to 32% of the former (National Bureau of Statistics of China, 2012). Furthermore, poverty eradication is still a huge challenge for China. By the end of 2011, the poverty-stricken people in China's rural areas numbered more than 90 million, with the per capita annual net income less than 1500 Chinese Yuan (US\$ 238) (Xiao, 2010).

4.2. Rapid urbanization leads to emission growth

In the population structure of China, the proportion of the urban population has been rising as the total population has increased. The urban population rose from 31.9% in 2000 to 51.3% in 2011 (National Bureau of Statistics of China, 2012), an increase of 19.4% in 12 years. According to developed countries' experience, the urbanization rate for an industrialized country needs to reach 70% plus. China is expected to complete its urbanization in 2030 based on the current rate of 1% per year. Data show that urban per capita energy consumption is 1.8 times (National Bureau of Statistics of China, 2010) the rural per capita energy consumption. The accelerated development of cities will inevitably lead to the growth of energy consumption. As a result, urbanization and the income gap caused by urbanization are bound to encourage energy consumption growth.

4.3. Industrialization and embodied energy export

China is experiencing a critical period of industrialization. The Chinese economy has been growing by 10% on average during the past 30 years of reform and opening up. Its industrialization has now shifted from a labor- to a capital-intensive stage. In 2010, China's raw steel output reached 627 million metric tonnes; cement 1.87 billion tonnes, accounting for about 50% of the global production (China News, 2011). China has earned its reputation as the "factory of the world." China's rise to become, according to some reports, the largest single emitter of GHGs is closely linked to its economic growth, and particularly the export sector that has driven this growth. Export volumes accounted for 26% of GDP in 2010 (Ma, 2011), with the majority consisting of intermediate or consumption goods destined for developed countries' markets. Under current accounting rules, the emissions associated with these exports are fully attributable to China, since they took place within its territory. Given China's status as the world's factory, the energy used in the production of exports account to 26% of total emissions in 2006 (Chen et al., 2008), and this is unlikely to be changed before 2030. China therefore faces a long struggle to reduce emissions.

4.4. Resource endowment and difficult adjustment of energy structure

Compared with most developed countries, China is still heavily reliant on coal, which takes up 72% of its total energy consumption in 2010 (National Bureau of Statistics of China, 2011), far exceeding the world average of around 30%. On the other hand, oil and natural gas takes up 20% and 4.6% (National Bureau of Statistics of China, 2011) of total energy consumption, respectively. Regarding nuclear and other renewable energies, the percentage is only around 3.5% (National Bureau of Statistics of China, 2011), including hydro, lagging far behind France (39.1%) and the world average (6%). Coal still retains its position as China's primary source of energy and coal-driven energy consumption pattern is unlikely to change in the near future. China's energy resource endowment has greatly limited its ability to decrease its carbon emissions per unit of energy. Lack of advanced technology, including energy technology patents, has caused the very high cost of investment for developing new energy sources.

4.5. Inefficient technology with lock-in effect of technologies

Backward technology for energy production and utilization in China is one of the main reasons for China's low energy efficiency and high GHG emission intensity. On the one hand, there are relatively large gaps between China and the developed countries in terms of technologies of energy exploitation, supply and transformation, transmission and distribution, industrial production and other end-use energy; on the other hand, out-of-date technologies still account for a relatively high proportion of production in China's key industries. For example, the overall energy consumption per tonne of steel in large-scale iron and steel enterprises is about 200 kgce (kilogram carbon equivalent) lower than that in small enterprises, and the overall energy consumption per tonne of synthetic ammonia in large or medium enterprises is about 300 kgce lower than that in small enterprises. Owing to the lack of advanced technologies as well as the large proportion of out-of-date processes and technologies, China's energy efficiency is about 10% lower than that of the developed countries, and its per unit energy consumption of energy-intensive products is about 40% (National Development and Reform Commission of P.R. China, 2007) higher than the advanced international level. As China is now undergoing large-scale infrastructure construction for energy, transportation and buildings, etc., employment of inefficient technologies will lead to a lock-in effect, which will persist for the next few decades and keep China in an inefficient energy-consuming mode. This poses severe challenges to China in addressing climate change and mitigating GHG emissions.

5. Prospects for the Durban Platform Negotiations

The construction of the post-2020 international climate regime has significance in global climate governance and global climate security. Like negotiations in other international agreements, the Durban Platform negotiation must be built on the basis of mutual respect and equity in accordance with respective responsibilities. Only with mutual understanding and compromises can the Durban Platform negotiation forge ahead effectively.

A single-track negotiation process does not equate to an assumption of undifferentiated responsibilities and obligations among Parties. Climate change is the result of historical GHG accumulation in the atmosphere.

Developed and developing countries have made different contributions to the cumulative GHG emissions in the atmosphere. It is a common understanding under international climate governance that developed countries face the biggest responsibility for action to address climate change. The debate about a single or double negotiation track in international climate negotiations is a procedural issue that cannot and should not become a plea to blur the unequivocal distinction between developed and developing countries in climate change responsibilities and obligations. Developing countries, under single-track negotiation, should not be required to bear the burden of emission reduction targets and actions equivalent to those adopted by developed countries.

Issues of equity and justice need to be addressed under the Durban Platform. The essence of international climate governance is to share the responsibility to address climate change taking account of Parties' respective historical emissions and financial and technological abilities to take action. And a fair responsibility-sharing mechanism prepares the ground for ongoing negotiations. The Kyoto Protocol is a paradigm that captured the international consensus that developed countries bear a greater historical responsibility to lead emission cuts under a total emission cap and developing countries voluntarily take emission cut actions consistent with their respective abilities and development needs. However, in recent years, some Parties have sought to redefine the meaning of equity and the "common but differentiated responsibilities" principle, thereby advocating undifferentiated emission reduction commitments and actions across developed and developing countries. However, is it fair, just or even realistic to require a country with US\$ 3,000 annual per capita income and 3 tonnes CO_2 emission per capital to commit and share the same emission target with a country that with US\$ 30,000 annual per capita income and more than 20 tonnes CO_2 emission per capita? If the Durban Platform cannot serve as a fair and just platform and drive the climate regime toward an appropriately differentiated end, then widespread resistance might be expected.

Setting emission reduction actions is more feasible than setting reduction targets for developing countries. The Durban platform was designed for the post-2020 international climate change negotiation. For developing countries that follow an unconventional development trajectory, it is not feasible to set GHG emission targets, even to 2025, based on social and economic development and energy demand projections estimated under hypothetical scenarios. Hence, rather than seeking to impose aggressive and unfeasible emission reduction targets on developing countries, the Durban Platform should focus more on mitigation actions that help developing countries to curb GHG pollution.

Concrete commitments to establish effective finance and technology support mechanisms are the key. To curb GHG emissions and achieve low-carbon development in developing countries require political commitments as well as funding and technology support from the international community. Advanced technology increases energy efficiency and thereby reduces energy use and GHG emissions. However, the acquisition, upgrade and promotion of technology needs to mobilize a huge amount of investment, and the application of renewable energy such as wind and solar energy has a much higher cost than does the use of coal and fossil fuel. Along these lines, international cooperation to achieve GHG reductions cannot be established without a sharing mechanism for climate-friendly technology and an effective access to finance and a funding guarantee mechanism.

References

Chen, Y., Pan, J.H. & Xie, L.H. (2008). Energy embodied in goods of international trade in China: Calculation and policy implications. *Economic Research Journal* **7**(003), 11–25.

China Climate Change Info-Net (2006). Eleventh Five-Year Plan Realizes Energy Saving of 630 Million Tons of Coal Equivalent which Equal to 1.46 Billion Tons of Carbon Dioxide Emissions Reduction. Available at: http://www.ccchina.gov.cn/cn/NewsInfo.asp?NewsId=29078 Accessed 11 April 2012.

China News (2011). The Output of Industries Such As Steel and Cement Increased in 2010. Available at: http://www.chinanews.com/cj/2011/01-28/2818410.shtml. Accessed 14 April 2012.

International Monetary Fund (2010). World Economic Outlook Database. Accessed 12 April 2012.

Ma, J.H. (2011). National Economy Performance Well in General. Available at: http://www.stats.gov.cn/tjfx/jdfx/t20110120_402699441.htm. Accessed 14 April 2012.

National Bureau of Statistics of China (2010). Residential energy consumption per capita. *China Energy Statistical Yearbook*

National Bureau of Statistics of China (2011). Total energy consumption and composition. *China Energy Statistics Yearbook*.

National Bureau of Statistics of China (2012). Macroeconomic Data. Available at: http://finance.chinanews.com/cj/2012/01-17/3610037.shtml. Accessed 11 April 2012.

National Development and Reform Commission of P. R. China (2007). China's National Climate Change Programme. Issued on June 4 2007. Available at: http://www.china.org.cn/english/environment/213624.htm. Accessed 15 April 2012.

Xiao, M. (2010). China Reset the Poverty Standard with Annual Income of 1500 Yuan in 2011. Available at: http://finance.ifeng.com/news/20101224/3107328.shtml. Accessed 11 April 2012.

Chapter 4

Sustainable Growth and Climate Change: Evolution of India's Strategies

Ruth Kattumuri and Darshini Ravindranath
India Observatory and Asia Research Centre,
London School of Economics and Political Science,
London, UK

With its population of over 1.2 billion and vulnerability to climate change, its history of low emissions and because of its democratic, cultural, political and scientific strengths, India is a key player in the global climate change debate. It has been playing an increasingly constructive role in international climate change negotiations. India's domestic climate policy is also becoming more ambitious as India progresses toward its 12th Five-Year Plan objectives for faster, sustainable and more inclusive growth. The country's objectives are achievable but will require faster and stronger action; efficient implementation strategies; greater co-ordination between states and among sectors; strengthening of public–private partnerships; and enhancing international collaborations.

1. Introduction

The *UNEP Year Book* (2009) states that, "one of the most pressing and complex challenges facing our generation is the search for a workable synthesis of economic relations and environmental realities". India is especially vulnerable to the impacts of climate change due to a large fraction of its population living in coastal areas, pressures on water supply, dependence on the Himalayas, erratic monsoon patterns, and the presence of many populous countries along its northern borders. Stern *et al.* (2012) reiterate that low-carbon growth is necessary in the developing world for overcoming poverty and managing climate change.

The scientific evidence of the scale of climate change and the risk of delaying action clearly exists (Stern, 2012). The history of emissions is unarguably inequitable; a population consisting of 1 billion from the rich countries (about 15% of world population) are responsible for more than

60% of current greenhouse gases (GHGs) concentrations. As an increasingly connected "global village", it is for everyone's mutual benefit to learn to avoid past mistakes, mitigate the damage already done as well as limit further damage, and adapt to sustainable growth. This has to be done through co-operation, collaboration, and integrated action to accelerate designing of low-carbon growth and development models, technologies and policies that can support the aspirations of the growing populations of the developing world while sustaining the requirements of the developed world.

The debate for a global framework that is effective in proportion with the scale of the challenge, efficient in keeping the cost of emissions down, and equitable, remains ongoing. There has been consistent discussion, since the 15th Conference of Parties (COP) in Copenhagen, on the contribution to GHG emission savings from developing countries. Developments at COP 16 (Cancun) and COP 17 (Durban) require governments and international organizations within developing countries to make increased efforts to incorporate the climate change agenda within their core processes.

India's stated priority was to avoid unnecessary and costly emission restrictions that can reduce its ability to grow and to reduce poverty. The debate on Common but Differentiated Responsibility (CBDR) was highlighted and equity outcomes were argued. Nearly 80% of India's population of over 1.2 billion (about 800 million) still survive on less than US$ 2 a day (Ghosh, 2009). Notions of equity would point to the rich countries supporting investments to cut emissions elsewhere, particularly in the poorest developing countries, as well as making radical cuts in their own.

Green growth is now a necessity with legally binding emissions cuts likely to be introduced by 2020, under the Durban agreements. At the United Nations Conference on Sustainable Development (UNCSD) or Rio+20 in June 2012, negotiations concluded with a Rio outcome document, titled "The Future We Want". The strategy document establishes a roadmap for a green economy, in the context of sustainable development and poverty eradication.

With its large population high dependence on climate vulnerable sectors, history of low emissions and because of its democratic, cultural, political and scientific strengths, India is a key player in the global climate change debate. India is part of the G77 and China Group, a member of the BASIC group, along with Brazil, China and South Africa. In line with its international importance, India's domestic climate policy landscape is also becoming more ambitious. According to Atteridge et al. (2012), Indian climate diplomacy is now being woven into wider foreign policy objectives, particularly its strategically important relationships with the United States and China. A desire to foster these relationships has encouraged India to introduce some flexibility to its previously fixed negotiating positions.

Influenced by international negotiations, the domestic policy dialogue is now shifting in India in important ways toward a more "internationalist" and proactive approach (Vihma, 2011). For instance, the recent commitment, through the Copenhagen Accord (2009), to reduce carbon intensity of the economy by 20–25% by 2020 with respect to 2005 shows some departure from a climate policy position focussed exclusively on emissions per capita. India is searching for win–win options that would allow it to reduce emissions while enhancing development (Walsh *et al.*, 2011). In a review of India's performance in the 11th Five-Year Plan (FYP) and consideration of future priorities, Ahluwalia (2011) identified four critical challenges for the 12th FYP (2012–2017), all of which relate to climate change. These are managing energy requirements; managing water resources; addressing likely problems from rapid urbanization; and ensuring protection of the environment in a manner that facilitates rapid growth.

There is growing awareness and knowledge of vulnerability to climate change in India and the need to manage it actively. This chapter attempts to understand the evolution of India's strategies to address climate change in the context of sustainable growth and development. It is hoped that the analysis will highlight more clearly the key opportunities and challenges faced by India in the formulation of its future climate policy together with low-carbon growth and poverty reduction. It is expected that studying India's evolving climate policies will help contribute to better understand existing and future rhetoric on the regional perspectives of climate change.

2. Climate Change in India

2.1. *India's emissions*

As India's economy has been growing rapidly in recent years, its emissions have also been increasing. A report by the Indian Network of Climate Change Assessment (INCCA), instituted by the Ministry of Environment and Forests (MoEF), indicates that emissions have increased by nearly 58% between 1994 and 2007 and are projected to grow to 70% by 2020 (INCCA, 2010a) (Figure 1). Emissions from energy (including electricity, transport, residential, and others) accounted for the major proportion of 58% of total emissions, while industry (mainly from mineral and metal industries) and

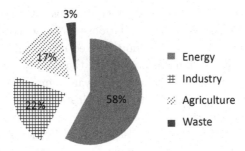

Figure 1.   Percent of net CO$_2$ emissions in India by Sector (2007).
Source: INCCA (2010a).

agriculture (owing mainly to methane emissions from livestock and rice paddy cultivation) were the other major contributors, at 22% and 17% respectively.

The IPCC (2007) predicts that India will experience the greatest increase in energy and GHG emissions in the world if it sustains its current high annual economic growth rate. International Energy Agency (IEA) forecasts that India will become the third largest emitter of GHGs by 2015.

India's emissions intensity of GDP (2005) was around 760 tonnes of CO$_{2e}$ per million dollars of GDP. This is only slightly higher than the US (600 tonnes) but well below China (1,400 tonnes). Overall, India accounts for only 2% of cumulative energy-related emissions since 1850. On a per capita basis, India's emissions are 70% below the world average and 93% below those of the United States (Pew Centre, 2008).

2.2. Vulnerability to climate change

Climate change may alter the distribution and quality of India's natural resources and adversely affect the livelihoods of its people. With an economy closely tied to its natural resources such as agriculture, water, and forestry, India may face major threats because of the projected changes in climate (Prime Minister's Council on Climate change (PMCCC), 2008). A study by National Communications (NATCOM) highlights these sectors as most vulnerable to the projected changes in surface temperate, precipitation patterns and rising sea levels (MoEF, 2004).

A report by the Planning Commission of India (2007) indicated that many regions in India are highly vulnerable to natural and other disasters on account of geological conditions. About 60% of the landmass is susceptible to earthquakes, 68% is susceptible to drought, and over 8% is prone to floods. Of the nearly 7,500 kilometers long coastline, approximately 5,700 kilometers is prone to cyclones. With urbanization and concentration of population in metropolitan cities, more people are becoming vulnerable to locational disasters. Another study published by MoEF in 2010 projects the climate and impacts on four eco-sensitive zones till the 2030s, covering major regions in India, i.e. Himalayan region, the North-Eastern region, the Western Ghats, and the Coastal region. The sectors covered are agriculture, forests and biodiversity, water resources, and coastal zones. This study suggests that the four eco-sensitive regions are vulnerable to projected climate change in the short to medium term. Table 1 evidences India's vulnerability to climate change.

India has several agro-ecological zones with varying degrees of natural resource endowment, rainfall patterns, social and economic vulnerabilities.

Table 1. Summary of climate change projections for India.

Indicator	Climate change projections
Temperature variability	An overall warming with a net increase in annual temperatures in the 2030s ranging between 1.7 and 2.2°C, with extreme temperatures increasing by 1–4°C, with maximum increase in coastal regions.
Precipitation variability	All regions are projected to experience an increase in precipitation (annual mean increase of 7–20%) in the 2030s and the increase is highest in the Himalayan region and lowest in the North Eastern region.
Extreme events — drought	A sharp drop in groundwater tables across the entire Indo-Gangetic plain. The Ganga, Narmada, Krishna, and Kaveri rivers are expected to experience seasonal or regular water stress, impacting western, northern and eastern India.
Extreme events — flooding	All the regions are likely to experience flooding exceeding the existing magnitude by 10–30% and a sea surface temperature rise of 2–4°C, which is expected to induce a 10–20% increase in cyclone intensity in the Indian Ocean (by 2030).
Rising sea level	Sea level along the Indian coast has been rising at the rate of 1.3 mm/year and is likely to rise in consonance with the global sea level rise (SLR). Significant coastal inundation is already observed with a 1 m SLR, especially in the low-lying areas.
Environmental health risk	Increased occurrences of environment-related health risks, due to extreme temperatures, flooding, and SLRs.

Source: Derived from scientific and policy studies by Chaturvedi *et al.* (2011), Gosain *et al.* (2011), Krishna Kumar *et al.* (2011), INCCA (2010b), Aggarwal *et al.* (2009), Revi (2008) and IPCC (2007).

O'Brien *et al.* (2004) depicted varying climate change vulnerability in India, through district-level mapping of climate change vulnerability, measured as a composite of adaptive capacity and climate sensitivity under exposure to climate change. Districts were ranked and presented as quantiles.

O'Brien and colleagues (2004) have shown that the magnitude of impact and vulnerability of the population are likely to vary greatly by region and sector. The distributional consequences of climate change within India will continue to pose major challenges to India's development goals. Hence, policies need to be proactive to incorporate both climate change mitigation and adaptation programs across India with particular focus on most vulnerable districts.

3. Key Climate Change Strategies up to the Eleventh FYP

Mapping the evolution of climate change development policy in India is difficult due to changing priorities and perspectives of the Government over the years. Furthermore, the sheer variety of physical geography, social structures, ecological zones and political leaderships ensure limited cohesive information and analyses on India's evolving perceptions of climate change and the impacts on national policy development. An attempt is made in the following section to track key junctures leading to recent climate policy proliferation in India.

3.1. *The Stockholm UN Conference*

India's presence was first felt at the *Stockholm United Nations Conference on the Human Environment* in 1972, which was the first major conference on international environmental issues. Linnér and Selin (2003) comment on the legacy of the 1972 UN conference and the scientific conferences preceding it, as having a real marked impact in paving the way for global environmental policies. The polluter pays principle was debated at this conference. The then Prime Minister Indira Gandhi (only head of state to attend this conference) spoke of the link between poverty and environmental degradation when she attributed pollution primarily to poverty and underdevelopment. Rogers (1999) stated that on hearing this statement, made by the head of state of a developing country such as India, many countries attending the conference expressed concern that environmental goals could detract from their development objectives.

Early policies in India revolved around the problem of energy scarcity and energy conservation. Following from this conference, some efforts were made to address environmental issues in India in 1972 and the MoEF was set up at the Centre. This was instrumental in enactment of the Wildlife Protection Act and the Forest Conservation Act; project Tiger was initiated; and awareness campaigns were set up, which promoted advertisements and distribution of posters and other printed material.

3.2. The UNFCCC

The 8th (1992–1997) and 9th (1997–2002) FYPs were critical to the development of climate change policy in India and brought about considerable change in addressing energy efficiency.

The *United Nations Conference on Environment and Development* (UNCED), popularly known as the Earth Summit, held in Rio de Janeiro (1992) was a turning point in global and Indian efforts to address climate change. The underlying theme of the summit was that integration and interrelation were at the heart of sustainable development and to achieve this, the Rio declaration emphasized a new and equitable global partnership, and priority to be given to the special situation and needs of developing countries (Principle 6 of the Rio declaration agenda, agenda 21). This ultimately led the way toward the principle of CBDR (UNFCCC, 1992):

- The largest share of historical and current global emissions of GHGs has originated in developed countries.
- Per capita emissions in developing countries are still relatively low.
- The share of global emissions originating in developing countries will grow to meet their social and development needs.

Under United Nations Framework Convention on Climate Change (UNFCCC), developing countries such as India do not have binding GHG mitigation commitments in recognition of their small contribution to the greenhouse problem as well as low financial and technical capacities. India agreed to and signed UNFCCC on 10 June 1992 and ratified it on 1 November 1993.

3.3. Kyoto Protocol

Government of India agreed to the Kyoto Protocol (KP) toward the beginning of 10th FYP in August 2002 and it was ratified in 2005. The major distinction between KP and the 1992 Convention (UNFCCC) is that while the Convention encouraged industrialized countries to stabilize GHG

emissions, KP commits them to do so (UNFCCC, 2012). As a signatory
to the KP, India benefits from investment through the Clean Development
Mechanism (CDM). This provides private sector funds for projects that
reduce emissions, via carbon-trading schemes. About a third of the projects
registered by CDM executive board were from India. Projects registered by
the Indian National CDM Authority have facilitated investment of over
US$ 26 million (Stern et al., 2010).

Bidwai (2012) suggests that the domestic impact of the shift caused
by KP is even more significant than its global impact. MoEF initiated
NATCOM in response to KP for assessing anthropogenic GHG emissions
from various sources and their removal by sinks not controlled by the
Montreal Protocol. The first report was submitted in 2002 and the second is
currently in progress. NATCOM process comprises comprehensive scientific
and technical exercises for estimating GHG emissions from different sectors;
attempt to reduce uncertainties in current estimations; development of
sector-and-technology-specific emission coefficients pertinent to India; and
assessment of the adverse impacts of climate change and strategies for
adapting to these impacts. GHG inventory for the country being prepared,
with base year 1994, will cover five sectors: (i) energy, (ii) industrial
processes, (iii) agriculture, (iv) forestry, and (v) waste (MoEF, 2004). This
exercise involves detailed work on estimation of sectoral GHG emissions
and identification of country-specific emission factors. Vulnerability and
adaptation assessment is also part of the NATCOM project.

Additionally, the 10th FYP (2002–2007), prepared with the backdrop
of Orissa cyclone, Gujarat earthquake, and end of the International Decade
of Natural Disaster Reduction, recognized disaster management as a
development issue for the first time. The government also realized the
importance of promoting energy efficiency to meet the growing energy need,
to power economic growth. The Integrated Energy Policy report was set up
to review and recommend ways to meet the demand for energy services
of all sectors through safe, clean and convenient forms of energy at least
cost and in a technically efficient, economically viable and environmentally
sustainable way (Planning Commission, 2006).

3.4. The 11th FYP

By the start of the 11th FYP (2007–2012), India's climate policy had
matured from concerns about energy conservation to energy efficiency. By
the end of the 10th FYP and the beginning of the 11th FYP the growth rate

had increased to 9.1% from a 5.3% growth rate in the 9th FYP (Planning Commission, 1997).

In recognition of the dangers posed by India's large population, economic growth and ever-increasing demand on natural resources such as energy and water, the government realized the urgent need to balance its growth strategies with climate change. While the period around the 10th FYP brought about many positive changes for India in terms of policy planning, the 11th FYP was to build on this experience by integrating environment considerations into policy-making in all sectors of the economy — infrastructure, transport, water supply, sanitation, industry, agriculture, and anti-poverty programs. The Planning Commission was also committed to strengthening the regulatory framework for environment management so that development decisions do not impinge adversely on sustainability. The key themes highlighted in the 11th FYP were:

- Afforestation and Joint Forest Management
- Improving Air Quality
- Water Quality
- Waste Management
- Biodiversity
- Environmental Research and Development
- Disaster Management

The plan developed a number of sector-specific policy targets, such as, to reach 33% forest and tree cover requiring an additional coverage of about 10–11 million hectares of forestland; and to achieve WHO targets of air quality in all major cities by 2011–2012. The 11th FYP included an indicative target of increasing energy efficiency by 20% by 2016–2017. The aim was to increase the installed capacity for renewable power (excluding large hydropower) by 14,500 MW, i.e. 20% of the overall increase in installed utility-based capacity (78,577 MW). The 11th plan had also set a goal of cutting emissions by 20%.

The 11th plan clearly strategized that, since a substantial adverse change in climate is unavoidable even with the optimal mitigation response, the process of adaptation to climate change must have priority (Ravindranath *et al.*, 2012). The plan recognized the need to incorporate adaptation responses in relevant programs, including those relating to watershed management, coastal zone planning and regulation, forestry management, agricultural technologies and practices, and health.

3.5. *National action plan on climate change*

Prime Minister Manmohan Singh launched India's National Action Plan on Climate Change (NAPCC) on 30 June 2008. Prepared by the specially constituted Prime Minister's Council on Climate Change, the document was intended to detail India's plans for combating climate change. The approach suggested by NAPCC for India is, "a directional shift in the development pathway" that promotes development objectives while additionally yielding co-benefits for addressing climate change effectively."

NAPCC identified eight missions to address climate change mitigation, adaptation, and knowledge management. The focus of these missions is on "promoting understanding of climate change, adaptation and mitigation, energy efficiency, and natural resource conservation". The missions and their status are highlighted in Table 2.

To address the multiplicity of issues for a large, diverse, and democratic country such as India through a single national climate change policy can be extremely challenging. The NAPCC provides a comprehensive policy framework to address the relevant issues to tackle climate change in India including the creation of strategic knowledge mission. It provides the framework for the various stakeholders and states to engage with the respective missions to build on, develop, expand, enable and implement the required regional and sectoral programs and strategies. This requires tremendous effort from all concerned — public sector, private sector, knowledge leaders, non-governmental organizations (NGOs), civil society, and local communities, to consolidate and collaborate to enable the implementation of these Missions.

Most recently, a detailed analysis of the missions have been conducted using a "modified Delphi method", with the authors adopting a process of expert interviews for each of the eight missions (Byravan and Rajan, 2012). The study concentrates largely on the design of the missions; as it is still too early to evaluate the implementation. A majority of the experts interviewed presented the view that the context, pressures and challenges in developing the national climate policy have resulted in certain tensions that run through the missions. They, however recognize and hope that the mission designs will be dynamic and will be revised with the learning that comes from implementing the programs.

Table 2.   Eight missions of national action plan on climate change.

Mission	Goals	Status
Solar	• The NAPCC aims to promote the development and use of solar energy for power generation and other uses, with the ultimate objective of making solar competitive with fossil-based energy options. • Rural applications are to be pursued through public–private partnership.	• A target of delivering 80% coverage for all low temperature (<150°C) applications of solar energy in urban areas, industries, and commercial establishments. • A target of 60% coverage for medium temperature (150 to 250°C) applications. • A target of 1,000 MW/annum of photovoltaic production from integrated facilities by 2017 as well as 1,000 MW of concentrating solar power generation capacity. • The deadline for achieving this is the duration of the 11th and 12th FYPs to 2017.
Enhanced energy efficiency	• Wide and diverse range of policy instruments to overcome the barriers to adoption of energy-efficient options in residential and commercial sectors. • Highlight the need for a more competitive market for energy-efficient products and advocate involving all stakeholders. • The need for technology transfer from developed countries.	Current initiatives are expected to yield savings of 10,000 MW by 2012.
Sustainable habitat	To promote energy efficiency as a core component of urban planning (i.e. buildings, waste management, transport, and fuel economy standards).	Information not available.
Water	• To conserve water, minimize wastage, and ensure more equitable distribution through integrated water resource management.	The mission aims to optimize water use by increasing water use efficiency by 20%, recycling of wastewater, and implementation of Integrated Water Resource Management (IWRM).

(Continued)

Table 2. (*Continued*)

Mission	Goals	Status
	• To tackle variability in rainfall and river flows such as enhancing surface and underground water storage, rainwater harvesting, and more efficient irrigation systems like sprinklers or drip irrigation.	
Sustaining the Himalayan ecosystem	The plan aims to conserve biodiversity, forest cover, and other ecological values in the Himalayan region, where glaciers that are a major source of India's water supply are projected to recede as a result of global warming.	Not available.
Green India	Aims at enhancing ecosystem services such as carbon sinks.	Goals include the afforestation of 6 million hectares of degraded forest lands and expanding forest cover from 23 to 33% of India's territory.
Sustainable agriculture	The plan aims to support climate adaptation in agriculture through the development of climate-resilient crops, expansion of weather insurance mechanisms, agricultural practices, and improving productivity of rain-fed agriculture.	Not available.
Strategic knowledge for climate change	To gain better understanding of climate science, impacts, and challenges, the plan envisions a new Climate Science Research Fund, improved climate modeling, and increased international collaboration. It also encourages private sector initiatives to develop M&A technologies through venture capital funds.	Not available.

Source: Compiled from Prime Minister's Council on Climate Change (2008) and Lead International (2012).

3.6. State action plans on climate change

Following from NAPCC, all Indian states and union territories have been urged to prepare state action plans on climate change (SAPCC), detailing sector specific plans to adapt and mitigate climate change at the state level. Some states have initiated studies and aim to identify the most vulnerable sectors and regions to projected climate change and also to develop adaptation projects. The state action plans also aim at assessing GHG emissions and identifying potential mitigation programs and projects.

Thus far, a majority of states and union territories (16 out of 28) including New Delhi, Himachal Pradesh, Orissa, Uttaranchal, Karnataka, Chandigarh, Haryana, West Bengal, and all north-eastern states barring Tripura are in the process of working their plans on climate change. Some plans are being developed through a broad participatory planning process (GTZ, 2011). Some studies have analyzed preliminary state action plans and conclude that most of the initial documents and drafts have been prepared without targets, timelines, financial implications and allocations that do not prescribe the period of operation (Jha, 2011).

The development of comprehensive and rigorous state action plans requires all major stakeholders, including government officials from various government departments, policy-makers, academics, NGOs, scientists, the private sector, civil society and local communities to collaborate to develop actionable plans and ensure their implementation.

The states action plans are still works in progress and no doubt require capacity and skills for the development and implementation for climate change action plans. The Bangalore Climate Change Initiative — Karnataka (BCCI-K) is an example of an initiative, which is a collaboration of national and international consortia of policy-makers, practitioner researchers and donors who support the government of Karnataka to formulate the official SAPCC (BCCI-K, 2011).

4. 12th FYP

India is planning to progress beyond the objectives of faster, inclusive growth of 11th FYP to faster, sustainable and more inclusive growth in the 12th FYP (2012–2017). The Approach Paper for 12th FYP clearly states the need to meet the challenges of climate change through management of water, forests, land and energy requirements. This chapter also calls for implementing the activities outlined under various missions of NAPCC and a low carbon mitigation strategy (Planning Commission, 2011a).

The Planning Commission had drawn up "Twelve Strategy Challenges" to initiate consultations and engage with state governments and the general public for preparation of 12th FYP. The strategy challenges refer to core areas that require new approaches to produce the desired results and include the following environment-related issues:

- Managing the environment and ecology
- Markets for efficiency and inclusion
- Decentralization, empowerment and knowledge for sustainable development
- Technology and innovation
- Rural transformation and sustained growth of agriculture
- Improved access to quality education
- Managing urbanization

The government of India is of the view that an effective strategy for addressing climate change should permeate the planning process at three levels.

1. In articulating the overall approach of the FYP, considerations of sustainable development and low-carbon inclusive growth should be integrated in all sectors.
2. In specific sectors, which are considered particularly vulnerable to climate change, a climate change adaptation strategy should be built into their respective plans.
3. In the environment and forests sector, specific schemes and programs should be launched to strengthen the capacity for making scientific assessment, GHG measurement and monitoring, and achieve environmental protection through a coherent strategy of adaptation and mitigation actions.

Integrating the objectives of NAPCC and SAPCC in addition to domestic mitigation goals in the development strategy of the respective sectors is considered an optimal strategy (Planning Commission, 2011b). To be effective, the plan has to be implemented through an appropriate mechanism that should decide, finance and administer the process of achieving the domestic mitigation goals. The government with the help of Planning Commission is therefore revising their overall strategy to respond to these new priorities. A number of strategy documents relevant to sustainable low-carbon growth have been released in the initial stages of the 12th FYP. Mainstreaming climate considerations, particularly in sectors that will impact the long-term development of the country is considered vital and the 12th plan period is likely to bring welcome structural changes to policies in India.

4.1. *Low-carbon growth strategy*

In January 2010, Prime Minister Manmohan Singh constituted a 26-member expert group, chaired by Kirit Parikh, to inform the Planning Commission to help develop a low-carbon growth strategy for India as it sets out the framework for 12th FYP. Members of this group were drawn from government, industry, academia, and civil society and the interim report was released in May 2011. This report set out options and policies for reducing emissions intensity across power, transport, industry, buildings, and forest sectors.

The report indicates India may be able to reduce emission intensity of GDP by around 25% over the period 2005–2020. It suggests that intensive efforts, including new policies and technologies, would ensure India could achieve both 8% economic growth through the year 2020, and a reduction of emissions intensity by nearly 35%. The projections are in line with India's Copenhagen Accord commitment, to reduce emissions intensity of its GDP 20–25% by 2020 (from 2005 levels).

The interim report considered two scenarios of 8% GDP growth rate as well as 9% GDP growth rate until 2020 (Table 3). Within each scenario, it analyses what can be achieved on a sectoral basis through "determined" measures (vigorous and effective implementation of policies that are already in place or being contemplated by the government) and "aggressive" measures (implementation of current policies plus design and implementation of new policies, along with significant deployment of new technologies and increased innovation). In these scenarios, the projections for emissions intensity reductions by 2020, over a 2005 baseline, vary from as low as 23.88% (9% growth rate and determined effort) to 34.40% (8% growth rate and aggressive effort).

4.2. *Sustainable development policies and programs*

The earlier sections have attempted to document India's evolving framework for sustainable development since the UN conference in 1972. Table 4 consolidates key policies and programs introduced progressively by the government in the last decade. The most recent schemes, such as MGNREGA, Greening India, NAPCC, have been formulated to incorporate environmental policies with sustainable growth and indicate strong commitment to inclusive social and economic development. A majority of the policies and programs are ongoing and will contribute greatly to the country's sustainable development, which will become evident in the next 5 to 10 years.

Table 3. Projected emission intensity reduction over 2005 levels.

SI.	Growth scenarios Higher and lower ends of the range	2005 emissions	2020 with 8% GDP growth		2020 with 9% GDP growth	
			Determined effort	Aggressive effort	Determined effort	Aggressive effort
1	Emissions at 2005 levels (MT CO_2-eq)	1,433	4,571	4,571	5,248	5,248
2	Actual and projected emission (MT CO_2-eq)	1,433	3,537	3,071	4,016	3,521
3	Emissions intensity (grams CO_2-eq/ Rs. GDP)	56.21	42.47	36.87	42.79	37.51
4	Percentage reduction in emission intensity	—	24.44%	34.40%	23.88%	33.27%

Source: Planning Commission (2011c).

The prioritization and commitment to sustainable development programs are also evident in the increased government spending. Data from Union Budget and economic survey reports of India indicate that allocation for sustainable growth and development has grown substantially. For example, since the early 1970s, total planned allocation of resources has increased from INR 394 billion in the 5th FYP (1974–1979) to INR 36,447 billion during the 11th FYP (2007–2011). These resources are provided to key economic sectors, such as agriculture and allied activities, rural development, energy, industry, and minerals and social services. Two sectors in particular, whose shares have significantly increased over the years, are energy and social services (Table 5).

Table 4.   Sustainable development — Key policies and programs.

Key policies and programs, year instituted	Key characteristics
National Environment Policies	
National Environmental Policy, 2006	• Intended to be a guide to action: in regulatory reform, programs, and projects for environmental conservation. • Asserts that the most viable basis of environmental conservation is to ensure that people gain better livelihoods from the act of conservation of natural resources than from environmental degradation.
National Action Plan on Climate Change, 2008	• Strong linking of development and climate change. • Eight missions of NAPCC that focus on solar energy, energy efficiency, sustainable habitat, water, sustaining the Himalayan eco-system, Green India, sustainable agriculture, and strategic knowledge for climate change. • Currently being implemented by the nodal ministries to address vulnerability to climate change and enhance capacity at central and state levels.
Ecosystems and ecology	
National Forest Policy, 1988	• Issue necessary resolutions and guidelines to initiate stronger institutional framework. • Involve local communities through Joint Forest Management.
National Forestry Action Programme, 1999	• A comprehensive 20-year strategy and long-term work plan formulated to address issues underlying the major problems of the forestry sector.
National Afforestation Programme, 2002	• Flagship program of the National Afforestation and Eco-development Board (NAEB). • Provision of physical and capacity building support to Forest Development Agencies (FDAs), which are the implementing agencies. • Promote plantations in degraded forest land.
Integrated Watershed Management Programme, 2009	• Restore the ecological balance by harnessing, conserving, and developing degraded natural resources such as soil, vegetative cover, and water.
National Mission for a Green India, 2011	• Double India's afforested areas by 2020, adding an additional 10 million hectares. • Enable forests to absorb 50–60 million tonnes of CO_2 annually, offsetting about 6% of India's annual emissions.

(Continued)

Table 4. (*Continued*)

Key policies and programs, year instituted	Key characteristics
Mission Clean Ganga Initiative, 2012	• Ensure effective abatement of pollution and conservation of river Ganga by adopting a river basin approach for comprehensive planning and management.

Agriculture and Food

National Agricultural Policy, 2002	• The policy seeks to promote technically sound, economically viable, environmentally non-degrading, and socially acceptable use of country's natural resources — land, water, and inherent endowment to promote sustainable development of agriculture.
Fodder and Feed Development Scheme, 2005	• Centrally Sponsored Fodder Development Scheme ensuring efficient use of available fodder/feed. • Instruments for interventions include: (i) strengthening of feed testing laboratories; (ii) introduction of chaff cutters; (iii) establishment of silage making units; and (iv) demonstration of Azolla cultivation and production units, among others.
National Food Security Mission, 2007	• Enhance production of rice by 10 million tonnes, wheat by 8 million tonnes, and pulses by 2 million tonnes by the end of the Eleventh FYP. • The approach is to bridge the yield gap with respect to these crops through dissemination of improved technologies and farm management practices.

Urban sustainability

National Urban Transport Policy, 2006	• Incorporating urban transport as an important parameter in urban planning. • Ensuring more equitable allocation of road space with people rather than vehicles as the main focus. • Encouraging greater use of public transport and non-motorized modes of transport. • Overall, ensuring safe, affordable, quick, comfortable, reliable, and sustainable access to the growing numbers of city residents.
National Urban Housing and Habitat Policy, 2007	• Promoting sustainable development of habitat in the country with a view to ensuring equitable supply of land, shelter, and services at affordable prices to all sections of society.

(*Continued*)

Table 4. (*Continued*)

Key policies and programs, year instituted	Key characteristics
National Urban Sanitation Policy, 2008	• Generate awareness. • Promote integrated citywide sanitation. • Encourage safe disposal and proper operation and maintenance of all sanitary installations.

Energy, Trade and Transport

Technological Upgradation Fund, 1999	• Promote imports of capital goods for certain sectors under the Export Promotion Capital Goods (EPCG) scheme at 0% duty.
Auto Fuel Policy, 2002	• Identify a road map to vehicle and fuel norms in India. • Encourage fuel economy based on levying of differential tax on two wheelers and passenger cars/jeeps.
Integrated Energy Policy, 2008	• The vision is to create an environment that can help reliably meet the energy demands of all sectors. • According to the Planning Commission, this would require India to pursue all available fuel options, in addition to working toward competitive energy markets, transparent subsidies, improved efficiencies across the energy chain, and policies that reflect the externalities of energy consumption.
Perform, Achieve and Trade (PAT), 2012	• PAT is a market-based mechanism — through tradable energy saving certificates (ESCerts) — to enhance energy efficiency in "designated consumers" that are large energy-intensive industries and facilities.

Equitable and Inclusive policies

National Policy for Empowerment of Women, 2001	• To enable advancement, development and empowerment of women.
Mahatma Gandhi National Rural Employment Guarantee Scheme (MGNREGA), 2005	• Enhancing the livelihood security of people in rural areas by guaranteeing minimum 100 days of wage-employment in a financial year, to a rural household whose adult member is willing to work. • Failing this, the person will be provided with a daily unemployment allowance (one third to half of the minimum wage).
National Rehabilitation and Resettlement Policy, 2007	• Minimize displacement from development activities and protecting the rights of weaker sections of society. • Design adequate rehabilitation packages.

(Continued)

Table 4. (*Continued*)

Key policies and programs, year instituted	Key characteristics
National Disaster Management Policy, 2009	• A vision of building a safe and disaster resilient India by developing a holistic, proactive, multi-disaster oriented, and technology, driven strategy through a culture of prevention, mitigation, preparedness, and response.
National Rural Livelihood Mission, 2009	• Reducing poverty among rural BPL by promoting diversified and gainful self-employment and wage employment opportunities which would lead to an appreciable increase in income on sustainable basis.
	• In the long run, it will ensure broadbased inclusive growth and reduce disparities by spreading out benefits from the islands of growth across regions, sectors and communities.

Source: Adapted from MoEF (2011) report on sustainable development.

Table 5. **Recent government spending on major sustainability programs.**

Programs	Actual (INR million) 2009–2010	Revise (INR million) 2010–2011	Budgeted (INR million) 2011–2012
Mahatma Gandhi National Rural Employment Guarantee Scheme (MGNREGS)	3,35,394	4,01,000	4,00,000
National Rural Livelihood Mission/Swarna Jayanti Gramin Swarojgar Yojana (SGSY)	22,280	26,830	26,216
Indira Awas Yojana — Housing for Poor	87,999	93,335	89,960
Swarna Jayanti Shahari Rozgar Yojana (SJSRY) — employment for urban unemployed	4,850	5,362	0
Forest Conservation, Development and Regeneration	820	567	567
National Afforestation and Eco-development Programme	3,430	2,595	2,530
Renewable Energy for Rural Applications	138	1,620	1,760
Renewable Energy for Urban, Industrial and Commercial Applications	647	370	100
National Rural Health Mission (NRHM)	1,47,027	1,35,403	1,61,407
Provision for Urban Amenities in Rural Areas (PURA)	—	662	900
Jawahar Lal Nehru National Urban Renewal Mission (JNNURM)	200	200	800
Integrated Low Cost Sanitation Programme	96	10	10

Source: MoEF (2011).
Note: INR 1 million = approximately GBP 11,000.

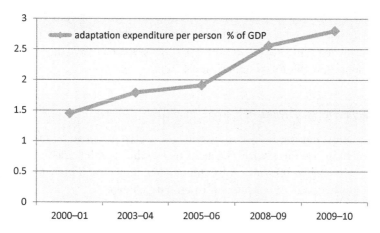

Figure 2. Expenditure on adaptation-oriented programs, India.
Source: Derived from data sourced in MoEF (2011).

The Government of India estimates for adaptation expenditures related to agriculture, water supply, health and sanitation, coastal zones, forests, and extreme weather events, show that the country's expenditure on adaptation oriented schemes has doubled in the last 10 years from 1.45% of GDP in the year 2000–2001 to 2.84% during 2009–2010 (Figure 2).

India's strategy for enhancing environmental quality and promoting adaptive capacity to climate variability is reflected in many of its social and economic development programs, highlighted above. Whilst there is limited information on implementation, the number of programs and allocated funding is proof of government's progressive commitment to combating climate change.

5. Opportunities and Challenges for a Sustainable Future

The global negotiations from Copenhagen (COP 15), Cancun (COP 16), Durban (COP 17), and Doha (COP 18) are re-conceptualizing notions of equity and differentiation. It is evident that by the 12th FYP, India has matured from a climate policy entirely focussed on energy sufficiency to a comprehensive framework incorporating the various factors involved in addressing climate change.

The government of India has taken cautious steps toward incorporating climate change mitigation and adaptation within its overall policy design. Despite some criticisms that none of the policies and programs emphasize targets and judge consequences, there is enough scope within the stated climate agenda to achieve sustainable development in the next five years with commitment and strong action. We discuss some critical opportunities and challenges in the following sections.

5.1. Technology diffusion

As a developing nation, India can benefit from actively enforcing sustainable development procedures with the help of existing technologies as well as through investing in innovation to enhance technologies. This will provide additional advantage of adaptation to climate change.

The pressures on infrastructure, transport, and housing are escalating with rapid urbanization. Hence, it is crucial for India to invest in programs to increase energy efficiency in major carbonintensive industries, and these will additionally yield financial as well as developmental benefits for the country.

India is blessed with natural and renewable resources, such as solar, gas, and wind energy. Renewable resources contribute about 11% to India's electricity generation; of that, solar energy comprises merely 0.01% or about 18 MW per year; this offers great potential for expanding solar power and second generation bio-fuels. Under US$ 19 billion National Solar Mission, launched in 2010, India hopes to generate 1,000 MW of solar power annually by 2013, and as much as 20 GW by 2022. Several companies have been encouraged to invest in solar energy through government subsidies and incentives. Harvey and Segafredo (2011) suggest that India could eliminate blackouts by 2014 and increase the value of national output by around 50% by 2017 through strong energy-efficiency standards.

India's highly developed skills in science and technology offer the potential for innovation and development of energy-efficient low-carbon technologies including solar, biogas, hydroelectric, halting deforestation, carbon capture, and storage. India's skilled human capital provides great opportunities for international collaboration.

Some studies have attempted to forecast the technological changes that will be necessary to sustain India's emissions (McKinsey, 2009; TERI, 2008; UNFCCC, 2007). These include renewable sources such as solar PV, wind, and biomass technologies, in addition to higher thermal efficiency coal plants and energy-efficient building technologies. While the ability for technology transfer as a means to achieve GHG emission reduction is established, there are likely to be significant costs involved. There is a need for innovative financial mechanisms to support the growth in technology diffusion.

5.2. *Innovative finance mechanisms*

McKinsey (2009) estimate that the overall incremental capital expenditure (CAPEX) required in India under the "abatement case" would be approximately US$ 750 billion to US$ 950 billion from 2010 to 2030. The estimates are based on assumptions about the declining costs of certain technologies such as solar energy and LED lighting. The report also highlights that about two-thirds of the abatement potential comes from opportunities that entail a net economic cost to make them viable. This would require fund flows of roughly US$ 16 billion annually between 2010 and 2020, and then US$ 30 billion annually over the decade to 2030. In the power generation sector, TERI (2008) estimated that if India moves along the business-as-usual pathway, the cumulative investment required in the power generation technologies, from 2001/2002 to 2036/2037, would be US$ 1.4 trillion. However, if India were to move along a low carbon pathway, these investment requirements are expected to increase by four to seven times.

International financial mechanisms instituted by the UNFCCC such as the CDM and the Global Environment Facility (GEF) have had mixed results. While India has benefitted from these mechanisms relative to other developing countries, financing has not been available adequately to deliver the scale of transformative change needed to shift India's emissions trajectory.

On the other hand, traditional bilateral and multilateral development funding (including Official Development Assistance (ODA)) has played a complementary role in supporting GHG reductions in India. It has been used to support projects in the clean energy, energy efficiency, urban infrastructure, and forestry sectors. India and other developing countries maintain that ODA financing in climate change should only be viewed as a co-benefit of the finance toward development projects, as they are sensitive to ensuring ODA commitments are not shifted from development projects to fund climate initiatives (Atteridge *et al.*, 2009).

India has also benefitted from investments through private sector funds. Additional global private sector financial flows for investment in carbon-finance, clean coal technologies will enhance entrepreneurship, technical expertise, and innovation and have universal benefits.

While the Indian government has already initiated some ambitious policy measures — particularly pertaining to solar energy and energy efficiency — the effectiveness of international finance mechanisms and other forms of international partnership will be crucial in determining the success of mitigation efforts (Atteridge *et al.*, 2009). This could be done through reforming existing mechanisms such as CDM; improving on the approval process which tends to be long and cumbersome; a drive toward a more sector-based approach that is demand-driven. There is also scope for ODA to continue to play a key role in funding such opportunities with newer paradigms of inclusive development being brought to the fore.

5.3. *Mainstreaming climate change into development programs*

In order for climate change adaptation and mitigation to be sustainable and applicable on a wide scale, it must be incorporated, integrated or "mainstreamed" into the policy apparatus of governments. Mainstreaming in the context of climate change refers to incorporation of climate change considerations into established or ongoing development programs, policies, or management strategies, rather than developing adaptation and mitigation initiatives separately (FAO, 2009). Revising "growth-centric" development plans to respond to the duality of climate change and sustainable development is necessary.

This would also aid in addressing the varying distributional aspects of climate change within India. Policy must consider the fragmented nature of the impacts of climate change on a country as diverse as India (see Table 1). Inclusive, developmental policies and programs that target vulnerable groups such as women should be enhanced. The understanding of distributional implications of climate change at the sub-national level is inadequate and poses a challenge for the development of targeted policies (see also Jacoby *et al.*, 2011). Thus, there is a need for greater research and understanding of the distributional consequences of climate change. This requires that national and regional governments to ensure adequate funding support for undertaking research and analyses at state and local levels for better understanding, which can subsequently enable the development of targeted policies and programs for adaptation and mitigation.

The government of India is mainstreaming both climate change mitigation and adaptation within its developmental framework through policies and action plans. The 12th FYP is a large step in the right direction, as are the sustainability initiatives introduced through programs such as the MGNREGA and NAPCC missions. Government with the aid of the Planning Commission is revising the overall strategy to incorporate low-carbon growth for sustainable development in the 12th FYP. A well-defined implementation strategy can be adopted by the 12th FYP to help in achieving the objective of the various NAPCC missions across all sectors that will impact development so as to move toward a more inclusive long-term sustainable growth. Effective implementation of MGNREGA also offers multiple opportunities for creation of green jobs.

Managing its natural forests and vibrant animal life (tigers, elephants, dolphins, etc.) and restoration of degraded land and low-till agriculture will enable India to achieve its development objectives as well as provide auxiliary benefits to the economy, such as enhancing tourism prospects.

5.4. *Global governance*

India has been playing a more constructive role in recent international climate change negotiations. Moving on from the not very constructive discussions at UNFCCC COP 15 in Copenhagen in 2009, India's delegation to UNFCCC COP 16 in Cancun in 2010 was co-ordinated and purposive. They were instrumental in both setting a better atmosphere for discussion and in achieving progress on specific issues, especially on Monitoring, Reporting, and Verification (MRV). Developing countries agreed to produce biennial update reports on their GHG emissions, which will be reviewed under an international consultation and analysis (ICA) process. India's constructive participation in international negotiations was critical to progress during the international negotiations in Cancun. At COP 16, Indian negotiators were able to get the backing of the EU and G-77 countries and succeeded with their proposal to set up a mechanism for technology transfer to deal with climate change. Similarly, India showed that it has the ability to participate and influence global governance debates at the COP 17 in Durban and the latest UNCSD held in Rio in June 2012. At COP 18 in Doha (November 2012), the four countries of Brazil, South Africa, India, and China (known as the BASIC bloc) released a joint ministerial statement highlighting the need for more ambitious targets by developed countries. India is a key member of the BASIC, given its strategic importance geopolitically. India's role is also crucial to help unlock the US–China deadlock that creates stalemate in the progress toward a legally binding international agreement (Olsson *et al.*, 2010).

This is a strong platform that can be used to bridge deep-seated gaps in climate change strategy in the global and national arena. For instance, the voluntary commitment made by Prime Minister Manmohan Singh in June 2007 at Heiligendamm, that India's per capita emissions level will never exceed the average per capita emissions of developed countries. This implies that India will attempt to go further than the committed measures (Stern *et al.*, 2012). At the national level, India has made a number of voluntary emissions reduction commitments. Dr Singh also signed the Major Economies Forum (MEF) leaders declaration that recognized that global temperature rise "ought not to exceed 2°C" and the need for a "global goal" to reduce "global emissions by 2050". A voluntary target of a reduction in emissions intensity (emissions per unit of output) of 20–25% over the period 1990 to 2020 was also announced in relation to the Copenhagen Accord (December 2009), and the Cancun agreement at UNFCCC (COP 16) in December 2010.

Also critical to India's global governance framework is the implications of the special vulnerabilities acquired through spillover effects from neighboring states such as Bangladesh, Nepal, and Maldives. The most obvious spill-over effect India faces is the large-scale migration from highly vulnerable, disaster prone states like Bangladesh and Maldives into India. Particularly sensitive is the border between India and Bangladesh; which covers a mangrove forest of 10,000 sq. km. and is home to endangered Bengal tigers; 60% of which is in Bangladesh and the rest in India (WWF, 2013). A large number of refugees regularly migrate into India as a result of livelihood loss and problems of water sharing, which is often caused by cyclones and other impacts of climate change. This region of India is highly vulnerable to climate change and dealing with the influx of people from neighbouring countries poses additional burden on the country.

It is apparent that cross-border migration due to climate change might increase the susceptibility of people to climate change in both countries (Panda, 2010). Without adequate bilateral and multilateral institutional arrangements in place to protect climate migrants, it will pose greater risks to India. India's policies and laws on refugees are however not equipped to protect the rights of migrants due to climate change The issue is largely dealt with politically when circumstances arise and there has been minimal support for cross-border migration as an adaptive strategy to deal with the impacts of climate change. More recently, India has shown a willingness to address the issue through forums such as the Indo-Bangladesh Sundarbans Ecosystem Forum (2010), championed by former Environment Minister Jairam Ramesh. Such forums are important for countries in the region to work together and devise new policies to deal with disaster management on a large scale. Due to its prominence in the region and vested interest in the issue, India could take a lead to formalize such deliberations and help facilitate sharing of knowledge, information, and capacity-building programs.

5.5. *Implementation, accountability, and governance*

Implementation, accountability, and governance have been stated as overarching challenges that require much greater attention in the 12th FYP. While India has been developing comprehensive plans at the national level, the development of state level plans has not been fast enough. Inefficiency in implementation and shortage of capacity in the public sector are major challenges.

Managing the developmental needs of 1.2 billion people and tackling climate change in the largest democracy of federal republic of 28 diverse states and 7 union territories where elections happen every year in several state assemblies, is extremely challenging. Disruptive coalition politics and dysfunctional democracy where arguments are taken to the streets rather than debated in parliament impedes progress.

Corruption is rampant in many of the key sectors. It is particularly prevalent in the electricity sector and comprises a major problem for state electricity boards (Gulati, 2006). Transmission and distribution losses in power sector are estimated to be about 50%, out of which about 30% is attributed to theft in connivance with Electricity Boards employees. Clean energy development and deployment in India has shown how information asymmetry, limited regulatory, and public oversight and the calculation and rolling out of incentives and subsidies can cloud decision-making in the sector (WRI, 2011).

India needs to exercise stronger action for emissions reduction across all sectors. Stern (2012) argues that delay increases the risk we would need to undertake radical, rapid and expensive decarbonization in two or three decades, which would result in the scrapping of vast amounts of "'locked-in" capital. He states that if India delays strong action until 2030, then very rapid transition consistent with 450 ppm post-2030 — would need to scrap between US$ 20 and 70 billion of coal plant in India (35–140% of current value).

Expansion of programs based on micro-finance and other innovative financial instruments are required for promoting low-carbon development opportunities for poorer communities through public–private partnerships as well as working in partnership with MDBs.

As described in Table 5 expenditure and funding allocated to programs and policies related to sustainable development have been steadily increasing, which indicates growing commitment by government to tackle climate change and achieve sustainable development. Effective implementation and accountability is required to ensure expenditure is targeted in the right direction.

India is progressing in the right direction in its 12th FYP objectives for faster, sustainable, and more inclusive growth. The country's objectives are achievable but will require faster and stronger action; efficient implementation strategies; greater co-ordination between states and sectors; strengthening public–private partnerships; and enhancing international collaborations.

5.6. *Knowledge management*

Awareness and knowledge has been growing among policy-makers, business community, and general public in recent years. Information, education, and communication (IEC) efforts need to be intensified to enable greater understanding and choices for sustainable behaviors.

In a country with vast and complex geographical, social, and economic systems, there is high regional and sector variability in climatic patterns. This necessitates in-depth regional and sector treatment of vulnerability, adaptation, and mitigation to climate change. Systematic observation networks and research to estimate GHG emissions; sector-specific estimates; developing high-resolution climate scenarios whilst looking into measures and a consultation process on climate change policy formulation are all essential for India (Ravindranath, 2010).

Public, private institutions, and NGOs should work together to scale up the development and implementation of IEC programs to create awareness about climate change and knowledge about adaptation and mitigation across all sections of the population.

A sub-section within the approach paper for India's 12th FYP indicates the need for strengthening scientific research capacity and strategic knowledge for climate change observation and assessment. This requires to be pursued rigorously.

6. Conclusions

The main concerns during the 1970s and 1980s were fuel scarcity and energy conservation. The notion of climate change as a global environmental crisis, with serious economic implications has led both developed and developing countries to pay closer attention. This advent was mainly led by scientific studies that were heralded and that spurned further assessments. India is seemingly at the center of the climate debate.

India's per capita emissions are among the lowest in the world. It is however crucial to inherently adopt sustainable low-carbon growth for its own benefit and maintain emissions at manageable levels. The government of India is aided by increasing recognition of the importance of, and opportunities available from, pursuing sustainable low-carbon growth. Support from developed countries, on both finance and technology, will help India strengthen and achieve its stated objectives. Additionally, India could build on its existing human capital with competence in science and technology and invest further to enhance innovation. International collaborations through knowledge and resource sharing offer opportunities for both developed and developing countries.

Overall, India's intentions, plans, and voluntary targets, and its aim to include a more ambitious strategy for low-carbon growth in its 12th FYP, will further India's standing in the international community and increase its positive influence in moving forward international collaborations and agreement.

It is crucial for India to be proactive in designing and effectively implementing policies for low-carbon growth in order to achieve inclusive and sustainable development for the benefit of its own current population as well as its future generations.

References

Aggarwal, P.K., Pathak, H. & Kumar, N. (2009). *Global Climate Change and Indian Agriculture: A Review of Adaptation Strategies, Trust for Advancement of Agricultural Sciences*, New Delhi, August 2009.

Atteridge, A., Kumar, M.S., Pahuja, N. & Upadhyay, H. (2012). Climate policy in India: What shapes international, national and state policy? *Ambio*, **41**(1), 68–77.

Atteridge, A., Axberg, G.N., Goel, N., Kumar, A., Lazarus, M., Ostwald, M., Polycarp, C., Tollefsen, P., Torvanger, A., Upadhyaya, P. & Zetterberg, L. (2009). *Reducing Greenhouse Gas Emissions in India Financial Mechanisms* and *Opportunities for EU-India Collaboration.* Stockholm, Sweden: Stockholm Environment Institute (SEI).

Ahluwalia, M.S. (2011). Prospects and policy challenges in the twelfth plan, *Economics and Political Weekly*, **46**(21), Special Article.

BCCI-K, (2011). *Bangalore Climate Change Initiative — Karnataka*, An analytical report submitted to Government of Karnataka. Available at: http://www2.lse.ac.uk/asiaResearchCentre/_files/KarnatakaCCactionPlanFinal.pdf. Accessed 30 March 2012.

Bidwai, P. (2012). *The Politics of Climate Change and the Global Crisis: Mortgaging our Future.* New Delhi: Orient Black Swan.

Byravan, S. & Rajan, S.C. (2012). *An Evaluation of India's National Action Plan on Climate Change*, July 2012. IIT Madras: Centre for Development Finance (CDF), IFMR and Humanities and Social Sciences.

Chaturvedi, R.K., Gopalakrishnan, R., Jayaraman, M., Bala, G., Joshi, N.V., Sukumar, R. & Ravindranath, N.H. (2011). Impact of climate change on Indian forests: A dynamic vegetation modeling approach, *Mitigation and Adaptation Strategies for Global Change*, **16**(2), 119–142.

FAO (2009). *How to Mainstream Climate Change Adaptation and Mitigation into Agriculture Policies*, Major Economies Forum (MEF) Leaders Declaration signed at the G8 Summit, L'Aquila, Italy, 2009.

Ghosh, J. (2009). The unnatural coupling: Food and global finance, *Journal of Agrarian Change*, **10**(1), 72–86.

Gosain, A.K., Rao, S., & Arora, A. (2011). Climate change impact assessment of water resources of India, *Current Science*, **101**(3), 356–371.

GTZ (2011). *Tackling Climate Change in India*, Deutsche Gesellschaft fürInternationale Zusammenarbeit (GIZ). New Delhi: GmbH.

Gulati, S. (2006). *Deterring Corruption and Improving Governance in the Electricity Sector.* Washington, DC: The World Bank.

Harvey, H. & Segafredo, L. (2011). *Policies that Work: How to Build a Low-Emissions Economy.* San Francisco, California: Climate Works Foundation.

INCCA (2010a). *India: Greenhouse Gas Emissions 2007.* Ministry of Environment and Forests (MoEF), Government of India.

INCCA (2010b). *Climate Change and India: A 4 * 4 Assessment — A Sectoral, Regional Analysis for 2030s.* Ministry of Environment and Forests (MoEF), Government of India.

IPCC (2007). *The Fourth Assessment Report, Climate Change 2007: Synthesis Report.* Geneva, Switzerland.

Jacoby, H., Rabassa, M. & Skoufias, E. (2011). *Distributional Implications of Climate Change,* Policy Research Working Paper 5623, The World Bank, April 2011.

Jha, A.K. (2011). *Much ado about the State Action Plans on Climate Change; Its business as Usual for the Governments*, PAIRVI Occasional Paper Series, August 2011.

Krishna Kumar, K., Patwardhan, S.K., Kulkarni, A., Kamala, K., Koteswara Rao, K. & Jones, R. (2011). Simulated projections for summer monsoon climate over India by a high-resolution regional climate model (PRECIS), *Current Science*, **101**(3), 312–326.

Lead International (2012). *India's National Action Plan on Climate Change*. Available at: http://www.climate-leaders.org/climate-change-resources/india-and-climate-change/indias-national-action-plan-on-climate-change. Accessed 10 September 2010.

Linnér, B. & Selin, H. (2003). *The Thirty Year Quest for Sustainability: The Legacy of the 1972 UN Conference on the Human Environment*. Paper presented at Annual Convention of International Studies Association, Portland, Oregon, USA, 25 February–1 March 2003, as part of the panel "Institutions and the Production of Knowledge for Environmental Governance".

McKinsey (2009). *Environmental and Energy Sustainability: An Approach for India*. Mumbai, India: McKinsey.

MoEF (2004). *India's Initial National Communication (NATCOM) to the United Nations Framework Convention on Climate Change*. Ministry of Environment and Forests, Government of India.

MoEF (2011). *Sustainable Development in India: Stocktaking in the run up to Rio+ 20*. Government of India, New Delhi.

O'Brien, K., Leichenko, R., Kelkar, U., Venema, H., Aandahl, G., Tompkins, H., Javed, A., Bhadwal, S., Barg, S., Nygaard, l. & West, J. (2004). Mapping vulnerability to multiple stressors: climate change and globalization in India. *Global Environmental Change*, **14**(4), 303–313.

Olsson, M., Atteridge, A., Hallding, K. & Hellberg, J. (2010). *Policy Brief — Together Alone? Brazil, South Africa, India, China (BASIC) and the Climate Change Conundrum*. Stockholm Environment Institute (SEI) International.

Panda, A. (2010). *Climate Induced Migration from Bangladesh to India: Issues and Challenges (6 September 2010)*. Institute for Social and Economic Change.

Pew Centre on Global Climate Change (2008). *Climate Change Mitigation Measures in India*, International Brief 2, PEW Centre and TERI, New Delhi.

Planning Commission (1997). *India's Ninth Five Year Plan 1997–2002* Government of India.

Planning Commission (2006). *Integrated Energy Policy*. Government of India.

Planning Commission (2007). *India's 11th Five Year Plan*. Government of India.

Planning Commission (2011a). *Faster, Sustainable and More Inclusive Growth — An Approach to the 12th Five Year Plan*, October 2011. Government of India.

Planning Commission (2011b). *Climate Change and 12th Five Year Plan — Report of Sub-Group on Climate Change*, October 2011. Government of India.

Planning Commission (2011c). *Low Carbon Strategies for Inclusive Growth — An Interim Report*, May 2011. Government of India.

Prime Minister's Council on Climate Change (PMCCC) (2008). *National Action Plan on Climate Change* (NAPCC). Government of India.

Ravindranath, D., Chaturvedi, R. & Kattumuri, R. (2012). Mainstreaming adaptation to climate change in Indian policy planning, *International Journal of Economics and Econometrics*, Special Issue, Working Paper.

Ravindranath, N.H. (2010). IPCC: Accomplishments, controversies and challenges, *Current Science*, **99**(1), 26–35.

Revi, A. (2008). *Climate Change Risk: An Adaptation and Mitigation Agenda for Indian Cities*, IIED Environment and Urbanisation.

Rogers, A. (ed.) (1999). *Taking Action — An Environmental Guide for You and Your Community*, UNEP.

Singh, M. (2012). *Need to Reduce Fiscal Deficit, Improve Investment Sentiment*, Speech when chairing meeting to discuss 12th five-year plan). Available at: http://profit.ndtv.com/news/economy/article-need-to-reduce-fiscal-deficit-improve-investment-sentiment-says-pm-full-speech-310863. Accessed 15 September 2012.

Stern, N., Kattumuri, R. & Nilekani, N. (2010). A global deal on climate change: A possible role for India. In *India's Economy: Performance and Challenges*, S. Acharya and R. Mohan (eds.), Oxford: Oxford University Press, pp. 430–463.

Stern, N., Kattumuri, R. & Rydge, J. (2012). Low-carbon growth and development, In *The New Oxford Companion to Economics in India*, K. Basu and A. Maertens (eds.), New Delhi: Oxford University Press, pp. 310–317.

Stern, N. (2012). *What we risk can how we should cast the economics and ethics*, Lionel Robbins Memorial Lecture Series 1. Available at: http://www2.lse.ac.uk/asiaResearchCentre/_files/LR%20-%20Lecture%201%20FINAL.pdf

TERI (2008). *Mitigation Options for India: The Role of the International Community* New Delhi: The Energy and Resources Institute (TERI).

UNEP (2009). *UNEP Year Book — New Science and Developments in our Changing Environment.* United Nations Environment Programme.

UNFCCC (1992). *United Nations Framework Convention on Climate Change*, United Nations.

UNFCCC (2007). *Investment and Financial Flows to Address Climate Change*, United Nations.

United Nations Framework Convention on Climate Change (UNFCCC) (2012). Kyoto Protocol. Available at: http://unfccc.int/kyoto_protocol/items/2830.php. Accessed 12 July 2012.

Vihma, A. (2011). India and the global climate governance: Between principles and pragmatism, *Journal of Environment and Development*, **20**(1), 69–94.

Walsh, S., Tian, H., Whalley, J. & Agarwal, M. (2011). China and India's participation in global climate negotiations, *International Environmental Assessments: Politics, Law and Economics*, **11**(3), 261–273.

World Resources Institute (WRI) (2011). Emissions (tons of CO_2e) per unit of GDP (millions of International dollars, constant 2005 PPP).

World Wide Fund for Nature (WWF) (2013). *Status of Tigers in Sundarban Biosphere Reserve, WWF-India.* Available at: http://awsassets.wwfindia.org/downloads/status_of_tigers_in_24_parganas__south_forest_division_08_10_12.pdf. Accessed 22 May 2013.

Chapter 5

After Copenhagen and the Economic Crisis: Does the EU Need to Go Back to the Drawing Board?

Christian Egenhofer*
Associate Senior Research Fellow,
Centre for European Policy Studies (CEPS), Brussels

and

Monica Alessi
Research Fellow and Programme Manager,
Centre for European Policy Studies (CEPS), Brussels

For long, the EU has assumed leadership in advancing domestic and international climate change policy. Whilst pushing its negotiations partner in international negotiations, it has led the way in implementing a host of domestic measures including a unilateral legally binding target, an ambitious renewable energy policy, or a low-carbon technology deployment strategy. The centerpiece of EU policy however has been the EU Emissions Trading System (ETS), a cap-and-trade program launched in 2005. The ETS has been seen as a tool to ensure least-cost abatement, drive EU decarbonization, and develop a global carbon market. After an initial review of the ETS to come into force in 2013, there has been a belief that the new ETS is "future-proof", meaning being able to cope with the temporary lack of a global climate change agreement and individual countries' emissions ceilings. This confidence has been shattered by the simultaneous "failure" of Copenhagen to deliver a robust perspective toward a global (top-down) agreement and the economic crisis. The lack of perspective for national caps at international level has led to a situation where many member states hesitate to pursue ambitious climate change policies. The economic crisis, which led to a dramatic fall of the EU allowance price until at least 2020 if not beyond, means that the ETS will not be able to deliver the second and third objectives, i.e. drive decarbonization and develop a global carbon market. This has triggered a debate across the EU on whether, and if so, how and when to adapt the EU ETS to accommodate the changed circumstances. It has also triggered a more fundamental discussion on the need of a price management mechanism and about the role of the ETS.

---

*Visiting Professor, College of Europe (Bruges & Natolin), SciencesPo (Paris) and LUISS University (Rome).

1. Introduction

As is well known, the EU has identified tackling climate change as one of the world's greatest challenges. It has repeatedly confirmed its position that an increase in the global, annual, and mean surface temperature should not exceed 2°C above pre-industrial levels. After the US's withdrawal from the Kyoto Protocol, the EU has found itself being catapulted into global "leadership" on climate change. While few had bet at the time for the Kyoto Protocol to survive, not at least due to active EU diplomacy, Japan, Canada, and Russia ratified the Protocol to bring it into force in 2005. As a result, the EU has adopted numerous laws both to fulfil its commitments and to prepare the path for a new post-2012 agreement or at least a framework. Among them have been a host of policies to support renewable energy, improve energy efficiency, decarbonize transport, and a low-carbon technology deployment strategy. The centerpiece of EU climate change policy has been the EU Emissions Trading Scheme (EU ETS) that started in 2005. The outcome of the Copenhagen negotiations and beyond as well as the 2008/2009 economic crisis have triggered a rethinking of the EU strategy.

2. A Brief History of EU Climate Change Policy

Since 1996, the EU has pursued the goal to limit global temperature increase to a maximum of 2°C above pre-industrial levels. In order to achieve the medium-term greenhouse gas (GHG) emissions reductions required of developed countries, European heads of state and governments at their 8–9 March 2007 spring summit set a number of targets as well as a host of accompanying policies, generally referred to as "climate and energy package" or the "20 20 by 2020 targets".

(1) A binding absolute emissions reduction commitment of 30% by 2020 compared to 1990 conditional on a global agreement, and a "firm independent commitment" to achieve at least a 20% reduction.
(2) A binding target to reach a 20% share of renewable energy sources in primary energy consumption by 2020 (European Commission, 2009a).
(3) A binding minimum target of increasing the share of renewables in each member state's transport energy consumption to 10% by 2020 (this target initially focused solely on biofuels but was later widened to include other forms of renewable energy sources) (European Commission, 2009a).

(4) A 20% reduction of primary energy consumption by 2020 compared to projections (non-binding).

(5) A commitment to enable the construction of up to 12 large-scale power plants using carbon capture and storage (CCS) technology.

The "climate and energy package" was adopted in April 2009. It contains six principal elements, including a directive for the promotion of renewable energy sources, a revised EU ETS starting 2013, an "effort sharing" decision setting binding emissions targets for EU member states in sectors not subject to the ETS, a regulation to reduce by 2015 average CO_2 emissions of new passenger cars to $120\,g/km$, new environmental quality standards for fuels and biofuels (aimed at reducing by 2020 GHG emissions from fuels by 6% over their whole life-cycle), and a regulatory framework for CCS. Prior to that, the EU had already published the so-called *Strategic Energy Technology* (SET)-Plan to strengthen research, development and demonstration as well as early deployment help for new low-carbon energy technologies. Finally, the level and nature of allowed subsidies (or "state aid") for low-carbon was reviewed.

While climate change was the main driver, the "package" was equally meant to address energy policy challenges. Domestic energy resources have been dwindling at the same time that government intervention in the energy industry is on the rise in precisely those countries that could potentially fill the gap. While many supplier countries seem unable to increase production due to a lack of investment, the fact that other supplies are tightly controlled by governments in exporting countries raises the fear of "excessive" leverage of supplier countries such as Russia. Some supplier countries are hostile toward the West. Others are politically unstable. Many reserves will take years to develop because of problems of access, investments, and physical conditions. A prolonged tight market might increase political tensions and possibly some sort of "resource nationalism". The EU had realized that success in integrating Russia into a strategic energy partnership is very unlikely. Despite an institutionalized energy dialogue (since 2000) and some recent foreign investments in the Russian energy sector, the strategy aimed at opening the Russian market to European and other western enterprises and thus to gain large-scale access to Russian gas and oil reserves has largely failed and this is not expected to change in the foreseeable future.

In such a scenario, the EU and its member states have been examining domestic and external policy options to move to a more sustainable and secure energy supply. This includes, amongst others, investment in renewable energy sources, pushing CCS technology and investment in nuclear energy in member states that wish to do so. Renewables policy has been guided by the need for large-scale deployment to bring down costs of technology.

Additional real or perceived advantages of the EU climate and energy package included the following:

- The renewable energy policy can provide for technological leadership in sun-rise technologies.
- Renewable electricity can reduce long-term electricity prices and their volatility.
- Substitution of fossils combined with renewables may reduce pricing power by Russia (notably on gas).
- The introduction of the EU ETS led to the retention of some of the economic rent of producer countries.

To offset the higher prices both for industry and domestic consumers, energy efficiency was perceived as a central piece, certainly for the transition period until new technologies and new fuels become available on a large scale. With increasing prices, reducing consumption gives a reasonable prospect for keeping the energy bill constant.

There has been an additional aspect of the "20 20 by 2020" targets which is often overlooked. The first phase of the EU ETS has shown that setting a hard cap in GHG emissions in the EU is next to impossible without some sort of legally binding constraint. In a scenario of a post-2012 agreement *without* absolute caps, it was and still is difficult to see how the EU ETS could continue to exist in a meaningful way. Member states and the European Commission would most likely not be able to impose an ambitious emissions ceiling on industry without a legally binding constraint. The "20 20" targets were meant to address this risk.

At the heart of the agreement are the "20 20 by 2020" targets. In addition to the revised EU ETS which will allow for a 21% emissions reduction compared to 2005 in sectors covered by the EU ETS, the implementation of these targets has been operationalized by the introduction of legally binding national GHG emissions reduction targets (referred to as "effort sharing", ranging from −20 to +20%) for all sectors not covered by the EU ETS — such as buildings, transport, agriculture and waste — amounting to an overall reduction of 10% below 2005 levels by 2020 (European Commission, 2009b). The 20% renewable target by 2020 — which translates into a roughly 35% share of renewables in the power sector — has been broken

Table 1.   National overall targets for the share of energy from renewable sources in gross final consumption of energy in 2020 and member state GHG emissions limits in non-ETS sectors for the period 2013 to 2020.

Member state	Share of energy from renewable sources in gross final consumption of energy, 2005* (%)	Target for share of energy from renewable sources in gross final consumption of energy, 2020† (%)	Member state GHG emissions limits in 2020 compared to 2005 GHG emissions levels (from sources not covered by ETS) (%)
Austria	23.3	34	−16
Belgium	2.2	13	−15
Bulgaria	9.4	16	20
Czech Republic	6.1	13	9
Cyprus	2.9	13	−5
Denmark	17	30	−20
Estonia	18.0	25	11
Finland	28.5	38	−16
France	10.3	23	−14
Germany	5.8	18	−14
Greece	6.9	18	−4
Hungary	4.3	13	10
Ireland	3.1	16	−20
Italy	5.2	17	−13
Latvia	32.6	40	17
Lithuania	15.0	23	15
Luxembourg	0.9	11	−20
Malta	0	10	5
The Netherlands	2.4	14	−16
Poland	7.2	15	14
Portugal	20.5	31	1
Romania	17.8	24	19
Slovak Republic	6.7	14	13
Slovenia	16.0	25	4
Spain	8.7	20	−10
Sweden	39.8	49	−17
UK	1.3	15	−16

*Annex 1 of Directive 2009/28/EC on the promotion of the use of energy from renewable sources.
†Annex 2 of effort sharing Decision No 406/2009/EC.

down into differentiated national targets (Table 1) for the share of renewable energy sources in final energy consumption.

The climate and energy package also stands for a level of EU centralization, absent in other policy areas of shared competence like the environment. Such centralization, i.e. hard caps and binding renewable obligations, has only been possible as a result of a complex burden sharing, which essentially has been based on a mixture of efficiency and equity considerations. Hard targets for the EU ETS and the non-ETS sectors as well as for renewables have been set on the basis of an "efficiency approach", i.e. reflecting a least-cost approach for the EU as a whole, however, with some adjustment to ensure that costs for member states remain roughly similar in per-capita terms.

— *GHG reduction ("effort sharing") targets*: Countries with a low GDP per capita are allowed to emit more than they did in 2005 in non-EU ETS sectors, reflecting projected higher emissions due to higher economic growth.
— *Renewables targets*: Half calculated on a flat-rate increase in the share of renewable energy and the other half weighted by GDP, modulated to take account of national starting points and efforts already made.
— *In the EU ETS sector*: Uniform cap across member states and allocation based on EU-wide allocation methods. About 12% of the overall auctioning rights is re-distributed to economically weaker member states in Central and Eastern Europe. Another 2% of the total auctioning rights is distributed to eight countries that have already achieved significant reductions before 2005.

3. Cornerstone EU ETS: Designing a Regional System for an Uncertain Future

The EU ETS has been designed as a domestic policy, largely "protected" from carbon markets that at the time were seen as emanating from the Kyoto Protocol such as Clean Development Mechanism (CDM) and Joint Implementation (JI) or International Emission Trading. The principal reason has been concerns over compliance under the Kyoto Protocol and the Marrakech Accords. For an efficient trading system to work, there has to be guarantee that a "tonne is a tonne" and that compliance is ensured with a possibility of recourse to a court in case of litigation. This is possible only within a national or regional jurisdiction and not within a more loosely UN framework.

By covering currently some 2 billion tonnes of GHG emissions in the EU and the European Economic Area (EEA),[1] the EU ETS by most

---

[1]The EEA describes the EU's internal market consisting of the EU member states as well as Norway, Iceland, and Liechtenstein, which are fully integrated in this market.

estimates makes up some 80% of the global carbon market. Strictly speaking a regional carbon market, its size however means that prices for EU allowances (EUAs) under the ETS are price setters for the global carbon market. With demand from those countries that have ratified the Kyoto Protocol fast decreasing, the EU ETS will become — at least temporarily — an even more important component of the global carbon market. Therefore, despite being a regional market, the ETS remains the backbone of the global carbon market. Seen from within the EU's political economy, the EU's carbon market is first of all meant to serve EU interests, i.e. to "promote GHG reductions in a cost-effective and economically efficient manner" (Article 1 ETS Directive), and if one wants to believe policy-makers, to drive EU decarbonization. Only secondary are EU concerns of developing a global carbon market, once forcefully advocated, now somewhat more tempered after the US *de facto* abandoned attempts to develop a federal US carbon market and with progress slow in other regions, with the exception of California, Korea, and China where carbon markets are developed. Yet the domestic and international agendas cannot be separated (Box 1).

Box 1. The emergence of GHG emissions markets.

The emergence of GHG emissions markets was the direct result of the United Nations Framework Convention on Climate Change (UNFCCC) and the Kyoto Protocol, which included in its provision three articles that provided for the creation of offsets and the trading of these units. The Kyoto Protocol established that counties with emissions' targets so-called Annex I countries can buy and sell parts of their emissions' rights — Assigned Amounts in "Kyoto-speak" — or emission reduction units from projects with other Annex I countries, and buy certified emissions reductions (CERs) that are generated from project in developing countries (so-called non-Annex I countries). Trade can take place in various ways under three mechanisms.

- *Clean Development Mechanism (CDM)*: Article 12 establishes that Annex I countries (and firms in these) can transfer emissions reductions from projects in developing countries through so-called CERs.
- *Joint Implementation (JI)*: Article 6 allowed that Annex I countries (and firms in these) can transfer reductions in emissions compared to a baseline for individual projects through so-called ERUs (Emissions Reduction Units).

(*Continued*)

Box 1. (*Continued*)

- *International emissions trading*: Under Article 17 of the Protocol Annex I countries (and firms in these) can trade parts of the assigned amounts, i.e. emissions rights allocated under the Protocol (Assigned Amounts Units or AAUs).

- Each mechanism has a different function and rationale, particularly the CDM, which is meant to finance sustainable development and has more elaborate governance provisions. The tradable units from the mechanisms are interchangeable, however, which means that all three mechanisms work together in one international system.

The trading mechanisms were meant to become an integral part of and work side by side with other policy measures to provide flexibility to abate emissions where that can be done most cheaply and therefore as a means of reducing compliance costs. Behind this has also been the vision of a global carbon market and a single (global) price for carbon. To date, this has not been accomplished. There is a carbon market; however, it is fragmented and largely confined to the EU, Japan, and the developing countries. The Kyoto Protocol units have been used for trading and accounting in the EU and Japan. The rest of the world uses emerging, and until now, largely voluntary standards, which have little influence on the price for carbon. The decision of the US not to ratify the Kyoto Protocol, accompanied by a long delay by Australia and an official policy of inaction by Canada, led to the emergence of a Voluntary Carbon Market, mainly in North America and different trading systems.

The agreements struck during the global climate change negotiations in Durban, South Africa in November/December 2011 have launched a new process to consider the future of global carbon markets. This process will give an answer to the question whether the initial vision of a global carbon market and one single price for carbon, which emerged from the Kyoto Protocol, will prevail or whether the future will see a long period of building through a bottom-up approach, which may or may not lead to a unitary carbon market in the future.

3.1. *ETS beginnings*

The well-rehearsed initial problems were partly the result of the rapid speed with which the ETS was adopted, motivated by the EU's desire to show a strong determination to tackle climate change.[2] This should, however, not hide the fact that the ETS suffered from some serious design flaws (e.g. Egenhofer, 2007; Swedish Energy Agency, 2007), which were largely the result of two political choices: a high level of decentralization and free allocation based on grandfathering, i.e. historical emissions. Initial allocation of allowances by member states on the basis of National Allocation Plans led to a "race to the bottom", i.e. member states were under pressure by industries not to hand out fewer allowances than their EU competitors received (e.g. Ellerman *et al.*, 2007; Kettner *et al.*, 2007). This led to over-allocation, and ultimately to a price collapse. During the period when the EU allowance price was high, free allocation also generated "windfall profits", mainly but not only in the power sector (e.g. Keats and Neuhoff, 2005). Some of these issues were addressed in phase 2 (2008–2012) as a result of member state cooperation and the European Commission being able to reduce member states' allocation proposals (e.g. Ellerman *et al.*, 2010). Still, throughout both phases, by and large, the ETS has managed to deliver a carbon price. One result has been that carbon pricing has now officially entered board room discussions (Ellerman and Joskow, 2008).

In the absence of a global agreement, leading to "uneven" carbon constraints, concerns over competitiveness and carbon leakage have been high on the agenda. The essential answer by the ETS was free allocation. Free allocation constitutes a compensation or a subsidy, potentially creating an incentive to continue producing in Europe. At the same time, historical grandfathering in the first two phases has led to significant windfall profits.

The *ex-post* analyses on economic rents and windfall profits are relatively clear, while also more or less consistent with *ex-ante* studies that assessed the potential windfall profits for the ETS sectors at the time. Ellermann *et al.* (2010), the most authoritative *ex-post* study conducted so far, conclude that in total, the rents were substantial, even at a relatively modest carbon price of €12, and amounted to more than €19 billion in windfall profits, plus more than €10 billion of "informational"[3] rents, although with the caveat of surrounding uncertainties in the calculations.

---

[2] For a full overview of this period, see Delbeke, 2006 and Skjærseth and Wettestad, 2008.

[3] "Informational" rents describe the fact that during the first period of general over-allocation, which should have produced a zero price, the EU allowance price remained at around €12. Companies that have received allowances for free — both industry and the power sector — could make large trading profits by selling their allowances. This appears to be a one-off rent.

Other *ex-post* studies (e.g. Delarue *et al.*, 2010) and own calculations
(Egenhofer *et al.*, 2011) do not significantly disagree with this finding.[4]
During phase 1, all technologies and all participants included in the ETS —
power and industry alike — benefited from ETS-related rents. Those rents
for the power sector that accrued as a result of free allocation will disappear
with the auctioning in the ETS phase 3. This is not the case, however, for
those rents in the power sector of low-carbon power-generation technologies,
such as hydro or nuclear, which will enjoy additional revenues as a result
of higher power prices due to the ETS but do not face additional costs.
The benchmark-based allocation — in place as of 2013 — will reduce
potential rents, sometimes significantly. Still, different studies come to
diverse conclusions (e.g. CE Delft, 2010; De Bruyn *et al.*, 2010). This is
partly so because windfall profits depend on the ability to pass through
product price increases due to the ETS allowance price, an issue that
remains controversial.

3.2. Overhaul in two steps

Experiences from phase 1 and 2 have greatly helped the European
Commission to propose and adopt radical changes to the EU ETS, which
were not even thinkable before its initial adoption in 2003.[5] The principal
element of the new ETS is a single EU-wide cap, which will decrease
annually in a linear way by 1.74% starting in 2013. This linear reduction
continues beyond 2020 as there is no sunset clause.

The revised ETS Directive also foresees EU-wide harmonized allocation
rules. Starting from 2013, power companies will have to buy all their
emissions allowances at an auction with some temporary exceptions for
"coal-based" poorer member states. For the industrial sectors under the
ETS, the EU agreed that the auctioning rate will be set at 20% in 2013,
increasing to 70% in 2020, with a view to reaching 100% in 2027. The
remaining free allowances will be distributed on the basis of EU-wide
harmonized benchmarks, set on the basis of the average performance of
the 10% most GHG-efficient installations. Industries exposed to significant
non-EU competition and thereby potentially subject to carbon leakage,
however, will receive 100% of allowances free of charge up to 2020, based

---

[4]For a detailed overview, see Egenhofer *et al.*, 2011, 8–14.
[5]See e.g. Ellerman *et al.*, 2010; Skjærseth and Wettestad, 2010; and Egenhofer *et al.*,
2011 for a full overview.

on community-wide product benchmarks set on the basis of the average performance of the 10% most GHG-efficient installations.

Other changes include a partial redistribution of auction rights between member states, restrictions of the total volume of CDM/JI credits, the use of 300 million EU allowances to finance the demonstration of CCS and innovative renewable technologies and a general — non-legally binding — commitment from EU member states to spend at least half of the revenues from auctioning to tackle climate change both in the EU and in developing countries, including for measures to avoid deforestation and increase afforestation and reforestation in developing countries.

- The system will be extended to aviation, the chemicals, and aluminum sectors and to other GHGs, e.g. nitrous oxide from fertilizers and perfluorocarbons from aluminum.
- Member states can financially compensate electro-intensive industries for higher power prices. The European Commission has drawn up EU guidelines as to this end.

As already in the previous periods, access to project credits under the Kyoto Protocol from outside the EU will be limited. The revised ETS will restrict access to no more than 50% of the reductions required in the EU ETS to ensure that emissions reductions will happen in the EU. Leftover CDM/JI credits from 2008 to 2012 can be used until 2020.

Changes for phase 3 are not the end point of ETS reform.

First, several implementation provisions, e.g. on allocation or monitoring and reporting of emissions, have not been finally adopted or implemented. New gases and sectors have required amendment of the Monitoring and Reporting Guidelines (MRGs). Similarly, the auctioning regulation needed revision.

Second, the ETS Directive has also developed a framework for possible changes without amending the Directive. This includes, for example, the possibility for member states to opt-in new gases and activities under certain conditions, a clause that has already been applied in the past. A second possibility constitutes a kind of domestic offset schemes, the so-called community-level projects under Article 24a, where member states can issue credits for reductions projects outside ETS coverage. Another clause (Article 27) allows for the exclusion of small installations from the ETS. Finally, the ETS features an enabling clause for linking the ETS with other regional, national, or sub-nation emissions trading programs through mutual recognition of allowances (Article 25). Another — potentially contentious — issue will be the compensation of electro-intensive industries by member states. There is a risk of a new round of distortions to competition between industries in different member states.

Third, the revised ETS Directive explicitly foresees the possibility for a revision in the case of an international climate change agreement. Depending on the nature of the agreement, this could mean the lowering of the cap, for example if the EU decided to move to a unilateral EU reduction commitment of 30%. This move would trigger a whole number of implementation rules including notably an increase of the linear annual reduction factor of currently 1.74%[6] allocation rules, the role of flexible mechanisms, the inclusion of forestry credits, and land use changes. To date, there is little risk that this might happen soon both for lack of progress internationally and domestically, i.e. internal EU political reasons. The Conference of Parties to the UNFCCC held in Doha in December 2012 (COP 18) was meant to be largely procedural and did not as such work on reaching a global agreement, nor on setting ambitious targets for the 2nd commitment period of the Kyoto Protocol. Moreover, the lack of progress on the delivery of financial pledges is proving to be a major stumbling block. The financial crisis and a renewed "economic growth first" approach in many developed nations have reduced the interest of negotiating parties to address climate change or fulfill their pledges. In Europe itself, the position of the member states has shifted. For example, the present policy of support for renewable energy sources has been put into question by Poland, who argues that such policies are driving energy prices up. For other member states, price increases in the energy sector are politically very sensitive at a time where they are implementing demanding restructuring and austerity programmes.[7]

4. Toward Global Level Carbon Pricing in Aviation (and Maritime)?

Following the continuous lack of progress in international fora such as the UN or within the International Civil Aviation Organisation (ICAO) on

---

[6]Simple calculations reveal that in order to almost entirely decarbonize the power sector by 2050 — a precondition to meet the officially agreed 80–95% reductions of GHG emissions by 2050, the ETS linear annual reduction factor would need be in the order of 2.5% rather than the current 1.74%.

[7]This position has been defended by the Polish environment Minister in Warsaw on 17 May 2013 under the European Commission's initiative "A world you like with a climate you like".

international aviation emissions, from the start of 2012; emissions from all domestic and international flights that arrive at or depart from an EU airport will be covered by the EU ETS regardless of how long that flight is in EU airspace. Airlines will — as any other installation under the ETS — have to surrender allowances, which they receive for free or will be required to purchase.[8]

Coverage of international flights, especially by non-EU carriers, has been contested by many other countries by either political pressure or legal complaints. Most vocal opposition has come from China and the US. Chinese airlines have been threatening to boycott the scheme with support from the government. The United States is planning legislation to outlaw compliance with the scheme, and other countries have joined the lobbying efforts.[9] The issue has been more one of principle than actual impact. Experts have calculated that passengers on long-haul flights may be faced with additional costs of between €2 and €12 a ticket. It is interesting to note that all airlines have submitted emission and other data on time for the launch of the system.

On 21 December 2011, the European Court of Justice delivered its judgment in a legal case brought by some US airlines and their trade association against the inclusion of aviation in the EU ETS. The Court upheld the 2009 legislation, stating that the extension of the EU ETS to aviation infringes neither the principle of territoriality nor the sovereignty of third countries. It also stated that the EU ETS does not constitute a tax, fee, or charge on fuel, and so would not be in breach of the EU–US Air Transport Agreement. The Court concluded that the uniform application of the EU ETS to all flights that depart or arrive from the EU is consistent with provisions designed to prohibit discriminatory treatment between aircraft operators on nationality grounds, an issue also covered by this agreement. Nevertheless, the Court's decision did not stall the complaints of international carriers, and China in particular

---

[8] The total quantity of allowances to be allocated for the aviation sector (cap) in 2012 will be equal to 97% of the EEA-wide historical aviation emissions. In the period 2013–2020, this percentage will be reduced to 95%. The Directive 2008/101/EC foresees that in 2012, 85% of the allowances will be given for free to aircraft operators and 15% of the allowances will be allocated by auctioning. In the trading period 2013–2020, 82% of the allowances will be granted for free to aircraft operators, 15% of the CO_2 allowances will be assigned by auctioning, and the remaining 3% will remain in a special reserve for later distribution to fast-growing airlines and new entrants into the market.

[9] In cases of non-compliance, the airlines must pay a penalty of €100 per tonne in addition to surrender the allowances or eventually face a ban.

threatened to cancel Airbus orders. ICAO has accelerated its negotiation pace on this issue, indicating its willingness to progress toward a global solution. As a consequence of ICAO's actions, and maybe also due to the potential consequences on Airbus of Chinese retaliation, the EU decided to pause the introduction of ETS charges on flights to and from non-European countries. On 3 June 2013, ICAO backed a global post-2020 carbon offsetting scheme, and the EU agreed to cement the exclusion of flights to and from the EU from the EU ETS, on the condition that a satisfactory market-based mechanism (MBM) is approved by ICAO by September 2013 (see http://www.voxeu.org/article/should-eu-suspend-its-airline-emissions-charge). Another possible way out is that incoming flights to Europe with airlines from third countries may be exempted from the scheme if those airlines take "equivalent measures" of their own to reduce CO_2 emission. To benefit from this provision, China and other third countries must show the EU that they have "equivalent measures" in place.

In parallel, a similar approach to the one taken for aviation is being pursued for maritime transport emissions. The EU has confirmed its commitment to "include these emissions into the existing EU reduction commitment" should the UNFCCC processes fail to tackle them and has announced a proposal in this case.

Conceptually speaking, inclusion of aviation within the ETS would be comparable to using a "carbon border tax" to pursue a global "level" pricing of carbon. The past EU strategy has been one of scaling-up and reform of existing flexible mechanisms such as the CDM and the creation of new ones that ultimately would allow the establishment of a global carbon price. But this would require the cooperation of other countries, notably developing countries, which currently seems uncertain at best. A similar effect can also be achieved if the EU (alone or with other developed countries) were to impose an import tax on services or the content (i.e. including the embedded carbon) of CO_2 of all goods imported into the EU from countries that do not have their own cap-and-trade system or equivalent measures. From a purely economic perspective, this would be a straightforward way to move toward a global "shadow" carbon price even in the rest of the world (Helm *et al.*, 2012). Such an import tariff improves global welfare because it transfers, at least partially, via trade flows, carbon pricing even to those parts of the world where governments have so far refrained from imposing domestic measures of any magnitude. A key effect of such a tariff is that it would *always* lower global emissions (Gros and Egenhofer, 2011). The aviation could be seen as a test case, whether planned or accidental.

5. After Copenhagen and the Economic Crisis: Is the EU Emperor Naked?

At the time of the hard-won compromise of the ETS review for post-2012, there was a general conviction that the new ETS would be "future-proof", i.e. able to cope with the *temporary* lack of a global climate change agreement and address competitiveness, yet be able to drive decarbonization of the EU economy. The 2008/2009 economic crisis, however, has destroyed that confidence by bringing about a seemingly permanent dramatic lowering of EUA prices due to a rapid and dramatic decline in economic output. Ever since, EUA prices have been lingering around €5 per tonne of CO_2 and few expect EUA prices to climb much higher than €20 at best throughout the period up to 2020, largely because of the possibility of banking unused allowances between the second and third phase.

When measured against 2007 levels, the EU's current pledge of 20% compares poorly with pledges of other industrialized countries. The current −20% pledge is inferior in terms of effort required to the one of the US (e.g. Den Elzen *et al.*, 2009; Spencer *et al.*, 2010). Translated into CO_2 intensity improvements, the EU's target of reducing emissions[10] by about 13% over the horizon 2005–2020 — taking into account the reduction prior to 2005[11] — translates into an implied reduction of CO_2 intensity of roughly 2.4% per annum (or −30.7% over the whole period).[12] For comparison, the pledge submitted by the US in the context of the Copenhagen Accord (emissions reduction "in the range of" 17% in 2020 from 2005 levels) would amount to a CO_2 intensity reduction of about 3.2% per annum on average

---

[10]We assume a constant portion of CO_2 emissions in total absolute GHG emissions. In this case, the percentage changes presented in this section are valid for both total GHG emissions (absolute targets are announced in this metric) and for the CO_2 emissions (intensity targets have been announced in terms of CO_2).

[11]The target of −20% from 1990 levels corresponds to −13.1% from 2005 levels (own calculations) due to the 7.9% reduction based on 2009 data from the European Environment Agency (EEA) achieved by the EU until 2005 (EEA, 2009).

[12]This is the result of combining the fall in emissions (−0.9% p.a.) with a potential GDP growth rate of around 1.5% per annum on average. *Note that per annum averages are compound annual growth rates. GDP growth rates are own estimates based on the data and projections until 2014 by the IMF*; see, IMF (2009).

(or −38.3% for the period).[13] As a result, the US effort (going forward from 2005) is more ambitious than that of the EU — at least in the sense that the improvement in intensity terms would have to be about 0.8 percentage points higher, compensating for the slightly steeper improvement by the EU since 1990.

True, using a 2005 or later base year does not take into account the EU's previous efforts and obfuscates progress compared with 1990 — the Kyoto Protocol base year and global yardstick — yet it is a very useful indicator of the level of effort required. This is even more important as after Copenhagen, one of the main, if not the most important, drivers of climate change policy has become domestic progress to the low-carbon economy, also one of the essential narratives in the Europe 2020 strategy and following the 26 May 2010 European Commission climate change communication (European Commission, 2010a).

The implication of the lack of ambition goes beyond the EU's domestic decarbonization strategy. The EU's minimum target is likely to lie above the trajectory implied by a linear reduction from current levels toward a 2050 target to reach the long-term target of reducing "emissions by 80–95% by 2050 compared to 1990 levels", the EU's politically accepted objective. This would mean that an EU reduction target of 20% does not seem to allow the world to reach its envisaged objective under reasonable assumptions (e.g. Ward and Grubb, 2009). This has been indirectly acknowledged by the European Commission in the Staff Working Paper accompanying the 26 May Communication, which states that "internal reductions by 2020 at a higher level than the reference case (which achieves the −20% target internally) is more in line with a 2°C compatible scenario" (European Commission, 2010b).

A low level of ambition in the EU equally is unlikely to facilitate an ambitious international agreement consistent with long-term objectives and economic efficiency. The European Commission's own analysis already in

---

[13]This is because the potential GDP growth rate of the US is estimated to about 0.5% higher than that of the EU, i.e. at 2% per annum on average. Higher US growth rates would of course have to result in higher reductions of US CO_2 intensity if the US is to attain its target. If both the EU and the US were to attain their targets, the outcome would probably be quite comparable (in terms of intensity changes), taking 1990 as the base year, because over that longer 30-year period, the difference in the change in emission levels (−20% for the EU, versus only −3% for the US) would be offset by higher US growth. For comparison, see the corresponding World Resources Institute estimate of US (−37%) and EU (−30%) efforts in terms of GHG intensity improvement (including LULUCF) from a 2005 base year under slow growth, see, Levin and Bradley (2010).

2009 (European Commission, 2009) noted that a 30% reduction target combined with a carbon market for the group of developed countries would cut global mitigation costs by about a quarter. Sticking to a 20% target would forego these potential benefits.

Finally, a lack of ambition is in gross contradiction to the EU's rhetoric about the EU's thinking on how to generate financing for mitigation and adaptation to climate change in developing countries. The EU envisages the majority of these financial flows coming though the carbon market. Under a 20% reduction pathway and the possibility to import credits through the Kyoto Protocol flexible mechanisms, the resulting EU carbon price is likely to be too low to generate a significant portion of the US$ 100 billion p.a. post-2012 that has been agreed.[14]

6. Back to the Drawing Board?

The EU's low level of ambition affects its influence in international fora when discussing climate change policy. The emergence of new, important global players (in particular BRIC[15] countries) with a large potential to reduce emissions — and also to increase them if no action is taken — requires a delicate diplomatic effort, as well as willingness to support effectively a change of track. The share of EU emissions in global emissions is decreasing (due in large part to the increases in emerging economies), which in turn brings adverse domestic incentives and puts into question the EU's climate policy. There is thus a need to reconcile the EU's rhetoric with its own ambitions, first by getting its house in order and second by engaging more meaningfully with emerging countries willing to participate constructively in reducing emissions. This will require addressing at least the following three areas.

6.1. *Addressing EU's divisions*

A first step has been made. At the UNFCCC COP 18 in Doha (end of 2012), the EU made a "firm independent commitment" to achieve an average

---

[14]The 26 May 2010 European Communication (European Commission, 2010a) estimates the ETS price of €16 in 2020 (European Commission, *op. cit.*, footnote 2 on p. 48). Assuming an average annual emissions cap for the years 2013 until 2020 of around 1.8 billion tonnes of CO_2 and that around 60% of total allowances would be auctioned (i.e. all allowances of the power sector) member states would auction 1.1 billion allowances. At a price of €16 per tonne, this would amount to €17.6 per annum. Note that member states have "politically" at best committed to use half of these revenues for global transfers.
[15]BRIC refers to Brazil, Russia, India, and China.

Table 2. European Commission's estimate of the trajectory to reach the 20% by 2020 target of total allowed emissions under the 2009 Climate and Energy Package.

Year	2013	2014	2015	2016	2017	2018	2019	2020
Reduction vs 1990 (%)	−14	−15	−16	−17	−18	−19	−20	−21
Reductions vs base year (%)	−17	−18	−19	−20	−21	−22	−23	−24

Source: EC (2012a) *Commission Staff Working Document — Preparing the EU's Quantified Emission Limitation or Reduction Objective (QELRO) based on the EU Climate and Energy Package*, SWD (2012) 18 final.

reduction of at least a 20% over the period from 2013 to 2020, calculated as shown in Table 2.

A second step has been taken with a European Commission proposal[16] to stagger the release of EUAs to be auctioned, a practice that is generally referred to as "back-loading". Once adopted, this would mean that fewer EUAs are released for auction initially and more later, toward the end of the trading period in 2020, which in the Commission's view would be able to address this "temporary" market imbalance. At the same time, the European Commission has initiated a discussion on the need for "structural" measures, in particular to address the root cause of the current imbalance (European Commission, 2012b). Numerous options exist, including such one-off measures as cancelling a certain amount of allowances, introducing systemic adjustment measures or even creating new bodies (see e.g. Egenhofer *et al.*, 2012). Whatever the final political solution, decision-making may take years to complete. The development of the EU's international strategy cannot be seen in isolation from the intricacies of the international discussion, notably since there is no consensus on either the domestic or the international aspects. This is why the European Commission may have launched a consultation on the post-2020 EU climate change policy in the form of the Green Paper on "A 2030 framework for climate and energy policies". We should not expect first results to be coming into operation before 2014 or 2015.

---

[16]The proposal consists of the following elements: (i) a proposal to amend the EU ETS Directive and clarify the prerogative of the EC to make changes to the auctioning profile within a trading period through the Climate Change Committee; (ii) an amendment to the Auctioning Regulation that does not include the number; and (iii) a Staff Working Document (SWD) that outlines, in some detail, the rationale behind back-loading as well as at least three different options on how to implement such action. The SWD showed, by calculations using three different models, the potential impact of back-loading.

Differences of interest among member states within the Council are multi-faceted, and there is a cleavage between the "new" and "old" member states, i.e. those member states that were already members in 2004 when the new and newly "independent" member states of the former Soviet area of influence joined the EU. These internal differences bear some resemblance to tensions at the international level, and this is often not understood by negotiating partners. Generally, the new member states have a far lower GDP per capita than the older member states. The poorest EU member states recorded a GDP per capita at purchasing power parity of €12,600 (Romania) and €13,800 (Bulgaria). These are levels comparable to Brazil at €11,900 and South Africa at €11,100. In many cases, this is coupled with a power sector that is predominantly coal based. Poland is the most extreme example, with coal-based power production being responsible for a bit more than 90% of total power, which translates into 56% of total primary energy consumption. The Europe OECD average figures for comparison are 24% and 17% (Spencer, 2012). Finally, energy efficiency in industry is considerably below that in old member states. Polish energy intensity is about 2.2 times higher than the EU-27 average and 2.5 times higher than that in the old member states.[17] This situation represents a kind of contradiction between intra-EU developed versus developing countries.

6.2. The EU's share of emissions is falling fast

It is increasingly becoming clear that the EU's share of global GHG emissions — currently at around 13% of the global share — is decreasing fast and will fall to around 10% in 2020. This compares with shares for China of more than 20% and the US of around 15%. According to the International Energy Agency (IEA) in Paris, the EU's cumulative savings over the period 2008 to 2020 — the period for which the EU has capped its emissions — would represent around 40% of China's expected, annual CO_2 emissions (IEA, 2008).

6.3. Industrial competitiveness starts to matter ever more

Closely related to the differentiation between developed and developing countries is the lack of progress in "industrial competitiveness"[18] issues.

---

[17]This is based on Eurostat figures: Polish energy intensity is 373.859 kgoe/€1,000 GDP; that of the EU-27 is 167.99 and the EU-15 is 150.942.

[18]This term has never been defined, although roughly speaking "competitiveness" in the context of EU climate change policy and the ETS has assumed a micro (i.e. firm or

The risk of carbon leakage, whether real or perceived, will become an increasingly important impediment in the EU to raising its ambition level. Prior to Copenhagen, pressure from EU industry was relatively modest, essentially for two reasons. First, there was a prospect of some sort of global deal able to establish a "level playing field". Second, ETS design has been able, if not to address for good, at least to park the issue. With the prospect of a global deal pushed farther away, competitiveness has again become an important matter on the EU's agenda. Competitiveness issues will be further aggravated because more European industry will need to contribute to the "deep" costs of decarbonization or energy transition, such as for renewable intake and massive new investment in energy infrastructure. To date, industry in many member states has largely been exempted from contributing. But as costs rise, households will decreasingly be willing or able to cover the full burden.[19]

In the past, "competitiveness" was addressed by free allocation in the ETS. Free allocation constitutes a form of compensation, potentially creating an incentive to continue producing in Europe. Electro-intensive industries can be compensated by state aid for additional costs stemming from carbon-induced increases in power prices.

Carbon crediting mechanisms are a second tool to address competitiveness. The extent to which crediting mechanisms are able to positively affect the competitiveness of industry in Europe by reducing compliance costs remains complex and depends on numerous conditions.

A third possibility is to include importers in the ETS or to impose an import tax on the content (i.e. including the embedded carbon) of CO_2 of all goods imported into the EU from countries that do not have their own cap-and-trade system or equivalent pricing measures.

A fourth possibility to deal with competiveness is to reinforce innovation and innovation policy to facilitate the transition of an industrial sector toward a low-carbon future. Such a transition will require a focus on the new value chains that a low-carbon sector could unlock. The paper and pulp industry's *2050 Roadmap to a low carbon bio-economy* (CEPI, 2012) takes such an approach. According to the document, the "sector

---

sector-specific) perspective, meaning the ability to sell, keep, or increase market share, profits, or stock market value or all of these at once.

[19]In Germany as well as some other member states, costs related to the "energy transition" of the power sector are borne primarily by household and commercial customers and small businesses. In 2012, these costs to households amounted to almost a quarter of the retail electricity price.

has the ambition to be at the heart of the 2050 bio-economy, an essential platform for a range of biobased products and the recycling society". Transitions toward unlocking new value chains have happened and continue to happen in other sectors, such as steel and chemicals (see also CCAP, 2013).

7. The Way Ahead

Both the failure of the Copenhagen climate change negotiations and the economic crisis caught the EU offguard. Since the demise of the Kyoto-style top-down world of legally binding emission "targets" for developed countries and "actions" for developing countries, and the subsequent substitution by a bottom-up approach based on voluntary pledges (with or without review), the EU has struggled to find a new climate change consensus. Although support for climate change policy is still very high among politicians and citizens alike, discussions on the distribution of costs and benefits among sectors, regions, and member states have become more acrimonious.

The EU has also realized that "leadership" requires followers. In Copenhagen, there was little if any interest in the EU's offer to increase its ambition level to 30% GHG emission reductions in 2020 compared with 1990. The EU's negotiation partners were rather preoccupied with replacing the top-down architecture of the Kyoto Protocol with a bottom-up model of voluntary pledges.

While there might be a comprehensive and legally binding global climate change agreement that the EU had so hoped for, it will significantly fall short of the EU's declared ambitions. Hence, the matter of a level playing field for EU industry, especially in times of economic crisis and uncertainty, will become more important and may hold back a new EU consensus.

This will certainly make the EU a more difficult negotiation partner in the future. Yet this does not mean that the EU might not consider pushing for "raising the ambition level", and if not possible within the UN, then "outside" or "around" the UNFCCC. Renewables, aviation, possibly shipping, and short-lived climate pollutants (SLCPs) are examples in this regard. Other potential areas might be REDD+ or certain "green growth" themes as follows:

- The most important is support to renewable energy. As a whole, the EU is still on track to meet the 20% target for renewables, arguably by far the most expensive policy of the Climate and Energy Package. To date, it has been largely on track although investment appears to be slowing in some member states and despite considerable challenges in incorporating renewables into the power system.[20]

- As we have shown, the EU remains committed addressing the issue of aviation and shipping emissions. While we can only speculate about the extent to which the EU's inclusion of aviation into the ETS has triggered progress, there is no doubt about the EU's commitment.

- The role of SLCPs[21] under UNEP-based Climate and Clean Air Coalition (CCAC)[22] to address short-lived climate pollutants such as black carbon emissions, SLCPs from municipal solid waste, HFC alternative technology and standards, or methane and black carbon emissions from oil and natural gas production, and other measures is also supported by the EU.

- Another area that is gradually gaining support is the concept of "green growth", partly owing to the failures of international climate negotiations, and partly to the economic stagnation following the 2008 financial crisis. The notion of green growth in the EU increasingly seems as a possible way out of both the "economic" and "climate" crises. The shift to a low-carbon economy would unleash a wave of investment, innovation, and more jobs. Developed countries would re-establish economic competitiveness partly due to high-tech green technologies,

---

[20]20 Member States in 2010 achieved or exceeded the 2010 renewable energy targets contained in the National Renewable Energy Action plans ("Plans"). Most of them also achieved their 2011/2012 interim targets; unless their renewable energy shares decreased in 2011 and 2012, they are seemingly on track with their trajectory toward 2020. Overall, there is 4.8% additional RES capacity in excess to what was planned for 2012. However, the European Commission warns that the expansion capacity will reach its limits if no significant policy framework improvements are made, and expects a slowdown from 2014. The deployment of certain RES technologies is also missing its targets considerably. The expected shortfall in RES under the expected trajectory without significant policy actions is of 24.3% by 2020. In absolute terms, the most important measures for achieving the renewable energy targets are better framework conditions for wind energy and biofuels for transport (EC, 2013a, 2013b).

[21]Recent studies by the United Nations Environment Programme (UNEP) (2011 and UNEP & WMO, 2011) estimate that a portfolio of low-cost abatement measures of black carbon, tropospheric ozone, and methane can reduce temperature increases by 0.4–0.5°C between 2010 and 2050.

[22]The state members are Australia, Bangladesh, Canada, Colombia, Denmark, Finland, France, Germany, Ghana, Israel, Italy, Japan, Jordan, Mexico, Nigeria, Norway, Sweden, the UK, the US, and the European Commission. Other members include international organizations and NGOs.

while developing countries and emerging economies would move on to more sustainable paths of economic development (Zysman and Huberty, 2012).

• Reducing emissions from deforestation or forest degradation (REDD-plus) as part of the international negotiations remains controversial. Yet, within the EU, there is a consensus on the importance of attributing a value to environmental services, such as those avoiding deforestation. The importance of avoided deforestation was discussed in detail during the review of the ETS and is recognized in Article 10(3) of the ETS Directive. To date, the sovereign participation of EU member states in the international REDD+ market generally appears to be the most likely avenue for the EU and its member states than a link to the ETS or carbon markets in general.

Despite the current difficulties of the ETS, we should still expect that the principal direction for the EU's domestic and international climate change policy will be to establish a global carbon market as soon as possible. Although the ETS is in need for reform, it still enjoys large support by most member states. In addition, cap-and-trade programs to reduce GHG emissions, or at least as a substantial element of a climate change policy, are proliferating in many regions of the world. The Kyoto mechanisms of CDM and JI have created a constituency that is likely to promote the use of emissions trading.

For the EU, emissions trading has the following attractions:

• over time, it will create a global carbon price or at least a bandwidth of prices;
• such a price has the credible potential to address EU competitiveness concerns;
• carbon crediting mechanisms as an integral part of emissions trading operate in several ways; in the transition toward a global carbon price, they can address competitiveness concerns in the short term, they help capacity building, and they link different markets;
• a global net of emission trading systems — as long as they are linked — will go a long way toward meeting the EU's aspirations for a global framework;
• if properly regulated, emission markets are efficient tools to achieve climate change objectives;
• finally, they can be a major source of financial transfers to support least developed countries in their decarbonization efforts.

For the EU, it can be seen as a success that the international climate change negotiations in Durban in December 2011 opened the way toward the creation of new market mechanisms.

References

CE Delft (2010). *Why the energy-intensive industry will keep profiting from the EU ETS after 2012.* Policy Brief on findings of CE Delft work on ETS and its implications for European innovation and low-carbon growth, 6 October.

CEPI (2012). *Unfold the Future: The Forest Fibre Industry 2050 Roadmap to a Low Carbon Bio-Economy.* Brussels: Confederation of European Paper Industries.

CCAP (2013). *The New Deal: An Enlightened Industrial Policy for the EU through Structural ETS Reform.* Washington DC and Brussels: Center for Clean Air Policy.

De Bruyn, S., Markowska, A. & Nelissen, D. (2010). *Will the Energy-Intensive Industry Profit from ETS under Phase 3?* CE Delft, October.

Delbeke, J. (ed.) (2006). *The EU Greenhouse Gas Emissions Trading Scheme.* EU Energy Law, Volume IV. Leuven: Clays & Casteels.

Delarue, E., Ellermanand, D. & D'Haeseleer, W. (2010). Short-term CO_2 abatement in the European power sector: 2005–2006. *Climate Change Economics,* **1**(2), 113–133.

Den Elzen, M., Mendoza Beltran, M.A., van Vliet, J., Bakker, S.J.A. & Bole, T. (2009). *Pledges and Actions.* The Netherlands Environmental Assessment Agency, Report No 500102 032 2009.

Egenhofer, C. (2007). The making of the EU emissions trading scheme: status, prospects and implications for business. *European Management Journal,* **25**(6), 453–463, December.

Egenhofer, C, Alessi, M., Georgiev, A. & Fujiwara, N. (2011) *The EU Emissions Trading Scheme and Climate Policy towards 2050.* CEPS Special Report 2011.

Egenhofer, C., Marcu, A. & Georgiev, A. (2012). *Reviewing the EU ETS Review?* CEPS Task Force Report, October 2012.

Ellerman, A.D., Buchnerand, B. & Carraro, C. (2007). *Allocation in the European Emissions Trading Scheme: Rights, Rents and Fairness.* Cambridge: Cambridge University Press.

Ellerman, A.D. & Joskow, P. (2008). *The European Union's Emissions Trading System in Perspective.* Arlington, VA: Pew Center on Global Climate Change, May.

Ellerman, A.D., Convery, F. & de Perthuis, C. (2010). *Pricing Carbon: The European Union Emissions Trading Scheme.* Cambridge: Cambridge University Press.

European Commission (2009). *Stepping Up International Climate Finance: A European Blueprint for the Copenhagen Deal.* Communication from the Commission COM (2009) 475/3.

European Commission (2009a). Directive 2009/28/EC of the European Parliament and of the Council of 23 April 2009. *Directive 2009/28/EC on the promotion of the use of energy from renewable sources and amending and subsequently repealing Directives 2001/77/EC and 2003/30/EC*, L140/16.

European Commission (2009b). Decision No 406/2009/EC of the European Parliament and of the Council of 23 April 2009, *on the effort of Member States to reduce their greenhouse gas emissions to meet the Community's greenhouse gas emission reduction commitments up to 2020*, L140/136.

European Commission (2010a). *Analysis of options to move beyond 20% greenhouse gas emission reductions and assessing the risk of carbon leakage.* Communication from the Commission COM (2010) 265/3 (unofficial version).

European Commission (2010b). Commission Staff Working Document, accompanying the European Commission Communication, *Analysis of options to move beyond 20% greenhouse gas emission reductions and assessing the risk of carbon leakage.* Communication from the Commission, SEC (2010) 650/2; Background information and analysis Part II (unofficial version), p. 40.

European Commission (2012a). Commission Staff Working Document — Preparing the EU's Quantified Emission Limitation or Reduction Objective (QELRO) based on the EU Climate and Energy Package, SWD (2012) 18 final.

European Commission (2012b). *The State of the European Carbon Market in 2012.* COM (2012) 652. Accessed 14 November 2012.

European Commission (2013a). Green Paper, *A 2030 framework for climate and energy policies*, March, COM (2013) 169 final.

European Commission (2013b). Commission Staff Working Document accompanying the document Report from the Commission to the European Parliament and the Council. *Renewable energy progress report*, SWD (2013) 102 final.

European Environment Agency (EEA) (2009). *Annual European Community greenhouse gas inventory 1990–2007 and inventory report 2009: Submission to the UNFCCC Secretariat.* EEA Technical Report No 4/2009, EEA, Copenhagen.

Gros, D. & Egenhofer, C. (2011) The case for taxing carbon at the border *Climate Policy*, **11**(5), Special Issue, 1212–1225.

Helm, D, Hepburn, C. & Ruta, G. (2012) Trade, climate change and the political game theory of border carbon adjustments *Oxford Review of Economic Policy*, **28**(2), 368–394.

IEA (2008). *World Energy Outlook.* Paris: OECD/IEA.

IMF (2009). *World Economic Outlook Database*, International Monetary Fund, October 2009.

Keats, K. & Neuhoff, K. (2005). Allocation of carbon emissions certificates in the power sector: how generators profit from grandfathered rights. *Climate Policy*, **5**(1), 61–78.

Kettner, C., Köppl, A., Schleicherand, S. & Thenius, G. (2007). *Stringency and Distribution in the EU Emissions Trading Scheme — the 2005 Evidence.* Nota di Lavora 22.2007 FondazioneEni Enrico Mattei.

Levin, K. & Bradley, B. (2010). *Comparability of Annex I Emission Reduction Pledges*, WRI Working Paper, World Resources Institute, Washington, February 2010.

Skjærseth, J.B. & Wettestad, J. (2008). *EU Emissions Trading*, Aldershot: Ashgate.

Skjærseth, J.B. & Wettestad, J. (2010). Fixing the EU emissions trading system? Understanding the post-2012 changes. *Global Environmental Politics*, **10**(4), 101–123.

Spencer, T. (2012). Time for a grand bargain with Poland on energy and climate. *European Energy Review*, March 2012.

Spencer, T., Tangen, K. & Korppoo, A. (2010). *The EU and the Global Climate Regime: Getting Back into the Game.* The Finnish Institute of International Affairs, Briefing Paper No. 55, February 2010.

Swedish Energy Agency (2007). *The EU Emissions Trading Scheme after 2012.* Swedish Energy Agency and the Swedish Environmental Protection Agency.

Ward, M. & Grubb, M. (2009). *Comparability of Effort by Annex 1 Parties: An Overview of Issues.* London: Climate Strategies.

Zysman, J. & Huberty, M. (2012). Religion and reality in the search for green growth. *Intereconomics*, **47**(3), 140–146.

Chapter 6

The Scope for "Green Growth" and a New Technological Revolution

Alex Bowen

Centre for Climate Change Economics and Policy,
Grantham Research Institute on Climate Change and the Environment,
London School of Economics and Political Science

There is much evidence that high-carbon growth will eventually become a contradiction in terms, or, as Lord Stern puts it, "High-carbon growth would kill itself" (Stern, 2010a). This chapter considers the implications for growth of the findings of the literature on climate change mitigation costs and then considers the additional elements to the emerging "green growth" narrative. The broad conclusion is that well-designed action against climate change could improve well-being for people in the near term as well as over the longer term. A concerted attack on market and policy failures to halt climate change would increase static efficiency and might generate higher growth in the short to medium term as well as the longer term, especially if it stimulated innovation and investment. This perspective, if sufficiently convincing to negotiators, could make reaching an international agreement post-Durban easier, reducing the emphasis on burden-sharing. But the potential size of near-term gains is highly uncertain, and it may still make sense from an ethical perspective to make greater sacrifices now to underpin sustainable development in the future.

1. Introduction

Action to stop human-induced climate change is imperative. If economic development around the world remains dependent on the exploitation of fossil fuels, the greenhouse gases that would be produced would be sufficient to induce a dangerously large and unprecedentedly rapid increase in global temperatures. The technological options of carbon capture and storage and geoengineering are still largely unexplored, although enough is known about them to understand that, at scale, they would pose serious risks themselves.

As a result, policy-makers around the world have agreed in principle that deep cuts in greenhouse gas emissions are required. In December 2010, under the auspices of the UN Framework Convention on Climate Change

(UNFCCC) meeting in Cancun, a large majority of countries agreed that
"... deep cuts in global greenhouse gas emissions are required according
to science, and as documented in the Fourth Assessment Report of the
Inter-governmental Panel on Climate Change, with a view to reducing
global greenhouse gas emissions so as to hold the increase in global average
temperature below 2°C above pre-industrial levels, and that Parties should
take urgent action to meet this long-term goal, consistent with science and
on the basis of equity" (UNFCCC, 2011).

However, there is enough coal, oil and gas in the ground that could
be recovered profitably at today's energy prices with today's technologies
to take the world well above the ceiling of a 2°C global mean temperature
change. Developments in "fracking" (hydraulic fracturing of rocks to recover
natural gas and oil), deep-sea oil exploration and enhanced oil recovery
techniques have helped to ensure that market forces alone will not be
sufficient to keep cumulative greenhouse gas emissions low enough for the
ceiling not to be breached.

That puts the onus on policy-makers to take action against climate
change. But the global economic crisis triggered in 2008 has moved the focus
of political debate toward growth in the near term and away from long-term
risks. As a result, policy-makers anxious to build up support for urgent
action on climate change have turned to the concept of "green growth" to
win acceptance for strong efforts to slow and stop human-induced climate
change. They have also sought to tap into an older strand of argument
advocating sustainable development. A recent rallying call by the Organisation for Economic Co-operation and Development (OECD), bringing
together a large-scale analytical effort by the organization (OECD, 2011),
is a good example of this trend. It defines green growth as follows: "Green
growth means fostering economic growth and development while ensuring
that natural assets continue to provide the resources and environmental
services on which our well-being relies." UNEP has advocated "greening"
the global economy, by which it means improving "human well-being and
social equity, while significantly reducing environmental risks and ecological
scarcities" (UNEP, 2010), which requires "reconfiguring businesses and
infrastructure to deliver better returns on natural, human and economic
capital investments, while at the same time reducing greenhouse gas
emissions, extracting and using less natural resources, creating less waste,
and reducing social disparities."

To what extent is this new, or at least reconditioned, narrative a
reflection of valuable insights and to what extent is it just spin? Bowen

and Fankhauser (2011) argue that, "The attraction of the green growth narrative is both strategic and analytical. From a strategic point of view, green growth allows environmental protection to be cast as a question of opportunity and reward, rather than costly restraint." Analytically, the "green growth" narrative holds out the promise of broadening the focus of climate change economics from the game theory of international collaboration, direct mitigation costs and adaptation costs.

There are four main additional elements, operating over different time frames:

(1) In the short term, the scope for a directed demand stimulus at a time of aggregate demand deficiency.
(2) In the medium term, the scope for greater productivity from a more comprehensive assault on market and policy failures.
(3) In the longer term, the scope for triggering a long wave of innovation analogous to the Industrial Revolutions of the past.
(4) In the longer term still, the prospects of "backstop" energy technologies that would cap the real price of energy services despite continued economic growth.

This chapter rehearses briefly the evidence that high-carbon growth will eventually become a contradiction in terms, or, as Lord Stern puts it, "High-carbon growth would kill itself: first from the high prices of hydrocarbons that could result, and second, and more fundamentally, from the very hostile physical environment it would create" (Stern, 2010a). Then it considers the implications for growth of the literature on climate change mitigation costs. The chapter goes on to consider the additional elements to the "green growth" narrative. The broad conclusion is that well-designed action against climate change could improve well-being for people in the near term as well as over the longer term. But the potential size of near-term gains is highly uncertain and it may still make sense from an ethical perspective to make greater sacrifices now to underpin sustainable development in the future (Box 1).

Box 1. The evolution of the concept of green growth.

The evolution of the "green growth" concept can be traced to the first theories about the limits to growth and the meaning of sustainable development. The view that population growth would ultimately be limited

---

(*Continued*)

Box 1. *(Continued)*

by resource constraints was first put forward by Malthus in his *Essay on the Principle of Population* (1798). Since then, several economic theories on resource scarcity and constrained growth have been elaborated (in, for example, Mill, 1848; Hotelling, 1931; Barnett and Morse, 1963; Hardin, 1968; Solow, 1974 — see the interesting discussion in Tahvonen, 2000). One milestone was the publication of the book commissioned by the Club of Rome, *The Limits to Growth* (Meadows *et al.*, 1972), which examined the consequences of a rapidly growing world population and finite resource supplies. This attracted much discussion and numerous critiques (e.g. Cole and Pavitt, 1973; Nordhaus, 1973).

The concept of "sustainable development" was introduced explicitly only in the early 1980s (IUCN/UNEP/WWF, 1980). Its most famous formulation is that associated with the 1987 report, "Our Common Future," by the World Commission on Environment and Development, also known as the Brundtland Commission. The report defines sustainable development as "development that meets the needs of the present without compromising the ability of future generations to meet their own needs."

The Brundtland report did not use the term "green growth" but the phrase was being used by the late 1980s at the latest, for example in Colby (1989): "The positive vision of eco-development is for "green growth" and integrated co-evolutionary development of humans and nature." In political discourse, UK political parties contrasted "green growth" and "no growth." In the UK, as early as 1989, a Conservative politician, Michael Howard, argued that "Green growth, rather than no growth, must become the watchword of the Conservative Party" (*Guardian*, 1989).

The issue has been discussed subsequently in several national and international arenas. Most notably, the United Nations Conference on Environment and Development in Rio de Janeiro in 1992 gave a strong impetus to the search for sustainable development. The Conference approved its "Agenda 21," which included ambitious commitments by world leaders to ensure sustainable development in many areas and at all levels of society. Ten years later, political leaders endorsed the objective at the Johannesburg Summit on Sustainable Development.

(Continued)

Box 1. (*Continued*)

The goal of "green growth" was proposed in 2005, at the fifth Ministerial Conference on Environment and Development in Asia and the Pacific. This was not meant to replace the concept of "sustainable development," but rather to be a "subset" of it (OECD, 2011). In use, the term usually has a slightly narrower focus than does "sustainable development," with a stronger emphasis on economic policy-making and the links between economic growth and the environment and the aim of "getting the economy right."

Currently, several terms are often used interchangeably, such as green growth, green economy or, in its narrower climate change focus, the low-carbon economy. There is no universal definition, although those used tend to have several aspects in common. The United Nations Environmental Programme (UNEP, 2011) defines a green economy as one that results in "improved human well-being and social equity, while significantly reducing environmental risks and ecological scarcities." According to the OECD (2011), green growth means "fostering economic growth and development while ensuring that natural assets continue to provide the resources and environmental services on which our well-being relies." For the World Bank, green growth is about "making growth processes resource efficient, cleaner and more resilient without necessarily slowing them" (Hallegatte *et al.*, 2011).

Recent initiatives include UNEP's Green Economy Initiative, launched in 2008 to assist governments in "greening" their economies, the OECD's strategy toward green growth, published in 2011, and the World Bank's "Inclusive Green Growth: the Pathway to Sustainable Development" in 2012. The promotion of green growth in the European Union was also one of the top priorities of the Danish EU Presidency in the first half of 2012.[1] Renewed political commitment to sustainable development was sought at the Conference on Sustainable Development in Rio de Janeiro in June 2012 (often referred to as "Rio+20").

---

[1] See the Danish EU Presidency website: http://eu2012.dk/en/EU-and-the-Presidency/ About-the-Presidency/Program-og-prioriteter.

2. High-Carbon Growth: A Contradiction in Terms?

Indefinite high-carbon growth is likely to entail increases in global mean temperatures well above 2°C above pre-industrial levels. In order to provide a benchmark against which to measure gross climate change mitigation costs, economists have suggested a wide range of emission path scenarios for a counterfactual world in which temperatures increase but there is no feedback from climate change to growth (the "BAU NCC" counterfactual). These can then be compared with paths along which possible climate change damages and risks are factored in and paths along which expected mitigation costs are deducted from output. Recent projections suggest that the increase in global temperatures before the end of this century could be over 5°C — considerably higher than earlier estimates — but new scientific findings are likely to lead to frequent revisions of such estimates.

This is illustrated very well by an MIT report that notes:

> The MIT Integrated Global System Model is used to make probabilistic projections of climate change from 1861 to 2100. Since the model's first projections were published in 2003, substantial improvements have been made to the model, and improved estimates of the probability distributions of uncertain input parameters have become available. The new projections are considerably warmer than the 2003 projections; for example, the median surface warming in 2091–2100 is 5.1°C compared to 2.4°C in the earlier study. Many changes contribute to the stronger warming; among the more important ones are taking into account the cooling in the second half of the 20th century due to volcanic eruptions for input parameter estimation and a more sophisticated method for projecting gross domestic product (GDP) growth, which eliminated many low-emission scenarios. However, if recently published data, suggesting stronger twentieth-century ocean warming, are used to determine the input climate parameters, the median projected warning at the end of the twenty-first century is only 4.1°C (Paltsev et al., 2009).

The costs of unmitigated climate change are inevitably highly uncertain, given the lack of any precedent in recorded human history. For example, long-term projections of greenhouse gas emissions under business as usual are sensitive to assumptions about economic growth in advanced countries, the speed of convergence of emerging-market economies with today's wealthiest economies and the evolution of technologies using fossil fuels. The mapping between annual emissions of greenhouse gases and the accumulated stock in the atmosphere is uncertain because the rate at which they are removed from the atmosphere via carbon "sinks," such as the oceans and forests, and chemical processes, such as rock weathering, is variable and is likely to respond to climate change itself. The impact of global warming on local climates is difficult to assess accurately. And the impacts of local climate change on economic growth are likely to be many and varied, with uncertainty over magnitude. It is therefore a challenge to judge to what degree societies could adapt to the economic impacts in the relevant timescale.

The Stern Review (Stern *et al.*, 2007) illustrated this uncertainty by the use of fan charts. It concluded that unmitigated climate change could cost the welfare equivalent of a 20% fall in consumption, per capita, now and forever, relative to the counterfactual business-as-usual, no-climate-damages case. And this calculation assumed that there would be no additional climate change damages after 200 years — a simplifying assumption that has received rather less attention than the Stern Review's advocacy of a low pure rate of time preference.

Stern has emphasized the potential geopolitical risks from such large economic and social impacts, writing, for example:

> The map of where people could live would probably be radically redrawn. This could imply, for example, that some areas would become deserts, some would be inundated, and many subject to radical change in weather patterns or in the location and flows of rivers. This could mean in turn the movement of hundreds of millions or billions of people. History suggests that movements of people on such a scale would likely involve extended, severe, and global conflicts (Stern, 2010a).

Some economists have been more sanguine. Tol (2009a) reviewed estimates of the marginal social cost of carbon and concluded that a government that uses the same 3% discount rate for climate change as it does for other decisions should levy a carbon tax of US$ 25 per metric tonne of carbon (modal value) to US$ 50/tonnes C (mean value) (equivalent to US$ 6.82/tonnes CO_2 and US$ 13.64/tonnes CO_2 respectively) — well below the Stern estimates of US$ 91.67/tonnes C to US$ 110/tonnes C (US$ 25 to US$ 30/tonnes CO_2). As he also noted that a tax of at least US$ 50/tonnes C would be required to bring about substantial reductions in carbon dioxide emissions, one might conclude that he does not share Stern's apocalyptic view. But he acknowledges the great uncertainties, particularly about "extreme climate scenarios, the very long-term, biodiversity loss, the possible effects of climate change on economic development, and even political violence", and also the role extreme risks — catastrophe risks — could play.

Nordhaus (2008) is keener on urgent action on mitigation but takes the same broad approach to costs as does Tol. Some other economists are closer to Stern's view — see, for example, Ackerman and Stanton (2010) and Dietz (2011). It is also clear that the risks are larger for countries that are the least developed, because of their dependence on agriculture, the disproportionate number of least developed countries located in low latitudes and their limited adaptive capabilities.

Estimates of the economic costs of unmitigated climate change are very sensitive to the assumptions made about discount rates, people's aversion to risk and ambiguity and the likelihood of catastrophic outcomes. The Tol point of view implies that high-carbon growth will not be much slower than the counterfactual growth in a "no climate change" world, a point elaborated in Fankhauser and Tol (2005). Nordhaus' view is not that far removed from Tol's. Both assume that per capita growth rates will slowly decline toward zero under the counterfactual BAU NCC case. The Stern view envisages the substantial risk that, for at least some parts of the world, growth could be reversed. Weitzman (2009) argues that the uncertain risk of catastrophic and irreversible changes in the global climate system is likely to dominate rational decision-making.

Faced with the many uncertain factors that ought, in principle, to be taken into account in assessing the costs of untrammelled greenhouse gas emissions and setting a carbon price, what are policy-makers to do? They can pool their knowledge and understanding of these factors, however incomplete, discuss the issues and make a best guess about the global goal that is likely to result in the highest well-being. As more is learnt about the scientific, economic and ethical uncertainties afflicting climate change, the goal can be periodically adjusted.[2] In practice, policy-makers have done this through the UNFCCC process. To give a 50–50 chance of remaining below the 2°C ceiling requires that the concentration of greenhouse gases in the atmosphere is stabilized at around 450 ppm CO_2e. Estimates of the carbon price necessary to achieve this target vary but appear to be closer to ones suggested by the Stern Review perspective than the Tol perspective.

---

[2]Thus, the target should reflect economic and ethical considerations, not only scientific ones.

Adoption of the 2°C ceiling does not logically entail the view that high-carbon growth will kill itself — it might simply slow substantially, particularly in poorer countries. The question turns on the likely effects of temperature increases outside the range considered by most empirical estimates. However, it seems plausible to this author that a change of over 5°C, a temperature difference as large as the one that separates us from the last Ice Age, over two centuries, with a risk of a larger increase if greenhouse gases in the ocean floors and tundra are released, could have devastating effects on food production and water supply and thus undermine economic systems, let alone halt growth. Diamond (2005) has documented the capacity of civilizations to destroy themselves through environmental degradation. This remains speculative, but policy-makers have to take a view on the future risks that the world is incurring with its current economic model of high-carbon development.

3. The Costs of Mitigating Climate Change

Economic studies that conclude that meeting the 2°C climate goal is feasible suggest that it will entail gross costs of less than 5% of GDP and as low as 1% of GDP (some estimates sometimes specify GDP at a particular time horizon — say, in 2050 — while others express the net present value of future costs in terms of the net present value of future GDP). As this is an impact on the level of GDP, the impact on growth rates can look very much smaller. A policy that builds from a cost of zero today to 5% of GDP in 2050 would reduce the annual growth rate over 2012–2050 by only about 23 basis points. The gross costs do not include any estimate of the benefits of climate change mitigation and usually do not include offsets from any so-called "co-benefits" such as reduced particulate pollution. Nor do they usually include benefits from policy reforms designed to correct market failures standing in the way of climate change mitigation, apart from carbon pricing to address the central greenhouse gas externality. Debate continues about likely climate change mitigation costs (see Box 2). A significant impact on growth seems unlikely to this author but cannot be ruled out if a target of 450 ppm CO_2e is not to be missed. However, somewhat less ambitious targets, which would also require sharp and large reductions in annual emissions, would have very little effect on growth if carried out in a cost-effective way.

Box 2. Some evidence on the costs of adhering to the 2°C temperature change ceiling.

Bowen and Ranger (2009) reviewed evidence on the costs of climate change mitigation designed not to exceed the 2°C ceiling, noting the following:

- Stern *et al.* (2007) concluded that the costs of mitigation consistent with a stabilization target of 500–550 ppm CO_2e were likely to be of the order of 1% of annual GDP by 2050, within a range of ±3%.
- Studies of mitigation costs have suggested that they would not rise very sharply with increased stringency of the long-term target, up to a point when the required technological changes become infeasible. That point, Stern concluded, would very probably be reached if the target was as low as 450 ppm CO_2e, so it proposed that level as the lower bound of the range for the stabilization goal.
- Since the Stern Review was published, the IPCC Fourth Assessment Report (2007), has surveyed the literature, finding that estimates from integrated assessment models of costs in 2050 for stabilization at 650 ppm CO_2e ranged from 2% of GDP in 2050 to −1% (i.e. net non-climate benefits); for stabilization at 550 ppm CO_2e costs ranged from 4% to just under zero; and for stabilization at 445–535 ppm CO_2e costs ranged up to 5%.
- The work of the United States Climate Change Science Program (US CCSP) on scenarios for greenhouse gas emissions and atmospheric concentrations came to a similar conclusion about the rise in expected mitigation costs as the target becomes tougher (US CCSP, 2007). It reported that the costs in 2060 of heading toward a target of 450 ppm CO_2 (around 525 ppm CO_2e) ranged from 1.9 to 6.7% of GDP across the three IAMs that were considered. That compared with only 0.2–2.3% if the target was a less demanding 550 ppm CO_2 (around 670 ppm CO_2e).
- den Elzen *et al.* (2007) investigated a set of feasible multi-gas emissions paths for stabilization at 450 ppm CO_2e (peaking at 510 ppm CO_2e), 550 ppm CO_2e and 650 ppm CO_2e. They estimated that net present value (NPV) of mitigation costs across the century (with a discount rate of 5%) would range from 0.2% of cumulative GDP in the case of the highest target to 1% in the case of the lowest.

(*Continued*)

Box 2. (*Continued*)

- Knopf *et al.* (2009) considered five IAMs with different characteristics and found that ultimate stabilization at 450 ppm CO_2e, if feasible, would cost less than 1.5% of GDP (cumulated to 2100). Stabilization at 400 ppm CO_2e would be, at most, around one percentage point of cumulative GDP more expensive than stabilization at 450 ppm CO_2e; that could be regarded as the premium to be paid to reduce the likelihood of exceeding the 2°C ceiling by some 30 percentage points.

- Rao *et al.* (2008), using two other IAMs, found that the costs of aiming for stabilization at around 450 ppm CO_2e would be about 3% of GDP by 2050, and 5% by 2100.

- Edenhofer *et al.* (2009), after examining three IAMs, concluded that the discounted welfare costs of stabilizing at 410 ppm CO_2 (a target of broadly similar ambition to the 450 ppm CO_2e target) would be around 0.8–4% of baseline global GDP.

- Calvin *et al.* (2009) developed a scenario with strong policies on land use that meets a 450 ppm CO_2e target for stabilization,[3] but only with a very high carbon price.

- Some of the models included in the 22nd Stanford Energy Modeling Forum (EMF22) exercise are unable to generate paths consistent with a target of stabilizing concentrations at 450 ppm CO_2e even with the full participation of all regions in the world. Blanford *et al.* (2009), for example, find that a radiative forcing target equivalent to 450 ppm CO_2e "cannot be met even allowing for full participation [of all countries] and overshoot during the entire 21st century." They point out that this finding reflects the "speed limits" imposed in their model on the rate of transformation of regions' energy systems, the strong growth of "business as usual" emissions that they project and the absence of negative-emissions activities such as biomass with carbon capture and storage and afforestation.

- Tol (2009b) finds that the target of avoiding a temperature increase of more than 2°C is infeasible "under any but the most advantageous of assumptions." In his model FUND, a climate sensitivity of no more than 2.5°C per doubling of ambient CO_2 is required, together with a carbon tax starting at over US\$ 270/tonne CO_2 in 2013, applied to all greenhouse gases and all countries and rising at the discount rate.

---

[3]The target is actually expressed in terms of a radiative forcing of $2.6 \, \text{W/m}^2$.

The key factors determining cost estimates include:

- The rate of growth of emissions of greenhouse gases under "business as usual" — the more rapid this rate is, the bigger the challenge of decarbonization.
- The speed at which the productivity of low-carbon technologies increases with spending on research and development, investment, time and experience (or cumulative production) — some models still exclude induced innovation and endogenous growth, whereas models that include them tend to project lower costs of action.
- The scope for demand-side adjustments — in other words, the degree of substitutability of low-carbon goods and services for high-carbon ones in consumption and production: estimates of price elasticities of demand derived from past energy price shocks may not be a good guide to the elasticities in a world of credible, long-term carbon pricing.
- The scope for "free lunches" from greater energy efficiency without changing the pattern of final production.
- Whether marginal abatement costs are equalized across firms, sectors and countries.
- Whether land-use is subject to strong policies, with deforestation reversed and the use of land for food production and biomass prevented from crowding out forest "sinks."

It is important to note that even the optimistic estimates of costs do not consider the non-zero possibility of a breakthrough invention that transforms the outlook for energy and emissions (e.g. power from nuclear fusion, sequestration of greenhouse gases from the atmosphere). The full probability distribution of possible mitigation costs includes such scenarios, but also scenarios at the other end of the spectrum, in which much more of the burden of emissions reductions has to be carried by substitution of consumers and companies away from emissions-intensive products.

At the same time as modelers have been developing the analysis of the costs and feasibility of tougher targets, the economic environment has been evolving and key parameters in cost estimates have been subject to re-assessment. Global annual emissions of greenhouse gases have continued to push up the concentrations in the atmosphere — by around 2.5 ppm CO_2e per year last decade (until the global downturn arrived), which made any given target more difficult to achieve. Projections of "business as usual" emissions of greenhouse gases have tended to be revised upward, reflecting both observed trends in emissions this decade, and sharp upward revisions in the long-term prospects of China and India following their unprecedented recent growth rates. This has been associated with a more rapid increase in the use of coal (see, for example, Garnaut *et al.*, 2008; Sheehan, 2008). The probability of long-term, low-growth trajectories for world GDP in the absence of climate change may have been overestimated in the past (Webster *et al.*, 2008).

However, the global economic slowdown may lead to a reassessment. One modeling group has already revised down its long-term GDP projections (Paltsev *et al.*, 2009). These authors also note that renewable energy technologies appear to be more viable and are being deployed more rapidly than previously assumed. However, they argue that both nuclear power and carbon capture and storage are likely to be more expensive than previously thought. Overall, they conclude, the costs of meeting tough targets for emissions reductions are likely to be somewhat higher than they thought a few years earlier.

Blanford *et al.* (2009) found that upward revisions of the outlook for growth in the developing world over the long term more than outweigh the impact of even pessimistic assumptions about the consequences of the current global slowdown. It is clear that if the current growth aspirations of the developing world are to be met, the climate challenge to policy-makers is tougher.

4. The Keynesian Element of Green Growth

Considering first short-term horizons, advocates of "green growth" attempt to reconnect the issue of long-term sustainability with the concerns of economists and politicians about short-term macroeconomic fluctuations, unemployment, fiscal sustainability and global saving–investment imbalances. The calls for a green fiscal stimulus that were heard as the economic crisis intensified illustrate this effort (e.g. Pollin *et al.*, 2008; UNEP, 2009; Bowen and Ranger, 2009; Edenhofer *et al.*, 2009; Houser *et al.*, 2009). The view still has traction because of the fear of future downturns and the continuing low investment rates in many countries despite low real interest rates. The emphasis has moved toward the question of how to utilize the flow of private saving by stimulating private investment, motivated by the likelihood that, globally, planned saving would still exceed planned investment at full employment (Zenghelis, 2011). Increasing investment to decarbonize economies is preferable to equilibrating saving and investment by reducing incomes and hence saving flows.

The key insight is that if there are spare resources available in the economy, stimulating investment in the capital stock necessary for the transition to green growth could increase GDP (and hence, in the short run, GDP growth) through a Keynesian multiplier effect. There is continuing debate about the likely size of such a multiplier but it seems likely that it is larger in deeper downturns caused by a deficiency of aggregate demand and aggravated by tighter private sector credit constraints (IMF, 2012). Governments can make the best of a bad situation by opportunistically increasing their spending on social and environmental capital at such times (Bowen and Stern, 2010).

The case for green spending, as opposed to other sorts of spending, rests primarily on the proposition that, among problems warranting structural changes in economies, the world's environmental challenges are one of the most urgent. That in turn reflects the growing awareness of the risks posed by anthropogenic climate change, which has led to more attention than previously being paid to the environmental "pillar" of sustainable development. The case has also been buttressed by appeals to various forms of green spending that may have particularly attractive properties with respect to the size of the Keynesian multiplier process that amplifies their macroeconomic effect.

The contingent nature of this second line of argument is perhaps best illustrated by the debate about "green jobs." Perhaps the most serious social impact of severe economic slowdowns is in the labor market, with increases in involuntary unemployment and the consequent deterioration of human capital. That has led to an emphasis on gross job creation in green investment projects in much of the discussion of green growth proposals. But instead of focusing on the gross number of "green jobs" created, it would be more useful to consider what the net labor market effects of introducing green growth policies would be economy-wide, even though in practice it is very difficult to estimate these impacts (Bowen, 2011).

Three main factors are likely to determine those effects. First, workers need to be made available to the sectors where they are most needed — including the expanding environmentally friendly ones but also existing lower-carbon sectors such as business services — and assisted in moving from declining sectors such as fossil-fuel extraction. There are signs of skill shortages in a number of sectors that are likely to benefit the most from green growth (ILO/CEDEFOP, 2011).

Second, the original causes of downturn are relevant. If the unemployment arises from a deficiency of aggregate demand — in other words, a particular macroeconomic market failure — the transition to green growth is much more likely to lead to net job creation. But in circumstances of near-full employment, the net effect of the transition to green growth may be reduced overall labor supply, if real incomes are lower than they otherwise would be because of higher prices for carbon-intensive products (Goettle and Fawcett, 2009). If involuntary unemployment results from labor market rigidities such as inflexible real wages or difficulties in moving workers from one sector to another, the transition may exacerbate the impact of these rigidities.

Third, if new green technologies are more labor-intensive at prevailing wages, input costs and interest rates than the ones that they replace, gross job creation is more likely. This appears to be the case for electricity generation from renewable energy (Kammen *et al.*, 2004; Wei *et al.*, 2010) and energy-efficiency improvements, and also probably some forms of land management (e.g. re-afforestation). Carbon pricing is likely to induce a substitution of labor for capital and energy more generally, although there is some debate about the impact on the demand for capital goods (see, for example, the discussion in Kemfert and Welsch, 2000). But not all activities needed for green growth are likely to be particularly labor intensive (e.g. R&D on low-emission vehicles) and some may crowd out more labor-intensive activities elsewhere in the economy, especially if government spending is constrained (e.g. capital-intensive spending on electricity grids displacing spending on teachers and nurses).

The composition of a fiscal stimulus matters. Corporate tax cuts, personal tax cuts, targeted social security payment increases, and public sector investment are all likely to have different multiplier effects from each other and in different macroeconomic circumstances. Some fiscal stimuli can be calibrated and activated quickly and then unwound speedily when capacity utilization and employment have recovered — projects under this heading are often called "shovel ready." Others are slow to get going and unpredictable in their ultimate size. All may be difficult to unwind or fund from taxation when debt financing has to be reduced, so an explicit strategy for exiting from deficit financing is required. These considerations should influence which elements of a green growth strategy are accelerated to help to make up for sharp falls in private sector aggregate demand.

The relevance of the Keynesian perspective needs to be investigated further. Several economists have emphasized the importance of taking into account macroeconomic volatility in climate change policy-making (e.g. McKibbin *et al.*, 2008; Bowen and Stern, 2010). Yet the implications of business cycles for specific policy instruments have barely been investigated. Is it more relevant for developed market economies than low-income countries? How should environmental policy tools be adjusted in the face of macroeconomic shocks? What does the debate about the size of fiscal multipliers in different settings imply for environmental policies? Should investment in social capital benefiting generations as yet unborn be insulated from fluctuations in market interest rates?

The issue of macroeconomic fluctuations and the business cycle is intimately bound up with the question of how to narrow fiscal deficits and what criteria should be used to assess climate-related public spending. Climate-related investment flows and carbon markets are likely to be large enough to have effects on the imbalances between saving and investment within and between countries. They could also affect the level of aggregate demand and aggregate supply. Promoting a new, low-carbon, industrial revolution has the potential to reduce government debt by increasing environmental taxes and stimulating faster GDP growth (especially while there is spare capacity available), while flows of private funds to finance "green" investment could help to reduce global saving–investment imbalances (Zenghelis, 2011).

5. The Pigouvian Element of Green Growth

As the scope for green fiscal stimuli has narrowed, given mounting concerns about fiscal sustainability in many countries, more attention has been paid to the opportunities to improve static efficiency in the transition to green growth, recognizing the various market imperfections and policy failures that prevail. The search for ancillary benefits is not new (see, for example, Pearce, 1992), but the green growth paradigm takes a much wider and systematic view of market failures, including network externalities, information failures and asymmetries, problems in the provision of public infrastructure, and constraints to innovation as well as environmental externalities. It also considers definitions and measures of prosperity beyond conventional national income measures.

The promise is held out of large welfare gains from well-designed Pigouvian taxes and subsidies and, in some cases, from direct assaults on the sources of market failure (for example, by improving information flows, setting up niche public sector investment banks and refining intellectual property rights regimes). Policy failures, such as fossil fuel subsidies, also need to be tackled according to this perspective. Pigouvian measures in principle can lead to a step improvement in well-being, some — but not all — of which will be reflected in conventional measures of GDP. Thus a short-run fillip to growth can be generated. However, if ill thought out, adding green growth measures to the existing policy mix can also dent the overall effectiveness of policies (Fankhauser *et al.*, 2010; Fischer and Preonas, 2010).

This perspective suggests a different way of looking at many of the "co-benefits" of climate change mitigation policies, such as lower particulate pollution, greater energy security, greater access to energy services for the poor, and higher rates of innovation. Climate change is a sufficiently large threat that it may finally have raised the issue of market failures higher up the agenda of policy-makers, spurring them to act. But correcting market failures can have an impact across the whole economy, not only in the high-carbon sectors. So mitigating climate change, higher rates of innovation, and other benefits are in a sense all co-benefits of taking the economic causes of market failures seriously. This way of looking at the challenge links the Pigouvian and Keynesian elements if one thinks of Keynesian unemployment as a symptom of a very large market failure, resulting from price adjustment costs or rational inattentiveness.

In some cases, including importantly action on climate change, the benefits of intervention are likely to be generated in the long term while the costs have to be paid sooner. But why should people in poor countries be expected to pay toward the preservation of environmental capital that predominantly benefits their own wealthier descendants (and future generations in the currently rich countries)? A judicious mix of policies could make all generations better off, given that correcting market failures is a positive-sum activity — in economists' jargon, a Pareto-superior outcome is possible.

For example, if the current generation is persuaded by carbon pricing to leave future generations more natural capital and lower greenhouse gas concentrations, governments could offset the impact on the current generation's consumption by taxing non-climate-related investment and returning the proceeds to households to consume (for example, by an interest rate surcharge on non-green investment). Thus, the current generation would not necessarily have to bear net costs. Similarly, larger resource transfers from rich countries could accompany climate change mitigation by low-income countries, as UNFCCC negotiators have recognized.

6. The Schumpeterian Element of Green Growth

The economic changes required by the transition to green growth are unlikely to be marginal, as much of the mitigation literature implicitly assumes, but pervasive and quantitatively significant given the range and size of market failures that need to be corrected. The outcome may be more akin to a new industrial revolution (Stern, 2010b). New inventions, social changes, and economic developments can trigger such revolutions, opening up huge opportunities for new firms while imposing enormous challenges for established ones committed to the old ways.

The nature and importance of such revolutions have been explored by Perez (2010) who draws on a neo-Schumpeterian perspective in her analysis of "techno-economic paradigm shifts." The perspective also has something in common with the analysis of endogenous growth (e.g. Acemoglu *et al.*, 2009). There may be increasing returns to human capital, knowledge accumulation, and investment, particularly in infrastructure networks, partly because of the positive spill-over effects (externalities) that can be generated. Central is the notion that a non-marginal policy shift toward strong environmental policies could kick-start a prolonged period of higher growth, in both its conventional and green forms, through two mechanisms: first, the positive impact in competitive markets of novelty — new green products — on demand and innovation; and, second, the increased emphasis on innovation, which is necessary if high-carbon products are to be replaced by low-carbon substitutes, not simply priced out of the market place.

If there is to be a new green industrial revolution, it will be dependent to an unusual extent on new, credible, strong, and persistent policies being implemented around the world. One can foresee a number of potential obstacles (see Pearson and Foxon, 2012, for a discussion of some of the difficulties and the lessons available from past industrial revolutions). First, the energy sector, which will have to be at the heart of any transformation, may not be big enough to have such transformative effects, despite its pervasive links with the rest of the economy.

Second, the mechanism central to Schumpeter's own vision — intensified entrepreneurial competition leading to a plethora of competing novel products, stimulating both potential supply and demand, followed by failure of the unsuccessful innovators — may be difficult to engineer. From the point of view of the end-user, energy from renewable sources instead of fossil fuels will still be supplied primarily in traditional forms and often by monopolistic regulated utilities, which are not renowned for their entrepreneurship and innovation. However, the transition to green growth could be more revolutionary if combined with advances in information and communications technologies and materials science.

Third, high-carbon innovation and lower fossil-fuel rents may discourage low-carbon deployment, just as in the 19th century the innovation of steamships set off a burst of improvements in sailing-ship technology. The prospect of high carbon prices in the future could lead low-cost fossil-fuel producers to extract resources more rapidly in the near term, giving up some of the scarcity rents embodied in the price of fossil fuels, thus driving down the relative price of fossil fuels and undermining the impact of carbon pricing.[4]

Again, the Schumpeterian perspective to green growth raises a number of important new research questions. The implications of past government actions to mitigate market failures for "green" growth have yet to be fully explored. The dependence of green growth on the persistence of coherent and credible policy interventions over a long time period raises issues of policy-maker independence, pre-commitment, and time inconsistency familiar from the discussion of monetary policy frameworks. The implications of these debates for "green" innovation need to be teased out, drawing on, among other sources, the existing literature on promoting sustainable energy (e.g. Foxon and Pearson, 2007), which has stressed the need for systems analysis and drawn attention to the importance of enabling conditions such as the adequacy of supply of the appropriate skills.

7. The Georgian Element of Green Growth

Green growth can also be viewed as a way to loosen the constraints imposed by increasing resource scarcity. Substituting away from scarce resources such as fossil fuels and toward renewable energy, manufactured capital and knowledge might remove a constraint to long-term growth while preserving unique environmental resources for the future (Hepburn and Bowen, 2013). Utilizing geothermal energy and solar power holds out the promise of escaping the threat of increasing entropy over any timescale relevant to human civilization.

---

[4]This issue is discussed in the literature on the "green paradox" (Sinn, 2008). However, the relevance of the green paradox is disputed (e.g. van der Ploeg and Withagen, 2010; Edenhofer and Kalkuhl, 2011). If it is a real threat, side payments to fossil-fuel owners may be needed to persuade them to keep their resources in the ground.

Concerns about running out of natural resources are long-standing and go back to at least Thomas Malthus, although the view is perhaps most prominently associated with the Club of Rome (Meadows *et al.*, 1972). The Malthusian view has been challenged by thinkers who have emphasized the capacity of human ingenuity and good governance to allow humanity to escape from the trap of population growth outstripping resources. One of the earliest was the US political economist Henry George in the 19th century.

So far George's view has been borne out. Increasing efficiency of resource use in response to relative price increases, together with technical progress, has allowed continued growth despite physical limits on resource endowments — and the limits themselves have responded to economic stimuli. Economic systems, perhaps anticipating the problem, have so far managed to generate alternative products and production techniques before resource constraints have begun to bite. The challenge is for green growth policies to repeat this feat. As some ecological economists have argued (e.g. Jackson, 2009), it is by no means certain that it will be possible. But nor is it logically or empirically impossible. That is borne out by the analyses of the feasibility of stopping anthropogenic climate change, the biggest threat from resource constraints to date.

8. Conclusions

Green growth is not an oxymoron. It is feasible and more attractive than the alternatives, especially the prospect of untrammelled climate change. This is becoming more and more apparent to many policy-makers in both developed and developing countries. The development strategies promulgated by international development agencies are increasingly designed to engineer a transition to green growth. The short-run costs need not be high and may be offset in whole or in part by a range of co-benefits, especially starting in a time of global demand deficiency. Policies to stimulate green innovation are likely to be particularly beneficial and transformative. This perspective, if sufficiently convincing to negotiators, could make reaching an international agreement post-Durban easier, reducing the emphasis on burden-sharing and increasing the attention paid to practical policies to increase the co-benefits of action on climate change. The evolution of the Nationally Appropriate Mitigation Actions reported under the UNFCCC and the recognition that all countries must play a part in global greenhouse gas emission reductions suggest that progress is being made in this direction.

However, a transition to green growth will require more consistent and coherent collective action over a longer time frame and across more aspects of the economy than most economic challenges require. Many actions will have to be co-ordinated across borders if the costs of climate change mitigation are to be minimized. For example, it would be helpful if a uniform global price of carbon evolved and if cross-border transfers of knowledge about green technologies were promoted. Taking full advantage of the opportunities from the correction of market failures in many parts of the economic system will also depend on policies being well-designed — good regulation, not just more regulation. The costs of well-designed policies need not be large in economic terms but the obstacles to good policy-making are great. Collective action needs to be taken within transparent, credible, and ethically acceptable frameworks of governance, globally and nationally, and it needs to be monitored, assessed, and regulated by the citizenry. It may still make sense from an ethical perspective to make greater sacrifices now to underpin sustainable development in the future.

Acknowledgments

I am grateful to my CCCEP colleagues for comments and advice and especially to Sam Fankhauser and Nicola Ranger, who have allowed me to draw on past joint work with them. I would also like to thank Samuela Bassi for her assistance. I alone remain responsible for any errors.

References

Acemoglu, D., Aghion, P., Bursztyn, L. & Hemous, D. (2009). *The Environment and Directed Technical Change*, NBER Working Paper 15451, Cambridge, Massachusetts, October.

Ackerman, F. & Stanton, E.A. (2010). The social cost of carbon. *Real-World Economics Review*, (53), June, 129–143. Available at: http://www.paecon.net/ PAEReview/issue53/AckermanStanton53.pdf

ADAM project (2009). Adaptation and Mitigation Policies; Supporting European Climate Policies. Available at: http://www.adamproject.eu/.

Barnett, H. & Morse, C. (1963). *Scarcity and Growth*. Washington, DC: Resources for the Future.

Blanford, G.J., Richels, R.G. & Rutherford, T.F. (2009). Feasible climate targets: The roles of economic growth, coalition development and expectations. *Energy Economics*, **31**(2), December, S82–S93.

Bowen, A. (2011). *Green' Growth, 'Green' Jobs and Labor Markets*, Policy Research Working Paper 5990, Washington DC: World Bank.

Bowen, A. & Fankhauser, S. (2011). The green growth narrative. Paradigm shift or just spin? *Global Environmental Change*, **21**, 1157–1159.

Bowen, A. & Ranger, N. (2009). *Mitigating Climate Change through Reductions in Greenhouse Gas Emissions: The Science and Economics of Future Paths for Global Annual Emissions*, Policy Brief, Grantham Research Institute on Climate Change and the Environment, LSE, London, December.

Bowen, A. & Stern, N. (2010). Environmental policy and the economic downturn. *Oxford Review of Economic Policy*, **26**, 137–163.

Calvin, K., Patel, P., Fawcett, A., Clarke, L., Fisher-Vanden, K., Edmonds, J., Kim, S.H., Sands, R. & Wise, M. (2009). The distribution and magnitude of emissions mitigation costs in climate stabilization under less than perfect international cooperation: SGM results. *Energy Economics*, **31**(2), S187–S197.

Colby, M.E. (1989). *The Evolution of Paradigms of Environmental Management in Development*, Strategic Planning and Review Department Working Paper WPS313, Washington DC: World Bank, November.

Cole, H.S.D. & Pavitt, K.L.R. (eds.) (1973). *Models of Doom: A Critique of the Limits to Growth*. New York: Universe Books.

den Elzen, M., Meinshausen, M. & van Vuuren, D. (2007). Multi-gas envelopes to meet greenhouse gas concentration targets: Costs versus certainty of limiting temperature increase. *Global Environmental Change*, **17**, 260–280.

Diamond, J. (2005). *Collapse: How Societies Choose to Fail or Survive*. London: Allen Lane.

Dietz, S. (2011). The treatment of risk and uncertainty in the US social cost of carbon for regulatory impact analysis, *Economics* (e-journal), Discussion Paper No. 2011-30.

Edenhofer, O., Carraro, C., Hourcade, J.-C., Neuhoff, K., Luderer, G., Flachsland, C., Jakob, M., Popp, A., Steckel, J., Strohschein, J., Bauer, N., Brunner, S., Leimbach, M., Lotze-Campen, H., Bosetti, V., de Cian, E., Tavoni, M., Sassi, O., Waisman, H., Crassous-Doerfler, R., Monjon, S., Dröge, S., van Essen, H., del Río, P. & Türk, A. (2009). The Economics of Decarbonization, Report of the RECIPE project, Potsdam Institute for Climate Impact Research, Potsdam.

Edenhofer, O. & Kalkuhl, M. (2011). When do increasing carbon taxes accelerate global warming? A note on the green paradox. *Energy Policy*, **39**, 2208–2212.

Edenhofer, O., Stern, N. *et al.* (2009). Towards a Global Green Recovery: Recommendations for Immediate G20 Action, Report submitted to the G20 London Summit on behalf of the German Foreign Office, PIK and LSE, April.

Fankhauser, S., Hepburn, C. & Park, J. (2010). Combining multiple climate policy instruments: How not to do it. *Climate Change Economics*, **1**(3), 209–225.

Fankhauser, S. & Tol, R.S.J. (2005). On climate change and economic growth. *Resource and Energy Economics*, **27**, 1–17.

Fischer, C. & Preonas, L. (2010). *Combining Policies for Renewable Energy: Is the Whole Less than the Sum of Its Parts?* Discussion Paper DP 10-19, Resources for the Future, March, Washington DC.

Foxon, T. & Pearson, P. (2007). Towards improved policy processes for promoting innovation in renewable electricity technologies in the UK. *Energy Policy*, **35**, 1539–1550.

Garnaut, R. *et al.* (2008). The Garnaut Climate Change Review Final Report. Available at: http://www.garnautreview.org.au/index.htm and Cambridge University Press.

Goettle, R.J. & Fawcett, A.A. (2009). The structural effects of cap and trade climate policy. *Energy Economics*, **31**, S244–S253.

Guardian (1989). *Minister steps up attack on Greens*. Patrick Wintour, 28 June, London: The Guardian.

Hallegatte, S., Heal, G., Fay, M. & Treguer, D. (2011). *From Growth to Green Growth — A Framework*, Policy Research Working Paper Series 5872, Washington DC: The World Bank.

Hardin, G. (1968). The tragedy of the commons. *Science*, **162**, 1243–1248.

Hepburn, C. & Bowen, A. (2013). Prosperity with growth: Economic growth, climate change and environmental limits. Chapter 29. In *Handbook of Energy and Climate Change*, R. Fouquet (eds.), Cheltenham, UK.: Edward Elgar.

Hotelling, H. (1931). The economics of exhaustible resources. *Journal of Political Economy*, **39**, 137–175.

Houser, T., Mohan, S. & Heilmayr, R. (2009). *A Green Global Recovery? Assessing US Economic Stimulus and the Prospects for International Coordination*, Policy Brief PB09-3, Washington DC: World Resources Institute.

ILO/CEDEFOP (2011). *Skills for Green Jobs: A Global View*. Geneva: ILO.

IMF (2012). *World Economic Outlook*. Washington DC: IMF, October.

IPCC (2007a). Summary for policymakers. In *Climate Change 2007: The Physical Science Basis. Contribution of Working Group I to the Fourth Assessment Report of the Intergovernmental Panel on Climate Change*, S. Solomon, D. Qin, M. Manning, Z. Chen, M. Marquis, K.B. Averyt, M. Tignor & H.L. Miller (eds.), Cambridge, UK, and New York, USA: Cambridge University Press.

IUCN/UNEP/WWF (1980). *World Conservation Strategy: Living Resource Conservation for Sustainable Development*. Gland, Switzerland: IUCN/UNEP/WWF.

Jackson, T. (2009). *Prosperity Without Growth: Economics for a Finite Planet*. Abingdon, UK: Earthscan Publications.

Kemfert, C. & Welsch, H. (2000). Energy-capital-labor substitution and the economic effects of CO2 abatement: Evidence for Germany. *Journal of Policy Modeling*, **22**(6), 641–660.

Keynes, J.M. (1929). The German transfer problem, 'The reparation problem: A Discussion. II. A Rejoinder, 'Views on the transfer problem. III. A reply. *Economic Journal*, **39** (March), 1–7, (June), 172–178, and (September), 404–408.

Knopf, B., Edenhofer, O. *et al.* (2009). The economics of low stabilisation: Implications for technological change and policy. Chapter 11 in Neufeldt, H. & Hulme, M. (2009). *Making Climate Change Work for Us: European*

Perspectives on Adaptation and Mitigation Strategies. Cambridge, UK, and New York, USA: Cambridge University Press.

Lane, P.R. & Milesi-Ferretti, G.M. (2000). *The Transfer Problem Revisited: Net Foreign Assets and Real Exchange Rates,* IMF Working Paper, Washington DC, July.

Malthus, T.R. (1798). *An Essay on the Principle of Population as It Affects the Future Improvement of Society.* London: Ward Lock.

McKibbin, W.J., Adelman, A.C. & Wilcoxen, P.J. (2008). *Expecting the Unexpected: Macroeconomic Volatility and Climate Policy,* Brookings Global Economy and Development Working Paper No. 28, November.

Meadows, D.H., Meadows, D.L., Randers, J. & Behrens III, W.W. (1972). The Limits to Growth. New York: Universe Books.

Mill, J.S. (1848). *Principles of Political Economy with Some of their Applications to Social Philosophy.* London: John W. Parker.

Nordhaus, W. (2008). *A Question of Balance.* New Haven: Yale University Press.

Nordhaus, W.D. (1973). World dynamics: Measurement without data. *Economic Journal,* **83**, 1156–1183.

OECD (2011). *Towards Green Growth.* Paris: OECD.

Paltsev, S., Reilly, J., Jacoby, H. & Morris, J. (2009). The cost of climate policy in the United States, MIT JPSPGC Joint Program Report Series No. 173, April.

Pearce, D. (1992). *The Secondary Benefits of Greenhouse Gas Control,* Working Paper GEC 92-12, Centre for Social and Economic Research on the Environment, University College London.

Pearson, P.J.G. & Foxon, T.J. (2012). A low carbon industrial revolution? Insights and challenges from past technological and economic transformations. *Energy Policy (Special Section: Past and Prospective Energy Transitions — Insights from History),* **50**, 117–127.

Perez, C. (2010). Technological revolutions and techno-economic paradigms. *Cambridge Journal of Economics,* **34**, 185–202.

Pollin, R., Garrett-Peltier, H., Heintz, J. & Scharber, H. (2008). *Green Recovery: AProgram to Create Good Jobs and Start Building a Low Carbon Economy.* Washington DC: Center for American Progress, and University of Massachusetts, Amherst: PERI, September.

Rao, S. *et al.* (2008). *IMAGE and MESSAGE Scenarios Limiting GHG Concentration to Low Levels.* Interim Report 08-020, International Institute for Applied Systems Analysis, October.

Rogner, H.H. (2000). Energy resources and technology options, Chapter 5. In *World Energy Assessment.* New York: UNDP.

Sheehan, P. (2008). The new global growth path: Implications for climate change analysis and policy. *Climatic Change,* **91**, 211–231.

Sinn, H.-W. (2008). Public policies against global warming: A supply-side approach. *International Tax and Public Finance,* **15**, 360–394.

Solow, R.M. (1974). The economics of resources or the resources of economics. Richard T. Ely Lecture, *American Economic Review,* **64**(2), Papers and Proceedings, 1–14.

Stern, N. (2010a). *Climate: What You Need to Know.* New York Review of Books, 24 June.

Stern, N. (2010b). *China's Growth, China's Cities and the New Global Low-Carbon Industrial Revolution*, Policy Brief, Grantham Research Institute, London School of Economics, November.

Stern, N. *et al.* (2007). *The Economics of Climate Change: The Stern Review.* Cambridge, UK: Cambridge University Press.

Tahvonen, O. (2000). *Economic Sustainability and Scarcity of Natural Resources: A Brief Historical Review.* Washington DC: Resources for the Future.

Tol, R.S.J. (2009a). The economic effects of climate change. *Journal of Economic Perspectives* **23**(2), 29–51.

Tol, R. (2009b). *The Feasibility of Low Concentration Targets: An Application of FUND*, ESRI Working Paper No. 285, March.

UNEP (2009). *Global Green New Deal.* Policy Brief, Geneva: UNEP, March.

UNEP (2010). *Green Economy Developing Countries Success Stories.* Geneva: UNEP.

UNEP (2011). *Towards a Green Economy: A Synthesis for Policy Makers.* Geneva: UNEP.

UNFCCC (2011). Decision 1/CP.16 The Cancun Agreements: Outcome of the work of the Ad Hoc Working? Group on Long-term Cooperative Action under the Convention. Available at: http://cancun.unfccc.int/

US CCSP (2007). Scenarios of greenhouse gas emissions and atmospheric concentrations (Part A) and review of integrated scenario development and application (Part B). A Report by the U.S. Climate Change Science Program and the Subcommittee on Global Change Research [Clarke, L., Edmonds, J., Jacoby, J., Pitcher, H., Reilly, J. Richels, R., Parson, E., Burkett, V., Fisher-Vanden, K., Keith, D., Mearns, L., Rosenzweig, C. & Webster, M. (Authors)]. Washington, DC, USA: Department of Energy, Office of Biological & Environmental Research.

van der Ploeg, F. & Withagen, C.A. (2010). *Is There Really a Green Paradox?* CESifo Working Paper No. 2963, February. Available at: http://hdl.handle.net/10419/30701

Webster, M., Paltsev, S., Parsons, J., Reilly, J. & Jacoby, H. (2008). Uncertainty in greenhouse gas emissions and costs of atmospheric stabilization. MIT JPSPGC Joint Program Report Series No. 165, November.

Wei, M., Patadia, S. & Kammen, D.M. (2010). Putting renewables and energy efficiency to work: How many jobs can the clean energy industry generate in the US?' *Energy Policy,* **38**(2), 919–931.

Weitzman, M. (2009). On modeling and interpreting the economics of catastrophic climate change. *Review of Economics and Statistics,* **91**(1), 1–19.

Zenghelis, D. (2011). *A Macro-Economic Plan for a Green Recovery*, Policy Brief, Grantham Research Institute, London School of Economics, March.

Chapter 7

Negotiating to Avoid "Dangerous" Climate Change

Scott Barrett

Lenfest-Earth Institute Professor of Natural Resource Economics
School of International and Public Affairs & Earth Institute
Columbia University

Ever since the Framework Convention on Climate Change was adopted in 1992, negotiation of emission limits has been intertwined with efforts to define a threshold for "dangerous" climate change. In this chapter, I explain the logic behind this framing of the collective action problem; show why this framing has failed to limit emissions so as to avoid "dangerous" climate change; and, finally, propose an alternative framing that can be expected to achieve more collective action.

1. Introduction

Ever since the Framework Convention on Climate Change was adopted in 1992, negotiation of emission limits has been intertwined with efforts to define a threshold for "dangerous" climate change. In this chapter, I explain the logic behind this framing of the collective action problem; show why this framing has failed to limit emissions so as to avoid "dangerous" climate change; and, finally, propose an alternative framing that can be expected to achieve more collective action.

Is it true that collective action has failed? Countries have agreed what they need to do collectively to avoid "dangerous" climate change. But they have failed to ensure that their agreed goal will be met. Analysis by Rogelj *et al.* (2010) shows that even an optimistic reading of the pledges made following the Copenhagen conference puts the world far off of the course needed to meet the temperature target these same countries agreed in Copenhagen. The negotiators evidently agree with these calculations. At the 2011 Durban conference they noted *"with grave concern* the significant gap between the aggregate effect of Parties' mitigation pledges in terms of global annual emissions of greenhouse gases (GHGs) by 2020 and the aggregate emission pathways consistent with having a likely chance of holding the increase in global average temperature below" the agreed threshold.

According to Rogelj *et al.* (2010, p. 1128), this behavior is "equivalent to racing toward a cliff and hoping to stop just before it," which is a useful metaphor for the reasoning I shall develop in this chapter. At a first look, the inconsistency in choosing a goal to avert "danger" and then failing to take the steps necessary to meet it seems irrational. Upon closer examination, the puzzle can be explained. When countries choose their collective target, they are focusing on their *collective* interests — what they know *all* of them ought to do together. When they pledge what *each* of them will do, they are focusing on their *individual* interests. Their collective interests pull them in one direction. Self-interest pulls them in another.

The pledges referred to above were made under the Copenhagen Accord, which is a voluntary (that is, a "political" rather than a "legal") agreement. The Kyoto Protocol is different. Being a treaty, Kyoto is binding under customary international law. The distinction seems important but is something of a mirage. First, knowing that they will be legally bound to comply with an agreement, countries will only participate in treaties that ask them to do what they want to do. In some cases, a treaty may simply codify what countries would have done anyway, in which case participation is compatible with self-interest but the treaty achieves nothing. In these cases, treaties are epiphenomena. Second, countries that become parties to a treaty and later decide that compliance is not in their self-interest can withdraw, and so cease to be bound by the requirements of the treaty. The same customary law that requires countries to comply with their treaty obligations also allows them to participate or not as they please. Canada became a party to the Kyoto Protocol, but it did not adopt the policies needed to fulfill its obligations. Rather than fail to comply, and thus violate their international legal obligations, Canada announced its intention to withdraw from the Kyoto Protocol. (Rather awkwardly, Canada did this within 24 h of the adjournment of the Durban conference.)

I am not urging cynicism, only circumspection. The legal nature of treaties matters; treaties can achieve a lot. In particular, they can cause countries to behave differently than they would if the treaty were not to exist (Barrett, 2003). But, to succeed, treaty negotiators must first understand what they are up against. They need to understand the reason collective action is not arising spontaneously. Then they need to do more than simply negotiate an outcome (a collection of emission targets, for example); they need to devise a mechanism for *getting to* and, most especially, *sustaining* the outcome. It is here that Kyoto failed. Kyoto refers to its emission limits as "commitments" as if by calling them this they will magically *become* commitments. Thomas Schelling (1960) taught us a long time ago that saying one is committed is very different from actually *being* committed.

There is a more important distinction to be made between Kyoto and Copenhagen than their legally "binding" natures. Kyoto was negotiated "in pursuit of" achieving the ultimate objective of avoiding "dangerous" climate change. But Kyoto failed to provide a concrete expression for this ultimate objective. When Kyoto was negotiated, countries had not determined, and certainly had not quantified, what "dangerous" climate change meant or how it could be avoided. Copenhagen, by contrast, recognizes "the scientific view that the increase in global temperature should be below 2°C." As I shall explain later, recognition of such a goal should, under the right conditions, suffice to enforce an agreement to meet the agreed goal. That is, identification of a threshold for "dangerous" climate change should succeed in doing what Kyoto failed to do; it should provide the mechanism for sustaining an outcome sure to make every country better off (relative, that is, to the alternative of each country acting independently). There is still the matter of "getting to" the desired outcome, but that, as I shall explain later, is something that treaties can arrange very easily. The real problem is enforcement.

As you might imagine, the success of this framing depends on "the right conditions" being met. These conditions do not depend on negotiating skill. They depend on science being able to predict, with near certainty, the consequences of policies to limit emissions, and this will never be possible. By definition, we are conducting an unprecedented experiment with the planet. Fundamental uncertainty is central to climate change. Science will improve, but there will always remain irreducible uncertainties. And so enforcement will remain as big a challenge as ever. We can improve on our efforts over the past 20 years. But to do that, we have to address the enforcement challenge from a different perspective. Durban has put the world on a path for another sequence of negotiations, with the aim of bringing into force a new climate treaty by 2020. The most important lesson of history is that if we continue to negotiate using the same approach as in the past, we will get the same result: no progress. If we want to obtain a different result, we need to try a different approach.

The most recent negotiations confirm this view. The Kyoto Protocol was amended in Doha in late 2012, to establish a new "commitment period" from 2013 to 2020. However, Canada, Japan, New Zealand, and Russia had all announced previously that they would join the US and not participate in this new agreement. The other parties went on to negotiate stricter allocation rules for 2013–2020, along with tough new rules limiting the use of "hot air" created by the original agreement. However, as a result of this, Ukraine, Belarus, and Kazakhstan threatened not to participate also. This behavior demonstrates that enforcement is the central challenge. If every attempt to tighten an agreement only causes further defections, this approach will never succeed in stabilizing concentrations.

If it were possible to overcome the collective action challenge completely — that is, if it were possible to sustain a "first best" outcome — we would have a chance of avoiding "dangerous" climate change. Some scientists believe that CO_2 concentrations need to be brought below 350 parts per million by volume (ppmv). They are already over 390 ppmv. To lower concentrations from today's level will require an emergency response, the equivalent of putting the world on a "climate war footing." The Durban agreement reflects a very different attitude — that there is no great rush. Durban allows continued growth in emissions through 2020 (the new Kyoto amendment only applies to countries accounting for about 15% of global emissions), and Hansen *et al.* (2008, p. 17) believe that this "practically eliminates the possibility of near-term return of atmospheric composition beneath the tipping level for catastrophic effects." Of course, Hansen and his coauthors (2008) could be wrong. But we cannot say for certain that they are wrong.

It is thus imperative that negotiators change their approach and begin to bring global emissions down immediately. Toward the end of this chapter, I shall outline a different approach — one that recognizes that enforcement is the central challenge, and that success depends not on trying to enforce obligations directly (something Kyoto has failed to do) but on strategically manipulating the incentives for countries to participate and comply with an agreement limiting emissions.

2. The "Scientific View" About "Dangerous" Climate Change

It is interesting to observe that negotiators want identification of the threshold for "dangerous" climate change to be a scientific matter. They do not want to have to identify the threshold themselves.

The word "science" does not appear in the Framework Convention or in the Kyoto Protocol. But when the threshold for "dangerous" climate change was first identified in the Copenhagen Accord, and later reaffirmed in the Cancun Agreement, it was portrayed as being "required according to science." The Copenhagen Accord says that,

> To achieve the ultimate objective of the Convention to stabilize greenhouse gas concentration in the atmosphere at a level that would prevent dangerous anthropogenic interference with the climate system, we shall, recognizing *the scientific view that the increase in global temperature should be below 2 degrees Celsius* [emphasis added], on the basis of equity and in the context of sustainable development, enhance our long-term cooperative action to combat climate change.[1]

The advantage in having "science" choose the overall goal is that it makes the negotiators' task much easier — it allows them to focus on negotiating individual shares for meeting the goal.

However, while scientists warned of "climate disaster" before the Framework Convention was adopted (see, in particular, Mercer, 1978), it is probably fair to say that the Framework Convention caused scientists to focus on this question at least as much as previous scientific research caused negotiators to focus on it.

Table 1 shows a number of prominent attempts to estimate a "threshold" for "dangerous" climate change. Copenhagen's use of the term, "*the* scientific view" [emphasis added], implies that there is strong agreement among scientists about the threshold. However, the table reveals a great variety of perspectives, not one. There even seems to be little

Table 1. Scientific thresholds for "dangerous" climate change.

Study	Threshold	Reason
IPCC Third Assessment Report (2001)	Reasons for concern, with "red" areas varying from 1–2°C, 2–3°C, and 4–5°C for different categories.	Risks to unique and threatened systems; risks to extreme events; distribution of impact; aggregate impacts; large-scale discontinuities.

(Continued)

---

[1]The Copenhagen Accord was written somewhat hastily, and this temperature target is identified without reference to a base level of temperature. In Cancun, the negotiators clarified that the temperature reference target was the pre-industrial level.

Table 1.   (*Continued*)

Study	Threshold	Reason
Smith *et al.* (2009)	Updating the above assessment, values from 0–1°C, 1–2°C, and 2.5°C	"...smaller increases in [global mean temperature] are now estimated to lead to significant or substantial consequences in the framework of the 5 'reasons for concern.'"
Rockström *et al.* (2009)	350 ppmv CO_2 and radiative forcing of $1\,Wm^{-2}$ above pre-industrial levels.	(i) Climate sensitivity ignores slow feedbacks; (ii) stability of large polar ice sheets; (iii) instability of Earth's sub-systems.
Hansen *et al.* (2007)	1°C relative to 2000 (or about 450 ppmv CO_2)	Ice sheets.
Hansen *et al.* (2008)	350 ppmv CO_2	Taking into account slow feedbacks, ignored by "climate sensitivity."
O'Neill and Oppenheimer (2002)	450 ppmv CO_2	"would likely preserve the option of avoiding shutdown of the [Thermohaline Circulation] and may also forestall the disintegration of [the West Antarctic Ice Sheet], although it appears to be inadequate for preventing severe damage to [coral reef ecosystems]...."
Oppenheimer and Alley (2005)	2–4°C	West Antarctic Ice Sheet.
Oppenheimer (2005)	2°C relative to 2005	More conservative value in above range.
Mastrandrea and Schneider (2004)	"optimal climate policy...can reduce the probability of dangerous anthropogenic interference from ∼45% under minimal controls to near zero."	Cumulative density function of the threshold for dangerous climate change, applied to DICE model.
Lenton *et al.* (2008)	Clusters of tipping points at 0.5–2°C and 3–6°C relative to 1980–1999.	Instabilities in geophysical sub-systems.
Lenton (2011)	Favors multidimensional approach, to include radiative forcing, rate of climate change, local temperature change, and non-GHG forcing agents.	Critical of "global warming" temperature targets, because physical systems respond to different metrics.

agreement about the appropriate *metric* for the threshold. Some scientists favor global mean temperature, others atmospheric concentrations. Still others emphasize radiative forcing, or local temperature, or probabilistic assessments, including economic analysis. Quantitative estimates, even for the same metric, also vary. The only "scientific view" that I detect in the literature is that thresholds are likely to exist.[2]

This reading of the science is consistent with the wording of the fourth assessment report of the Intergovernmental Panel on Climate Change (IPCC) (Metz *et al.*, 2007, p. 100): "The literature confirms that climate policy can substantially reduce the risk of crossing thresholds deemed dangerous." My interpretation of this literature is that we do not know precisely where the thresholds are, but we know that we are less likely to cross one if we do more to limit atmospheric concentrations. Put differently, limiting temperature change to 2°C would be better than limiting it to 2.1°C, but limiting it to 1.9°C would be even better. The negotiators in Cancun implicitly acknowledged this when they declared that it may be necessary to strengthen "the long-term global goal on the basis of the best available scientific knowledge, including in relation to a global average temperature rise of 1.5°C."

The uncertainties that matter are even greater than this. We do not know the concentration level that would bring about any particular temperature change; there is substantial "climate sensitivity" (Roe and Baker, 2007). Moreover, we do not know the quantity of global emissions (expressed, perhaps, as a cumulative sum) needed to meet any particular concentration target due to uncertainty in the carbon cycle (Archer, 2010). For example, there is uncertainty about how much of the CO_2 emitted will be taken up by soils and the oceans. What matters for the negotiations is uncertainty in the causal relationship between collective action (emission limits) and outcomes (climate change impacts).

3. Impacts versus Thresholds

Identification of thresholds is useful in distinguishing between "gradual" and "abrupt and catastrophic" climate change. What is the difference? Gradual climate change is a *linear* process: global emissions increase a

---

[2]Rapid changes in temperature have been observed in the paleoclimatic record, an example being the Younger Dryas; see Broecker (1997).

little, causing concentrations to increase a little, causing mean global temperature, following a lag, to increase a little, with the result that human impacts increase a little. Abrupt and catastrophic climate change is a *non-linear* process: global emissions increase a little, causing concentrations to increase a little, causing mean global temperature, following a lag, to increase a little, with the result that human impacts, near a threshold, increase *a lot*.

The link between temperature and human impacts is usually taken to be a geophysical feature. The first column in Table 2 gives a number of examples. How could a small change in global temperature cause an abrupt change in a geophysical subsystem? Consider the first "tipping element" in Table 2 — the loss of summer Arctic ice. Snow covered ice reflects solar radiation whereas darker open ocean absorbs it. If there is a lot of ice, solar radiation will be reflected, and local temperature will remain below freezing. If there is no ice, radiation will be absorbed, and ice will tend not to form. In between these extremes lies an unstable bifurcation — the threshold for this system. In this territory, there can be a positive feedback whereupon more warming causes more melting which in turn causes more warming. It is around such a threshold that a system can "flip" from one state (ice) to another (no ice). "Gradual" climate change causes ice to melt slowly. "Abrupt and catastrophic" climate change causes rapid transition to an ice-free Arctic.

I should underscore that the risk in the Arctic is to *summer* ice. If local temperature were to increase dramatically (due, perhaps, to substantial global warming), *annual* sea-ice cover could also disappear. It might even disappear rapidly. But the science of annual ice change is less well understood. It is also a more distant prospect. For both reasons, it is excluded from Table 2. Other possible catastrophe scenarios are also excluded from the table.[3] The ones shown in the table are simply better

---

[3]Lenton *et al.* (2008) identify the Indian Summer Monsoon as a possibly unstable system, but I have omitted it from the table because the proximate threshold is expressed in terms of planetary albedo (aerosols) rather than temperature, and my discussion ignores aerosols. These authors also discuss six other possible tipping elements, but these were not assigned a quantitative threshold for various reasons, such as that a global threshold could not be identified or global warming was not believed to be the only or even most important cause for abrupt change, or the trigger for change would not be pulled for a century at least, or the effects of crossing the threshold would take a millennium or more to materialize. Needless to say, there could well exist thresholds that are entirely unknown to us now.

Table 2. Possible thresholds and impacts due to global warming.

"Catastrophe"	Threshold	Threshold uncertainty	Impact	Impact uncertainty
Arctic summer sea-ice disappearance	0.5–2°C	A "critical threshold . . . may exist," and "could already have been passed."	Amplified warming, ecosystem change; transition could occur in 10 years.	Not discussed.
Greenland Ice Sheet loss	1–2°C	Compared to IPCC, a smaller lower bound and a narrower range, partly because models fail to explain observed melting.	2–7 m sea level rise; transition could occur in 300 or more years.	"If a threshold is passed, the IPCC gives a [greater than] 1,000-year timescale for . . . collapse."
West Antarctic Ice Sheet (WAIS) disintegration	3–5°C	The IPCC "declines to give a threshold . . ."	5 m sea level rise; transition in 300 or more years.	"Although the timescale is highly uncertain, a qualitative WAIS change could occur within this millennium."
Atlantic Thermohaline Circulation (THC) shutoff	3–5°C	IPCC "argues that an abrupt transition of the THC is 'very unlikely.'"	Regional cooling; transition about 100 years.	Not discussed.
El Nino-Southern Oscillation (ENSO) shift	3–6°C	The "existence and location of any threshold is particularly uncertain."	Drought in some regions; "transition happening within a millennium."	We "differ from IPCC and consider there to be a significant probability of a future increase in ENSO amplitude."

(*Continued*)

Table 2. (*Continued*)

"Catastrophe"	Threshold	Threshold uncertainty	Impact	Impact uncertainty
Sahara/Sahel and West African monsoon shift	3–5°C	Threshold depends on sea surface temperatures.	Could cause a "greening of the Sahara/Sahel ... a rare example of a beneficial potential tipping element," transition 10 years.	Decrease or increase in rainfall possible, as well as an increase in variability.
Amazon rainforest dieback	3–4°C	Depends on "complex interplay between direct land-use change and the response of regional precipitation and ENSO to global forcing."	Biodiversity loss, decreased rainfall; transition about 50 years.	Not discussed.
Boreal forest dieback	3–5°C	Studies suggest 3°C, "but limitations in ... models and physiological understanding make this highly uncertain."	Biome switch to grasslands; transition about 50 years.	Not discussed.

Source: Lenton *et al.* (2008). Note that the thresholds are calculated relative to the present temperature (specifically, 1980–1999).

understood, more immediate, and less tenuous than the others. The table does not give a complete picture of climate uncertainty.

I have so far focused on "threshold uncertainty." Another source of uncertainty concerns the *impacts* of crossing a threshold. What level of impact is needed for passing a threshold to be "dangerous" or "catastrophic"? The answer is not obvious. Nordhaus (2009) suggests that climate change would be catastrophic if it reduced world per capita consumption by half or more from today's level, but this definition is plainly arbitrary and arguably extreme.[4] At least some and possibly all of the catastrophic events shown in Table 2 would have a much smaller impact (of course, these impacts are additional to the impacts of "gradual" climate change). Indeed, individual events, such as a change to the Sahara/Sahel West African Monsoon, could be beneficial. (There can also be mixed effects. For example, while loss of Arctic summer sea-ice would threaten polar bears, infrastructure, and the way of life of native peoples, it would also open up the Northern Sea Route during the summer months, and facilitate access to oil and gas resources.[5]) Since the thresholds in Table 2 tend to cluster (see below), however, there is a strong presumption that the impacts of crossing a threshold will be negative overall. These clusters include and are probably dominated by global catastrophic events, such as those leading to global sea level rise.

It is not necessary that a threshold trigger abrupt change in a geophysical feature. The important non-linear response is to *impacts*. Until recently, it has been supposed that agriculture responds linearly to temperature changes. However, Schlenker and Roberts (2009) have shown that yields for corn, soybeans, and cotton in the US respond nonlinearly to temperature, around a threshold close to 30°C. Moreover, they find that the effects are much the same whether the focus is on time-series or

---

[4]Cavallo *et al.* (2010) define "local" natural disasters in terms of the number of people killed as a share of population. As examples, Hurricane Katrina killed 7 people per million in the US, the 2004 Indian Ocean Tsunami killed almost 2,000 per million in Sri Lanka, and the 2010 earthquake in Haiti killed over 20,000 per million in that country. They find that even the largest natural disasters have *no* significant effect on economic growth. However, other research finds that the effect is large and persistent; see Hsiang and Jina (2012).

[5]Taylor (2009) argues that there are three conditions for catastrophe: failures in governance, an ecological system exhibiting a tipping point, and an economy–environment interaction with positive feedbacks. He cannot find a compelling economy–environment positive feedback for climate change, but the opening up of the Arctic to hydrocarbon development is a clear example of such a feedback.

cross-sectional variations. Since cross-sectional variations can be interpreted as reflecting "adaptation" to climate change, their research suggests that the impacts of pushing temperature above the threshold will be huge. Indeed, by simulating their model for changes predicted under pretty standard emissions scenarios, they find that yields could fall 30–80% before the end of the century. It is often noted that agriculture is a small share of gross domestic product (GDP), implying that damages to agriculture do not really matter. Of course, in developing countries, agriculture can be a large share of GDP, especially in rural areas. But even leaving this point aside, there is a big difference between value (consumers' surplus) and GDP. If yields were to fall this much world wide, it would not be an exaggeration to say that the effects would be catastrophic.[6]

The important point is that impacts are determined by natural (that is, geophysical, chemical, biological, ecological) *and* social (including agro-economic) system changes. Loss of the Greenland Ice Sheet, for example, is expected to increase mean global sea level by 2–7 m over a period of from 300 to more than 1,000 years (Lenton *et al.*, 2008). If the loss is at the high end of this range (7 m) and rapid (occurring in a few centuries), the impact will be relatively large. If the loss is at the low end of this range (2 m) and occurs slowly (over more than a millennium), the impact will be relatively small. The magnitude of the loss will also depend on how society deals with these changes. Societies better able to adapt will experience a smaller loss.

4. Costs and Benefits

The thresholds shown in Table 2 tend to cluster around two global warming ranges, 0.5–2°C and 3–6°C, implying that the politically motivated 2°C target would avoid some but not all catastrophes.[7] Why choose 2°C? Why not choose 0.5°C? Perhaps even more importantly, why not choose 0°C? After all, we know what a world with no temperature change is like. Surely, this is the safest target.

---

[6]Agriculture is not the only vulnerable sector. Indeed, Hsiang (2010) has found that the impacts are much *greater* in non-agricultural sectors in the Caribbean and Central America, the reason being human (workers) vulnerability to thermal stress. There is also evidence that temperature change can trigger increases in civil conflict (Hsiang *et al.*, 2011). For the purposes of this chapter, what really matters is the non-linear response of impacts to temperature change — the reason for my focus on agriculture.

[7]Note that the temperature change referred to in the table relates to the "present," meaning 1980–1999. As noted before, the 2°C change target in the Copenhagen Accord is not specified with respect to a base period, while the Cancun Agreements express the 2°C target relative to pre-industrial temperature.

One reason for allowing temperature change to increase from pre-industrial levels is that it already has increased. According to the IPCC's fourth assessment report, mean global temperature has increased 0.76°C ± 0.19°C. Moreover, even if concentrations are capped at today's level, mean global temperature will continue to increase. Again, the IPCC's fourth assessment report says that global mean temperature might increase another 0.6°C through the end of this century if concentrations are held fixed. Very roughly, stabilizing concentrations at today's level might ensure that global mean temperature increases no more than about 1.5°C — the same level noted in the Cancun agreements. (According to Ramanathan and Feng (2008), holding concentrations at today's level through the end of this century would cause global warming of 1.6°C relative to today's temperature.) Note, however, that because of the many lags in the climate system, we cannot be sure that today's temperature is "safe" let alone that today's concentration level is "safe." However, we surely know that 1.5°C is safer than 2°C.

So, why not choose 1.5°C? The reason almost surely has to do with costs. It will be a lot more costly to limit temperature change to 1.5°C than to 2°C.

Of course, the costs may be worth incurring. It depends on the impacts that would be avoided by limiting temperature change to this level. The point is that it is not for science alone to determine the limit; economics is also relevant. Most importantly, deciding by how much to limit concentrations is a *social* choice. As noted by the IPCC's third assessment report, "decisions on what constitutes 'dangerous anthropogenic interference with the climate system'... are value judgments determined through socio-political processes ..." (IPCC, 2001, p. 2).

This is not to say that the economics of avoiding "dangerous" climate change will necessarily differ from the "scientific" view. For example, Keller *et al.* (2005, p. 236) use Nordhaus's well-known Regional Integrated model of Climate and the Economy (RICE; see Nordhaus and Boyer, 2000) to show that, limiting temperature change so as to avoid disintegration of the West Antarctic Ice Sheet "may well be an economically sound policy."

A great deal has been made of the effect of discounting costs and benefits on the economics of climate change policy.[8] Discounting matters a lot in a world with linear climate impacts and damages (with the benefits of limiting emissions being the avoided damages). It matters less in a world

---

[8] Contrast especially Stern (2008) and Nordhaus (2007).

with non-linear impacts and damages. If there existed a truly catastrophic threshold, one that posed an existential threat, say, then the economics and ethics of climate change policy would surely line up behind the scientific recommendation to avoid the threshold. Discounting would only play a minor role in determining the path to level that would avoid the threshold. As we get near to the threshold, discounting hardly matters at all. To avoid disaster, we would need to go on a "climate war" footing.

Martin Weitzman (2009) has offered a different perspective. He has argued that uncertainty about climate sensitivity — in particular, "fat tails" in the probability density function relating global mean temperature change to concentrations — should cause us to do everything possible to reduce emissions as quickly as possible, even though doing so cannot guarantee that catastrophe will be avoided.[9] He calls this result, appropriately enough, "the dismal theorem." Underpinning this result is the strong assumption that utility is unbounded.[10] If this assumption is relaxed, so that social preferences are not very risk averse as consumption approaches zero, a different outcome emerges, one that is consistent with Weitzman's policy recommendation of "*a relatively more cautious approach* [emphasis added]" to reducing GHG emissions (Weitzman, 2009, p. 13). This conclusion is reminiscent of the "precautionary principle," a controversial and generally poorly defined concept (Foster *et al.*, 2000).

However, we do not need to rely on this principle, let alone Weitzman's assumption about risk aversion, or extreme assumptions about discounting to show that radical action is warranted for limiting climate change.

Rockström *et al.* (2009) identify a "planetary boundary" in terms of atmospheric CO_2 concentrations of 350 ppmv. This value was chosen "to *ensure* [emphasis added] the continued existence of the large polar ice sheets." According to these authors, the paleoclimatic record implies "that there is a critical threshold between 350 and 550 ppmv." The suggestion here is that, if concentrations are limited to 350 ppmv, the ice sheets will be preserved. If concentrations rise to 550 ppmv, they will be lost. In between, there is a chance that the ice sheets will disappear, with the probability increasing in the concentration level.

---

[9]If the conditions that give rise to this result are relaxed even slightly, then the threat of catastrophe raises numerous policy issues; see Carolyn Kousky *et al.* (2009).

[10]Kenneth J. Arrow (2009, p. 94) notes that, for individuals, the assumption implies that "the value of statistical life is infinite, a conclusion clearly contrary to all empirical evidence and to everyday observation."

Rockström *et al.*'s (2009) recommendation makes no mention of economics, and implies application of the precautionary principle. However, it is easy to show that their conclusion can also be supported by economic analysis, even if social preferences are risk neutral. All that is needed is for the cost of reducing emissions so as to keep on the safe side of the uncertainty range to be low relative to the benefit of avoiding the threshold (Barrett, 2013).

5. Collective Action

Normally, collective action to address a problem like climate change is very difficult — possibly insurmountable. The reasons are due to costs being high and benefits being diffused. If the cost of reducing emissions is "high," every country will have an incentive to scale back on abatement, to save this cost. Of course, if they do, there will be more climate change; and no country will feel good about that. But from each country's perspective, most of the reduction in abatement benefits will be borne by other countries. Each country can therefore have a strong incentive to "free ride."

I have recently shown that concern about catastrophic climate change around a known threshold changes this calculus. Imagine that the world is far from avoiding the threshold. Then, no country on its own can ensure that the threshold is avoided, and it will pay each country to reduce its emissions just a little, to limit "gradual" climate change. This view is consistent with the conventional one noted above.

However, now imagine that every other country has pledged to reduce its emissions by a lot, so that your country can determine whether or not the threshold is avoided. Then, so long as the benefit to your country of avoiding the threshold is high relative to the cost, your country will want to act so as to avoid the threshold. Moreover, the same will be true for every country. Hence, what matters in this situation is not just the economics of abatement. What matters is the assurance that every other country will abate its fair share.

In the language of game theory, the existence of a known threshold changes the game from a "prisoners' dilemma" to a "coordination game." In a prisoners' dilemma, enforcement has to be achieved by the countries themselves. In this coordination game, with a known threshold, Mother Nature does the enforcing. What disciplines behavior in the coordination game is the certain knowledge that, should any country fail to reduce emissions, the threshold will be crossed, causing "catastrophic" damages.

Earlier in this chapter, I noted that treaties must first lead countries to a more desired outcome and then sustain this outcome. With a certain threshold, Nature does the sustaining. The treaty only needs to steer countries toward the mutual preferred outcome in which the threshold is avoided. This is the coordination challenge — a task for which treaties are supremely suited.

This explains why negotiators would want there to be a threshold for "dangerous" climate change, and why they would want this threshold to be determined by "science" — a threshold set by science has more credibility than a threshold set by the negotiators themselves.

Unfortunately, uncertainty about the threshold softens Nature's punishment to increasing emissions. As noted before, Rockström *et al.* (2009) argue that if concentrations are limited to 350 ppmv, the stability of the polar ice sheets will be preserved; catastrophe will be avoided. If this threshold were certain, no country would want to take a step from the edge of the cliff, for to do so would mean falling off for certain. However, if there is uncertainty about the threshold — if, as Rockström *et al.* say, the threshold lies somewhere between 350 and 550 ppmv — then taking another step does not cause the world to fall off the cliff for certain; it merely increases the probability of falling off the cliff by a little bit. If the costs of reducing emissions are "high," countries will have an incentive to take another step; they will have an incentive to "free ride." Uncertainty about the threshold transforms the game back into a prisoners' dilemma.

As noted before, the location of a threshold for "dangerous" climate change *is* uncertain. Hence, there is reason to believe that framing the negotiations around the need to avoid "dangerous" climate change will not have much effect on the incentives for countries to cooperate.

A recent experimental test confirms this hypothesis (Barrett and Dannenberg, 2012). Recasting the experiment in the context of the paper by Rockström *et al.* (2009), my coauthor, Astrid Dannenberg, and I found that, when people knew they should limit concentrations to 350 ppmv, they proposed that everyone collectively act so as to limit concentrations to about 400 ppmv.[11] They then pledged to limit their individual emissions so that, when summed over all players, concentrations would rise to around 450 ppmv. Finally, when the players made their actual choices, concentrations topped 550 ppmv, making catastrophe inevitable.

---

[11]The qualitative picture presented here is correct, but the numbers used in our experiment were different.

Another important prediction of the theory, also confirmed by the experiment, is that uncertainty about the impacts of crossing a threshold are of no consequence for behavior. It is only uncertainty about the location of the threshold that matters.

6. A Strategic Perspective on Treaty Negotiations

The preceding analysis teaches an important lesson. If avoiding "dangerous" climate change is a coordination game, climate treaties will be effective, and the worst climate outcomes averted. But the conditions that support this cheerful outcome depend entirely on Mother Nature. They depend especially on the threshold being certain, or nearly so. As already explained, this condition fails; climate change is inherently and irreducibly uncertain.

Might it be possible for negotiators to transform the prisoners' dilemma for abatement into a coordination game by some other means?

One suggestion would be to *make* the threshold certain. A Doomsday Machine could potentially do the trick. Imagine a huge stockpile of nuclear bombs being linked to a detonation device programmed to fire once atmospheric concentrations reached, say, 500 ppmv. If this device could not be deactivated or reprogrammed (so that the threat to punish deviations causing concentrations to exceed 500 ppmv would be credible), then the threshold for avoiding catastrophe would be certain, and we could be pretty confident that the world would pull out all the stops to limit concentrations.[12]

I am not proposing that we do this, but the suggestion is worth contemplating. For the device is an example of strategic manipulation. The Machine would be made in the expectation that it would not be used. Its purpose would be to alter every country's behavior, to change the rules of the game. This is what every good treaty needs to do (Barrett, 2003).

The Kyoto Protocol lacks a strategic design. The emissions targets and timetables were chosen in the expectation that they would be met. No consideration was given to whether the treaty created *incentives* for them to be met.

The Montreal Protocol, negotiated to protect the stratospheric ozone layer, was designed very differently. Remarkably, while the Montreal Protocol was not intended to reduce GHGs, it has been much more

---

[12]Of course, a similar proposal was made years ago to avert nuclear war. In that case, the plan (dreamed up by Herman Kahn, and never implemented) was for detonation to be triggered by a nuclear attack, guaranteeing "mutual assured destruction."

successful at doing this than the Kyoto Protocol. It turns out that ozone in the stratosphere is a GHG (protecting the ozone layer will thus add to climate change), as are the chemicals that deplete stratospheric ozone (reducing these emissions will thus help mitigate climate change) and many of their substitutes (use of these will thus add to climate change). Calculations by Velders *et al.* (2007) show that, by phasing out the ozone-depleting substances that double as GHGs, the Montreal Protocol has done four times as much to limit atmospheric concentrations as the Kyoto Protocol aimed to do.

Why did Montreal succeed where Kyoto failed? A key reason for its success is the threat to restrict trade — in particular, a ban on trade in controlled substances between parties and non-parties (Barrett, 2003). The most important motive for the trade restriction was to enforce participation in the agreement (Benedick, 1998, p. 91). If participation could be enforced, then trade leakage would be eliminated; moreover, compliance could also be enforced (Barrett, 2003). Crucially, the trade restrictions in the Montreal Protocol are a strategic device. Their purpose was not to be used; their purpose was to change behavior.

How do the trade restrictions work? Imagine that very few countries are parties to an agreement to limit emissions, and your country is contemplating whether or not to join. If you join, you will have to reduce your emissions. Your country will pay the cost, and the benefits will be diffused; the incentives to free ride will not be blunted. If, in addition, you are now also prohibited from trading with non-parties — the vast majority of countries — then you will be doubly harmed. By joining, you not only forfeit the benefits of free riding; you also lose the gains from trade.

Now imagine that almost every other country is a party to the same agreement. If you join, you still lose the benefits of free riding. But now you are able to trade with the vast majority of countries. If the gains from trade exceed the loss from free riding, your country will be better off joining. Put differently, if every country is a party to such an agreement, none will wish to withdraw. The agreement will sustain full participation by means of a self-enforcing mechanism — the trade restriction. Most remarkably, in equilibrium, trade will never be restricted, just as the Doomsday Device would never be detonated. It is the credible threat to restrict trade (detonate the device) that disciplines behavior.

Notice that a key feature of this strategy is that "enough" countries participate in the agreement. If too few participate, none will want to participate. If enough participate, everyone will want to participate.

Somewhere in between there exists a "tipping point" for participation. Once this tipping point has been identified, the treaty only needs to coordinate participation — something treaties can do very easily. As I said before, treaties need to ensure that countries are steered toward the desired outcome. In the Montreal Protocol, this was achieved by the minimum participation clause (Barrett, 2003).

Notice that the trade restrictions serve the same purpose as the Doomsday Machine. They both transform the prisoners' dilemma into a coordination game.

The Montreal Protocol could be amended to achieve more for the climate. Hydrofluorocarbons (HFCs) do not deplete the ozone layer, and so are not currently regulated by the Montreal Protocol. However, HFCs are a very potent GHG — one of the six gases controlled by the Kyoto Protocol. Kyoto has done very little to limit HFCs. In May 2011, the US, Canada, and Mexico proposed amending the Montreal Protocol to control HFCs.[13] If adopted, such an amendment would represent a significant departure from the approach taken so far to address climate change. It would mean addressing one piece of the problem, rather than all of it in a comprehensive way. And it would likely involve using trade restrictions for purposes of enforcement. I want to underline that the application of trade restrictions is purely strategic. Other proposals for trade restrictions in climate policy are very different; their purpose is to be *used*, not to alter behavior strategically (Barrett, 2011).

There are other opportunities for transforming the climate change game from a prisoners' dilemma into a coordination game, especially the application of technology standards (Barrett, 2003, 2006). My aim here is not to develop a comprehensive approach to future climate negotiations but to suggest a new direction. If the negotiators understood their job as needing to achieve coordination, and to think strategically, they would have better success.

7. Conclusions

If the threshold for avoiding catastrophic climate change were known, treaty negotiations would be an easy affair. Their only purpose would be to

---

[13]A similar proposal was submitted by the Federated States of Micronesia; see http://climate-l.iisd.org/news/us-canada-and-mexico-and-federated-states-of-micronesia-propose-hfcs-phase-down-under-montreal-protocol/.

coordinate emission reductions so as to avoid catastrophe. The treaty would not require an enforcement mechanism. Enforcement would be supplied free of charge by Mother Nature.

Uncertainty about the catastrophic threshold undermines this logic, transforming what would have been a coordination game with threshold certainty back into a prisoners' dilemma. As shown here, the threshold that could trigger climate catastrophe is uncertain. In particular, it is unavoidably and irreducibly uncertain. We are carrying out a huge experiment with the planet. We will not know how it will turn out until we throw the dice.

If Mother Nature will not help us, we will need to transform the game ourselves. The most important challenge for treaty negotiators is to devise strategies to transform the prisoners' dilemma of emission reductions into a coordination game. I offered one example here for how this could be done — the careful, selective, and (most importantly) strategic application of trade restrictions. Negotiators should shift their attention away from identifying thresholds for "dangerous" climate change and towards devising alternative strategies like this. It is only by this approach that we will have any hope of avoiding the cliff edge.

References

Archer, D. (2010). *The Global Carbon Cycle*. Princeton: Princeton University Press.

Arrow, K.J. (2009). A note on uncertainty and discounting in models of economic growth. *Journal of Risk and Uncertainty*, **38**, 87–94.

Barrett, S. (2003). *Environment and Statecraft: The Strategy of Environmental Treaty-Making*. Oxford: Oxford University Press.

Barrett, S. (2006). Climate treaties and 'breakthrough' technologies. *American Economic Review (Papers and Proceedings)*, **96**(2), 22–25.

Barrett, S. (2011). Rethinking climate change governance and its relationship to the world trading system. *The World Economy*, **34**(11), 1863–1882.

Barrett, S. (2013). Climate treaties and approaching catastrophes. *Journal of Environmental Economics and Management*, **66**(2), 235–250.

Barrett, S. & Dannenberg, A. (2012). Climate negotiations under scientific uncertainty. *Proceedings of the National Academy of Sciences*, **109**(43), 17372–17376.

Benedick, R.E. (1998). *Ozone Diplomacy: New Directions in Safeguarding the Planet*. Enlarged Edition, Cambridge, MA: Harvard University Press.

Broecker, W.S. (1997). Thermohaline circulation, the achilles heel of our climate system: Will Man-made CO_2 upset the current balance? *Science*, **278**, 1582–1588.

Cavallo, E., Galiani, S., Noy, I. & Pantano, J. (2010). *Catastrophic Natural Disasters and Economic Growth*, Inter-American Development Bank Working Paper IDP-WP-183.

Foster, K.R., Vecchia, P. & Repacholi, M.H. (2000). Science and the precautionary principle. *Science*, **288**, 979–981.

Hansen, J., Sato, M., Kharecha, P., Beerling, D., Berner, R., Masson-Delmotte, V., Pagani, M., Raymo, M., Royer, D.L. & Zachos, J.C. (2008). Target atmospheric CO_2: Where should humanity aim? *Open Atmospheric Science Journal*, **2**, 217–231.

Hansen, J. *et al.* (2007). Dangerous human-made interference with climate: A GISS modelE study. *Atmospheric Chemistry and Physics*, **7**, 2287–2312.

Hsiang, S. (2010). Temperatures and cyclones strongly associated with economic production in the Caribbean and Central America. *Proceedings of the National Academy of Sciences*, **107**(35), 15367–15372.

Hsiang, S. & Jina, A.S. (2012). *The Causal Effect of Environmental Catastrophe on Long-Run Economic Growth*. Columbia University: mimeo.

Hsiang, S., Meng, K.C. & Cane, M.A. (2011). Civil conflicts are associated with the global climate. *Nature*, **476**, 438–441.

Intergovernmental Panel on Climate Change (2001). *Climate Change 2001: Synthesis Report,, Summary for Policymakers*. Available at: http://www.grida.no/climate/ipcc_tar/vol4/english/pdf/spm.pdf. Accessed 20 November 2013.

Keller, K., Hall, M., Kim, S.-R., Bradford, D.F. & Oppenheimer, M. (2005). Avoiding dangerous anthropogenic interference with the climate system. *Climatic Change*, **73**, 227–238.

Kousky, C., Rostapshova, O. Toman, M. & Zeckhauser, R. (2009). Responding to threats of climate change mega-catastrophes. Resources for the Future Discussion Paper 09-45.

Lenton, T.M. (2011). Early warning of climate tipping points. *Nature Climate Change*, **1**, 201–209.

Lenton, T.M., Held, H., Kriegler, E., Hal, J.W., Lucht, W., Rahmstorf, S. & Schellnhuber, H.J. (2008). Tipping elements in the earth's climate system. *Proceedings of the National Academy of Sciences*, **105**(6), 1786–1793.

Mastrandrea, M.D. & Schneider, S.H. (2004). Probabilistic integrated assessment of 'dangerous' climate change. *Science*, **304**, 571–575.

Mercer, J.H. (1978). West Antarctic ice sheet and CO2 greenhouse effect: A threat of disaster. *Nature*, **271**, 321–325.

Metz, B., Davidson, O.R., Bosch, P.R., Dave, R. & Meyer, L.A. (eds.) (2007). *Contribution of Working Group III to the Fourth Assessment Report of the Intergovernmental Panel on Climate Change*. Cambridge: Cambridge University Press.

Nordhaus, W.D. (2007). A review of the stern review on the economics of global warming. *Journal of Economic Literature*, **45**, 686–702.

Nordhaus, W.D. (2009). *An Analysis of the Dismal Theorem*. Yale University: mimeo.

Nordhaus, W.D. & Boyer, J. (2000). *Warming the World: Economic Models of Global Warming*. Cambridge, MA: MIT Press.

O'Neill, B.C. & Oppenheimer, M. (2002). Dangerous climate impacts and the Kyoto Protocol. *Science*, **296**, 1971–1972.

Oppenheimer, M. (2005). Defining dangerous anthropogenic interference: The role of science, the limits of science. *Risk Analysis*, **25**(6), 1399–1407.

Oppenheimer, M. & Alley, R.B. (2004). The West Antarctic ice sheet and long term climate policy. *Climatic Change*, **64**, 1–10.

Ramanathan, V. & Feng, Y. (2008). On avoiding dangerous anthropogenic interference with the climate system: Formidable challenges ahead. *Proceedings of the National Academy of Sciences*, **105**(38), 14245–14250.

Rockström, J., Steffen, W., Noone, K., Persson, Å., Chapin III, S., Lambin, E.F., Lenton, T.M., Scheffer, M., Folke, C., Schellnhuber, H.J., Nykvist, B., de Wit, C.A., Hughes, T., van der Leeuw, S., Rodhe, H., Sörlin, S., Snyder, P.K., Costanza, R., Svedin, U., Falkenmark, M., Karlberg, L., Corell, R.W., Fabry, V.J., Hansen, J., Walker, B., Liverman, D., Richardson, K., Crutzen, P. & Foley, J.A. (2009). A safe operating safe for humanity. *Nature*, **461**, 472–475.

Roe, G.H. & Baker, M.B. (2007). Why is climate sensitivity so unpredictable? *Science*, 318, 629–632.

Rogelj, J., Nabel, J., Chen, C., Hare, W., Markmann, K., Meinshausen, M., Schaeffer, M., Macey, K. & Höhne, N. (2010). Copenhagen accord pledges are paltry. *Nature*, **464**, 1126–1128.

Schelling, T.C. (1960). *The Strategy of Conflict*. Cambridge, MA: Harvard University Press.

Schlenker, W. & Roberts, M.J. (2009). Nonlinear temperature effects indicate severe damages to U.S. crop yields under climate change. *Proceedings of the National Academy of Sciences*, **106**(37), 15594–15598.

Smith, J.E., Schneider, S.H., Oppenheimer, M., Yohe, G.W., Hare, W., Mastrandrea, M.D., Patwardhan, A., Burton, I., Corfee-Morlot, J., Magadza, C.H.D., Füssel, H.-M., Pittock, A.B., Rahman, A., Suarez, A. & van Ypersele, J.-P. (2009). Assessing dangerous climate change through an update of the intergovernmental panel on climate change (IPCC) 'reasons for concern'. *Proceedings of the National Academy of Sciences*, **106**, 4133–4137.

Stern, N. (2008). The economics of climate change. *American Economic Review: Papers & Proceedings*, **98**(2), 1–37.

Taylor, S. (2009). Environmental crises: past, present, and future. *Canadian Journal of Economics*, **42**(4), 1240–1275.

Velders, G.J.M., Anderson, S.O., Daniel, J.S., Fahey, D.W. & McFarland, M. (2007). The importance of the montreal protocol in protecting climate. *Proceedings of the National Academy of Sciences*, **104**(12), 4814–4819.

Weitzman, M.L. (2009). On modeling and interpreting the economics of catastrophic climate change. *Review of Economics and Statistics*, **91**(1), 1–19.

Chapter 8

Unilateral Measures and Emissions Mitigation[*]

Shurojit Chatterji
Singapore Management University

Sayantan Ghosal
Adam Smith Business School, University of Glasgow

Sean Walsh
University of Western Ontario

and

John Whalley
University of Western Ontario,
The Centre for International Governance Innovation and NBER

We discuss global climate mitigation that builds on existing unilateral measures to cut emissions. We document the extent of these measures and discuss the rationale arguing that such measures have the potential to generate positive spillover effects both within and across countries. We argue that while single countries on their own may never get to the point of switching completely to low emission activities, a learning process with positive spillovers across nations is more likely to deliver a global switch to low emissions. We also discuss the key features of a new global intellectual property (IP) regime that builds on the positive spillovers inherent in unilateral initiatives and accelerates global convergence to low emissions.

1. Introduction

This chapter studies the unilateral measures taken at national and lower levels of government to combat climate change, as well as the feasibility of these measures in terms of attaining stated emissions reduction/adaption

---

[*]We would like to thank participants ESRC funded Climate Change Workshops at Warwick in 2009 and 2010 for their helpful comments. E-mail addresses: shurojitc@smu. edu.sg; S.Ghosal@warwick.ac.uk; swalsh999@hotmail.ca; jwhalley@uwo.ca. The second two authors acknowledge financial support from the Ontario Research Fund (ORF).

goals in light of enforcement or measurement issues, and also issues caused by local conditions, such as excessive crime or political instability. We also examine the interplay between local measures and the multilateral United Nations Framework Convention on Climate Change (UNFCCC) negotiation and how they might affect one another from a post-Durban/Copenhagen and post-2020 perspective, including the possibility of a post-Kyoto regime based around unilateralism. The Copenhagen Accord, the text that came out of the Copenhagen meeting hosted by the UNFCCC in December 2009, while non-binding, sets out a possible foundation for an unilateral action-based framework that attempts to combine many unilateral initiatives into a larger effort. A question remains as to whether the unilateral efforts being made by various entities can be woven into a measurable whole and/or whether these climate change reducing actions will synergistically benefit from being put under a common umbrella. In this chapter, we sample and document the extent and variety of existing unilateral measures, including those covered under the Accord, and examine the implementability and impact of such measures, both locally and with respect to larger international negotiations.

The starting point of our analysis is to note that participation and compliance in a broad-based multilateral initiative that aims to go further than what some individual countries are unilaterally willing to commit has proved hard to achieve. Any broad-based global cooperation that requires nations to commit to emission cuts beyond what they are unilaterally willing to undertake is unlikely to be stable (Barrett, 1994) (i.e. immune to deviations by a nation or a coalition of nations) without strong enforcement measures that go beyond what is in the Kyoto Protocol. For the balance of the chapter, we assume such enforcement measures to be prohibitively difficult to agree and/or enact.[1] By delaying participation or by not complying with a global agreement to cut emissions, a deviating country or a coalition of such countries can continue capture the short-term benefits from continuing with high carbon economic activities but pass a significant portion of the costs to others (other countries, future generations) (see Coase, 1960). In other words, free riding in the presence of negative

---

[1]The negotiation of such enforcement mechanisms is beyond the scope of this chapter, but is an alternate path to stronger global action on climate change, but more focused on the top-down approach rather than unilateralism's inherent bottom-up nature. It should be noted though that the two approaches are not incompatible and can (and perhaps should) be pursued simultaneously.

externalities limits the scope of multilateral cooperation, particularly in the presence of weak property rights, and enforcement becomes problematic (Shapley and Shubik, 1969) and (Starrett, 1973) were among the first to make this point).

Although multilateral cooperation for a post-Kyoto deal has so far been hard to achieve, there are numerous unilateral initiatives underway to cut emissions. We document the extent, form and variety, at both a national level and sub-national (regional/urban/individual) level, of existing unilateral measures. Several examples of national measures are obtainable through National Plans or through the Copenhagen Accord documents (see Annex 1). Examples of sub-national measures include community-based programs as free bicycle plans, such as in Copenhagen, Denmark, or watershed renewal programmes, such as in rural communities bordering major rain forests, as in Mexico. Such unilateral measures consist of a mix of local adaptation together with increasing capacity in renewables and the reduction of energy consumption either directly and indirectly (via energy-saving techniques and increased efficiency).

Given their potential for positive spillovers, the breadth and scope of existing unilateral measures are such that it may make more sense to try to build on a unilateral-action-based path post-Kyoto, rather than to focus on a comprehensive global package. This unilateralism focus could perhaps be supplemented by a less ambitious multilateral agreement to facilitate such efforts, such as a follow-on agreement to the Copenhagen Accord or, minimally, an agreement simply to standardize measurement of emissions globally so that the effectiveness of unilateral initiatives could be accurately measured. This could then build up sequentially to a regime with the level of effectiveness required to keep temperatures limited to a 2°C rise from 1990. In a companion paper, Chatterji *et al.* (2013), we model unilateral measures and global learning over a connected network of nations and show the possibility of a global switch to a low carbon regime. The timeline for this build-up is unclear, however, and policy design would be critical in achieving that level of reduction in a timely manner.

To encourage the rapid spread of unilateral measures globally and to enhance their effectiveness to the point where we avert major damage from climate change, several elements would be useful to have from a global treaty. These include a platform for exchange of information (via subsidized monitoring), a stable market for innovation that lowers the relative cost of cutting emissions and a new global intellectual property (IP) regime involving relatively easy technology transfer of low carbon activities, in essence quite similar to what was proposed in paragraph 11 of the Accords by the G77. The key point will be to make unilateralism desirable to engage in for those not currently inclined to do so.

However, there are many barriers that must be traversed before the world can successfully create such a climate change regime. For instance, while the enforcement of a large overarching deal is assumed not to be viable, this does not mean enforcement will not be an issue for unilateralism. The nature and level of the enforcement to be employed (whether national or otherwise) and the method behind the verifiability of reductions are yet to be determined. A further issue is the venue for any unilateralism-related agreements. The Conference of Parties (COP) process under the UNFCCC did not adopt the Copenhagen Accord; rather the Parties merely took note of it and, in many but not all cases, later decided on their own to join. Because of this, and because the Copenhagen Accord was initially a China–US bilateral deal, which was then broadened to the BASIC countries, this process started in Copenhagen might progress further and more effectively in either their hands of the G20 or in the hands of the US and the BASIC countries than under the current UNFCCC process. Whether this is a politically feasible course to take remains to be seen, but in the following COP in Cancun, 2010, the value of the UNFCCC process was called into question and the UNFCCC only narrowly kept the discussion within its jurisdiction. Even after Doha (COP 18) in 2012, and the reinstatement of Kyoto as the global climate change mitigating regime, unilateralism may be the best short-term solution for combating climate change as the potential impact of this second Kyoto Phase is much less with the departure of key countries such as Japan and Canada from the agreement, and such unilateralism could also be discussed in alternative venues, which could include the World Trade Organization (WTO), the G20, or other international bodies.

The remainder of the chapter is structured as follows. Section 2 discusses the current use of unilateral measures; Section 3 examines various rationales for unilateral measures. Section 4 studies the conditions under which global learning, building on existing unilateral measures, leads to a low emissions world. Section 5 discusses the interplay between unilateral and multilateral initiatives while the last section concludes.

2. The Extent of Unilateral Measures for Emissions Mitigation

In this section, we attempt to document, characterize, and discuss the nature and extent of unilateral measures that have been taken worldwide toward climate change. In tandem with ongoing global negotiations, the major participant countries have also simultaneously launched national action plans for combating climate change, which involve extensive use of unilateral commitments. To an extent, these unilateral commitments may represent mechanisms for the implementation of proposed multilateral commitments (i.e. those of Annex 1 in the Kyoto Protocol), but in other ways they are quite different. Thus, in the European Union (EU), there is a commitment to a 20–20 program, which involves a 20% reduction in emissions and 20% of energy to come from renewables by 2020. This is separate from multilateral commitments, which stood at an 8% reduction from 1990 levels in Kyoto Phase 1 and 20% of base 2000 by 2020 in Phase 2. The EU has also offered to go further to a 30% emissions reduction if other entities will match. Similar initiatives can be found in the case of China, where there are extensive commitments to a 20% energy consumption reduction relative to 2005 by 2020, a 45% reduction in carbon emissions relative to gross domestic product (GDP) by 2020 and also a 20% commitment to renewable energy similar to that of the EU (China, 2010).

These forms of commitments, interestingly, also seem to involve deeper commitments by smaller countries. One striking case is Norway, which has committed itself to become a carbon-neutral economy by 2030.[2] Most of these types of national commitments predate the Copenhagen Accord but have since been listed within it by the various countries undertaking unilateral actions, possibly to capture some international merit or acclaim (useful in climate change negotiations) for an action that would have occurred in any case, albeit with a possibly expedited timetable to facilitate its inclusion in the Accord.

These unilateral examples are national but, on the face of it, go substantially beyond what countries are seemingly jointly willing to commit to multilaterally. And beyond the national level, there are also many further commitments being made by sub-national and local levels by governments, community-based organizations, businesses, and even by individuals. It is not unusual in Europe for individual cities now to have emissions reduction targets for specified dates. These could involve community-based programs such as free bicycle plans, as in Copenhagen, Denmark, or watershed renewal programmes, as in rural communities bordering major rain forests, as in Mexico, and community information monitoring schemes, using for example sophisticated software that tracks carbon emissions due

---

[2] As stated on the Norway government website, the timeline is for 9% reduction from 1990 by 2012, 30% by 2020, and full neutrality by 2030.

to individual houses based on lifestyle and energy use (the idea being that increased knowledge will change people's behavior). Commitments are also made at a business level, with new businesses offering what is needed for other businesses, communities and individuals to "go green".[3] Because of the wider social/political commitment to emissions reduction, it becomes good business to characterize products as emissions sensitive, contributing to significant emissions reductions. Finally, similar actions can be taken at an individual level, either through "greening" the living space in some way, or through social activism.

Unilateral actions being undertaken to combat climate change and reduce carbon emissions around the world are both diverse and in constant flux. The examples given in this chapter are representative samples of the levels and types of unilateral actions occurring.

2.1. *The Copenhagen Accord*

It is useful first to give a brief description of the Copenhagen Accord to avoid confusion since, while it is an international agreement, many unilateral commitments have become a part of it that should still be considered unilateral. The first thing to recognize is that the Accord is still in some sense "unofficial", as it has not been adopted in the UNFCCC process (the Kyoto Protocol (UNFCCC, 1992) being the favored negotiating track) and originated from a back-room meeting of a much smaller sub-set of countries, notably including the US and China, before being nominally adopted (support without specific commitments being made) by the G77 and a host of other countries.[4] Second, and more importantly it is entirely non-binding on any country that submits a "commitment" to be listed in the Accord and participation is voluntary (and many were already underway, or at least planned, before the Accord existed). Third, many articles within it only call for items to be discussed within the UNFCCC process, such as

---

[3]The size of green industry worldwide is seemingly difficult to measure because of definitional issues (lack of a clear definition of "green"), but, to give perspective, in 2010 global (public and private) investment dedicated to "green industry" was US$ 243 billion, a 39% increase over the previous year (http://www.bloomberg.com/news/2011-01-11/low-carbon-energy-investment-hit-a-record-243-billion-in-2010-bnef-says.html?utm_source=newsletter&utm_medium=email&utm_campaign=sendCarbonHeadlines).
By itself, this is just shy of half of the US$ 500 billion per year of financing the IEA has said will be required for the world to reach its goal of a 2°C limit on temperature increases.
[4]This has, however, not stopped negotiators from attempting to utilize it in post-Copenhagen UNFCCC negotiations to facilitate a post-Kyoto deal.

the proposed "technology mechanism" or the consideration of reducing the 2°C limit to acceptable temperature increase to 1.5°C.

The only portions of the Accord potentially requiring some sort of joint action are the creation of a Copenhagen Green Climate Fund by developed countries to aid with developing country adaptation and the creation of a discussion panel on how to initiate money flows into this Fund. This is self-contained and has no direct bearing on the unilateral measures submitted under the Accord unless the country in question is attempting to avail itself of some of this funding.[5] For these reasons then, we deem submitted actions to the Copenhagen Accord to be unilateral in nature.

2.2. *Unilateral measures by country*

In practice, national unilateral measures seemingly almost inevitably interact with multilateral negotiations. This is evident in the Copenhagen Accord document, which relies heavily on unilateralism to achieve any sort of emissions reduction. Many countries developed (or announced) unilateral measures in the lead-up to Copenhagen and, while such commitments could be interpreted as a way of simply staking out bargaining positions, the argument we put forward is that, by including them in the Accord, it increasingly causes the Accord to become a viable basis for an effective global climate change adaptation/mitigation framework. A matter of partic-ular interest is the question of whether, by committing to specific unilateral measures in the Accord, such nations positively alter the incentives for other nations to commit to new or more stringent measures — in essence causing a snowballing race to zero carbon on a wide scale. But, for now, we examine the breadth and scope of such unilateralism.

In addition to the examples of unilateral action already mentioned, a number of national governments and industries, particularly in Europe, are pushing for renewable energy in all its forms and renewables are gaining ground relative to other forms of power production, albeit from a very small base. For instance, Denmark stands out as the wind power capital of the world, with wind at 20% of total energy use.[6] This is especially notable

---

[5] Several Copenhagen Accord commitments by developing countries are contingent on available international support, and previous to the Accord's creation (and perhaps after as well) this support was to come from other international funds created for climate change initiatives.

[6] http://www.worldofwindenergy.com/vbnews.php?do=viewarticle&artid=32&title=ge-neral-information Also note that Denmark does not have the highest absolute wind power capacity.

since the push for the development of wind power there predates the Kyoto Protocol. Similarly, New Zealand has developed a major reliance on thermal power.

In some nations, there is also a push toward increasing capacity in the generation of nuclear power in addition to renewables. For example, in the UK, the national government, as part of its unilateral measures to cut emissions and achieve energy security, has supported a new generation of nuclear power stations.[7] The use of nuclear is a somewhat controversial move for at least two reasons. First, there is no reliable method for safely disposing of nuclear waste[8] and, second, given the large start-up costs involved, investment in nuclear power may crowd out investment in other forms of green power generation and use, such as energy efficiency and renewables. Also, a third reason, made clear by the recent Fukushima incident in Japan, is that we would be creating many more chances for a nuclear incident to occur down the road as plants age, particularly if climate change alters local conditions in ways power plant builders did not anticipate.

In the developing world, China has adopted a 45-20-20 plan[9] to reduce emissions intensity per unit of GDP by 45%, as well as achieving 20%[10] renewable energy use, both by 2020. A significant step toward this is the phasing-out of older inefficient coal plants, as well as an accompanying planned 20% improvement in energy efficiency by 2020. India, as part of its National Action Plan on Climate Change, is actively seeking to alter its energy sector to one that is "green" via improved efficiency, renewable energy sources (and nuclear power), attempting to forge a "green" development path, which will take environmental considerations and spillovers to other industries into account.

Sweden, Finland, the Netherlands, and Norway have all imposed carbon taxes, which have been in place since the 1990s. In South Africa, enforcement of existing environmental law has been an issue and hundreds of new environmental enforcement agents have been trained to ensure that prescribed environmental measures are implemented. In Brazil, there is

---

[7]http://news.bbc.co.uk/2/hi/uk_news/politics/7179579.stm.
[8]While this remains true, large steps to reduce the half-life of existing waste are underway in the form of promoting the use of waste to power in part thorium-based nuclear power plants. This potentially sets the half-life to 100–200 years rather than tens of thousands of years.
[9]China (2010) China's 12th Five-Year Plan (2011–2015).
[10]This is the national target. A 15% goal was recorded in the Copenhagen Accord.

the PROINFA plan, which aims to provide 10% of Brazil's production and consumption of energy by 2022 through renewables and also several biodiversity-related efforts concerning the preservation of the rainforest. With deforestation rates currently less than 70% of what they were in 2003, this is a large element putting Brazil on the track to reach their Copenhagen Accord commitment of ~37% emissions reduction four years early, in 2016.[11] Also there is Ecuador's 2007 Yatsuni-ITT proposal, which seeks to preserve rainforest despite it resting above a rich oil field and to wean Ecuador slowly off oil dependence, as indicative of the direction their government is taking. These actions seemingly directly benefit individual countries little relative to the effort involved.

Similarly, but much weaker, the US has reported under the Copenhagen Accord a target that sets out a 17% emissions reduction relative to 2005 by 2020 and an 83% reduction by 2050.[12] However, this is contingent on passing matching legislation in the areas of energy and climate, and actual reductions may be less or even nothing, depending on what passes in the House and Senate.

Many of these national-level unilateral actions, while reducing carbon, also serve more local climate needs (adaptation-based projects), adding a self-interest-based element to proposed actions. For instance, in Spain, as part of a push to halt desertification there, a government-led plan to plant 45 million trees over four years (2009–2012) is underway.[13] This serves to reduce carbon emissions and lessen the country's Kyoto shortfall but the need to halt desertification is the primary driver. A similar effort, with salt-resistant plants and de-salting plans as the weapons of choice, is underway against the more saline-based desertification progressing in Australia,[14] on top of their planned 60% greenhouse gas (GHG) reduction from 2000 by 2050. As an example of what may occur globally as extreme climate impacts occur (see IPCC, 2007), in the Maldives, former president

---

[11] Full progress report summarized here: http://www.brasil.gov.br/news/history/2010/11/17/brazil-announces-three-new-initiatives-to-advance-climate-change-policy-and-reduce-national-carbon-footprint.2/newsitem_view?set_language=en.

[12] This is exactly the same goal as in the Waxman–Markey Bill, which failed in the US Senate, so the plan set out in it may represent the pinnacle of emissions reduction the US foresees itself as capable of realistically achieving. However, there is still a significant base of US citizens who do not believe climate change is occurring and this hinders any efforts at reduction to the point where the Waxman–Markey Bill level of emissions cuts looks politically infeasible.

[13] http://www.abc.net.au/news/stories/2008/09/13/2363739.htm.

[14] http://www.planetark.org/dailynewsstory.cfm/newsid/37246/story.htm.

Mohamed Nasheed (2008–2012) set up a sovereign wealth fund specifically to buy a new homeland, should the islands become inundated[15] via sea level rise, saying, "We can do nothing to stop climate change on our own and so we have to buy land elsewhere. It is an insurance policy for the worst possible outcome." Thus, the phenomenon of unilateral actions with regard to CO_2 reduction, and to similar issues that cannot be explained by short-run self-interest, is likely to be limited in duration should climate change worsen and as more specific climate "damage" occurs.

The national unilateral initiatives not related specifically to the Copenhagen Accord mentioned thus far are summarized in Table 1, while Copenhagen Accord commitments are summarized in Annex 1. Note that some commitments in Table 1 are simply strengthened versions of a country's Copenhagen Accord commitments.

2.3. Unilateral measures by territories, states, and provinces

Unilateral measures also occur at the sub-national level. At the interstate levels of government in the US, we see multi-state agreements such as the Mid-West Greenhouse Gas Reduction accord, the Regional Greenhouse Gas Initiative, the Western Climate Initiative (WCI) and the Western Governors' Association: Clean and Diversified Energy Initiative. On the face of it, these initiatives are reactions to the US rejection of the Kyoto Protocol and the continuing lack of action on climate change since then. Setting restrictions on CO_2 emissions by specified dates is the content of all of these save the Clean and Diversified Energy Initiative, which sets a 30,000 MW production goal by 2015 for renewable energy among member states as well as more long-term goals. Many of these agreements, such as the WCI, are also not confined to the US. Several Canadian provinces have also signed onto some of these agreements, namely Ontario, British Columbia, Quebec, Manitoba and Alberta. Through the WCI, a cap-and-trade system is being designed to incorporate all members.

Individual state efforts in North America have the common thread that nearly all states and provinces have programs designed to improve energy efficiency and to reduce emissions directly, with the occasional case where both are rolled up into one policy. With a large amount of carbon emissions originating in the power generation sector and North America having the

---

[15]http://features.csmonitor.com/environment/2008/11/11/faced-with-rising-sea-levels-the-maldives-seek-new-homeland/.

Table 1. **Summary of *Non-Copenhagen Accord* country-wide measures.**[16]

Country/region	Type	Actions/goals
EU	Renewables	20% of region's power generated by renewables by 2020.
China	Energy efficiency/ renewables	20% improvement in energy efficiency relative to trend/20% of region powered by renewables — both to be achieved by 2020.
Norway	General emissions reduction	Zero carbon economy by 2030; carbon tax in place since 1990s.
Sweden	General emissions reduction	Long-standing carbon tax.
Finland	General emissions reduction	Long-standing carbon tax.
Netherlands	General emissions reduction	Long-standing carbon tax.
New Zealand	General emissions reduction	10–20% below 1990 levels by 2020, with a specific plan outlined for achieving this.
Costa Rica	Reforestation/ emissions reduction	No set goal, 1986–2006 added +30% forest cover to the country/zero carbon economy by 2021.
Denmark	Renewables	Top user and prominent exporter of wind power turbines to the rest of the world.
UK	Emissions reduction	Four new nuclear power stations being built; process slowed by Japan nuclear disaster.
India	Energy sector reform	Comprehensive efficiency and renewables (and nuclear) energy plan, attempting to create "green" development path.
Brazil	Renewables/ alternate fuels/ emissions reduction enforcement	7,000 MW production goal for renewables in 2022 (~10% of total power needs)/substantial ethanol production increase; Copenhagen Accord emissions goal (~37% reduction) inscribed into national law.
Ecuador	Forest preservation	Rainforest sitting on top of oil field protected by legislation.
Spain	Halting desertification	Four-year program to plant 45 million trees near desert edge underway.
Australia	Halting desertification; emissions reduction	Bioengineering salt resistant plants and building desalination plants to combat desertification; 60% reduction in GHGs from base 2000 by 2050 — aka "ClimateSmart 2050" plan.
Maldives	Adaptation measure	Sovereign wealth fund created to purchase new home should country be permanently flooded.
South Africa	Policy enforcement	Policing force for environment-related measures expanded.

---

[16]Note that some of these countries, for brevity, do not have all actions that they are taking listed. Other country-specific actions that were recorded in the Copenhagen Accord can be found in Annex 1 of the chapter.

most energy-intensive economy (per capita) of all major economies globally, these two activities seem to be both technical and political "low-hanging fruits" (Gupta *et al.*, 2007). The US states of California and Florida are notable for efforts to improve energy efficiency and CO_2 emissions reduction in numerous areas including all of industry, transit/autos and households, as well as opening the market and experimenting with all types of renewable energies. Further north in Canada, British Columbia is notable as the first Canadian province independently to impose a carbon tax.

In Australia, New South Wales has just finished (as of September 2011) a $170 million AUD plan to overhaul the homes of 330,000 low-income families to improve energy and water efficiency as a response to the likely increased energy costs associated with Australia's commitments under the Kyoto Protocol. Most other Australian provinces are also improving energy efficiency and some, such as Queensland, are also actively and independently funding research into renewable energy. Queensland's program has already provided over $7 million (AUD) to numerous projects on renewable energy production and efficiency improvements. This is most evident through a "lead by example" program aimed at all public institutions (and related vehicles) to reduce their carbon emissions anywhere from 20 to 100%.[17]

Even in China and India, where provinces by and large walk in step with the mandates passed down from the federal level, some regional initiatives already exist, such as solar power and biofuel projects in Karnataka, India.[18] Amazonas, Brazil has taken a rather blunt approach in their local efforts since law enforcement is touch-and-go when it comes to the environment and thus, in an effort to preserve rainforest, communities attend a training seminar on environmental awareness, which qualifies citizens for monthly grants of 50 reais (US$ 30), or alternately up to 4,000 reais (US$ 2,500) for full communities, for meeting a zero deforestation requirement — in essence attempting to make it more profitable to preserve rainforest than otherwise.[19] In Russia, on the other hand, perhaps due to the fact that it trivially met its Kyoto targets,[20] unilateralism among

---

[17]http://www.climatechange.qld.gov.au/whatsbeingdone/index.html.

[18]http://www.solarthermalworld.org/node/643.

[19]http://www.theredddesk.org/countries/brazil/info/activity/bolsa_floresta_program. An interesting point about this approach is that, in the larger community case, it encourages a community to enforce itself. Thus the payments may be thought of, save for inspection costs, a replacement for the costs of environmental policing.

[20]It was universally agreed that 1990 would form the starting point from which to measure CO_2 emissions in Kyoto. In Russia's case this meant that nothing had to be done to meet their targets since they suffered an economic collapse in the 1990s, resulting in a correspondingly large drop in emissions (over 33% drop). Business as usual in Russia

its federal constituents (Russia has various types of sub-national entities) is muted and mostly limited to data and information gathering.[21] There are some biodiversity preservation efforts underway in the Russian federal constituents, notably for the Siberian Tiger, but whether they are related to climate change is questionable.

Tables 2 and 3 summarize the unilateral initiatives discussed above. Again, this is just a sampling, rather than a full accounting of state-level measures.

2.4. *Unilateral measures by cities*[22]

City-level emissions mitigation efforts tend to lend equal weight to adaptation and mitigation, usually blending the two in proposed plans. In New York City, for example, a major initiative (PLANYC 2030) is underway to improve energy efficiency and reduce emissions of all sorts, including a 30% reduction in greenhouse gas emissions.[23] The focus is on replacing older infrastructure with new and more energy-efficient technology (including renewable energy generation), which will also prepare the way for any water, food, or natural disasters to be dealt with, and also to replace existing cars with more fuel-efficient ones and to increase the number of trees and parks within the city. Toronto, Canada, has also engaged in energy-efficiency upgrading for many of its buildings and infrastructure projects. Otherwise, its plan of action is very different, with Toronto seeming to prefer heavy promotion of green roofs and development of local sources of renewables over the larger infrastructure-upgrading projects. The Toronto emissions reduction target is 6% by 2012, 30% by 2020, and 80% by 2050 from 1990 levels.[24] Munich in Germany has a plan similar to Toronto's (save for different emissions targets), with the added financial innovation of weather derivatives regarding the weather's favorability for generating renewable power in order to help manage the risks involved.[25] Similarly, London, UK,

---

with no emissions cuts still fell far below the reduction target set out for them in Kyoto (which was zero — i.e. no reduction from 1990 needed but no further emissions per year allowed).

[21] http://earth.esa.int/workshops/envisatsymposium/proceedings/posters/3P9/463731fr.pdf.

[22] If information concerning a given city is not listed in this chapter, see http://www.gcp-urcm.org/Resources/CityActionPlans for a more comprehensive list.

[23] Baseline 2007 emissions, reduced 30% by 2030.

[24] Climate Change, Clean Air and Sustainable Energy Action Plan: Moving from Framework to Action (Phase 1).

[25] http://www.munichre.com/en/ts/innovation_and_insurance_trends/windmills_against_climate_change/default.aspx.

Table 2. Summary of intrastate emissions-reduction-related measures.

Regions/provinces/ states (country)	Type	Actions/goals
Rural communities in Southern Provinces (Mexico)	Watershed renewal/ preservation	Payment to farmers for preserving and maintaining forest area deemed ecologically critical (Up to roughly US$ 40/hectare/year).
Iowa, Illinoi, Kansa, Michiga, Minnesota, Wisconsin (US), and Manitoba (Canada)	General emissions reduction/cap and trade system	Midwest GHG reduction accord — works similarly to the EU model for emissions reduction/trading, only on a shorter 30-month timescale — mandates group and individual reduction targets for this time.
Connecticut, New Hampshire, Delaware, New Jersey, Maine, New York, Maryland, Rhode Island, Massachusetts, and Vermont (US)	General emissions reduction/cap and trade system	Regional Greenhouse Gas Initiative — caps power sector emissions at 188 million tonnes immediately, tightened by 10% by 2018 — member policing of each other — pure auctioning emissions trading system (ETS) with offsets allowed.
Arizona, California, Montana, New Mexico, Oregon, Utah and Washington (US), British Columbia, Manitoba, Ontario, and Quebec (Canada)	General emissions reduction/cap and trade system	Western Climate initiative — cap and trade approach modeled in phases as in the EU, focus on all institutes emitting over 25,000 tonnes of CO_2 annually, target is 15% emissions reduction from base year 2005 by 2020, enforced on a firm by firm basis rather than standard state basis.
Western Governors Association member states (US)	Renewables	Clean and Diversified Energy Initiative — 30,000 MW capacity goal in renewables for the group by 2015, 20% group energy-efficiency improvement goal by 2020.

has a plan that focuses most heavily on energy-efficiency upgrading, with projects on renewables.[26]

In China, Shanghai has invested 80 billion Yuan (US$ 11.6 billion) on environmental protection projects. The city, which is near to sea level, has

---

[26]http://www.london.gov.uk/priorities/environment/climate-change/climate-change-mitigation-strategy.

Table 3. Summary of individual state emissions-reduction-related measures.

Province/state (country)	Type	Actions/goals
Almost all provinces (Canada) and states (US)	General emissions reduction/ energy efficiency	Goals vary by state/province but most have a minimum of at least 10% improvement in energy efficiency and emissions reduction by various means by 2020.
California (US)	Various — focus on renewables and integration of them into infrastructure	Samples — Global Warming Solutions Act of 2006, Alternative and Renewable Fuel and Vehicle Technology Program, Solar Water Heating and Efficiency Act of 2007, The Clean Car Law, and an 80% GHG reduction target by 2050 from base year 1990.
Florida (US)	Various — focus on decentralizing power grid through renewables	Samples — 40% reduction target from base year 1990 by 2025, 80% by 2050, creation of Florida Climate and Energy Commission to oversee policy, banning of common energy saving devices prohibited, Florida Climate Protection Act, tax breaks for residential property with installed renewable power generators, Florida Energy Systems Consortium created to encourage R&D.
British Columbia (Canada)	Carbon tax	Revenue-neutral tax easing in from a $10 CAD carbon price equivalent tax in 2008 to a $30 one in 2012, specific goods taxed by average carbon content.
New South Wales (Australia)	Energy efficiency/ adaption preparedness	$170 million (AUD) program to help 330,000 low income households incorporate new technology into the home for improved energy and water efficiency — completed in 2011.
Queensland (Australia)	Renewables and efficiency R&D	$7 million (AUD) into various projects aimed at developing renewable technology and upgrading energy efficiency; these are spearheaded by government institutions, with public buildings and systems being overhauled to reduce emissions anywhere from 20–100%.
Karnataka (India)	Renewables	A "100,000 solar roofs" project centered around, but not limited to, the Bangalore area. To be achieved by 2013. Solar roofing currently and indefinitely mandatory for all new Bangalore area constructions >600 sq. ft.
Amazonas (Brazil)	Rainforest preservation	"Hands-off" approach to rainforest preservation — pays residents to abstain from rainforest cutting.

increased plant and tree coverage to help ward off erosion as the threat of flood increases and is also intensely focused on upgrading and installing infrastructure to ensure the city's water supply. The plan also provides incentives for promoting green industries within and around the city and also has the goal of decreasing the volume of vehicles on the roads by 65%.[27] Sydney, Australia, has created a "Sydney 2030" plan that will aim for 50% emissions reduction by 2030 (relative to 1990) and 80% of all public worker traffic to be public transit or cycling/walking.[28] Thus, the plan involves high attention to detail to city planning around links and access to transit.

Table 4 summarizes the various city-level unilateral initiatives discussed here. A common thread in these unilateral emissions reduction initiatives (direct and indirect) is a focus on renewables, energy-efficiency upgrading and infrastructure renovation at a city level within the global sphere. On the other hand, more so than at high levels of government, a clear focus on adaptive measures is also interwoven into these policies.

2.5. Unilateral measures by businesses and joint public–private partnerships

Unilateral measures are also being implemented by businesses and joint public–private partnerships. While efforts similar to those mentioned above are ongoing in Mumbai (India) and in Moscow (Russia), unlike in most large cities around the world, most of the efforts in these cities are often better described as business ventures than government efforts. This is because the deployment of clean development mechanism (CDM)-related projects in these cities has tended to overshadow the need for explicit climate change legislation in favor of legislation to manage a proliferation of CDM projects. These often take a form similar to other city efforts, focusing on renewables, energy-efficiency upgrading and infrastructure renovation, but with CDM projects subsidized by the carbon credits generated. These are not managed fully within the public sphere, nor are they specifically limited to city boundaries.[29] This makes CDM a common mechanism for the emergence of private–public partnerships in those areas where CDM projects are valid.

---

[27]http://en.chinagate.cn/development/environment/2008-12/15/content_16950071.htm.
[28]http://www.sydney2030.com.au/.
[29]http://www.articlearchives.com/energy-utilities/utilities-industry-electric-powerity/ 1816583-1.html and http://www.14000.ru/projects/city-climate/leaflet0908e.pdf and http://bangalorebuzz.blogspot.com/2006/12/emission-cuts-to-augur-well-for-bmtc.html.

Table 4. Summary of some large city-level emissions-reduction-related measures.

City	Type	Actions/goals
Copenhagen (Denmark)	Emissions and pollution reduction	City-wide public bike system; 20% reduction in 2005 base emissions by 2015 (base already low).
New York City (US)	Adaptation measures/emissions reduction/energy efficiency	PLANYC 2030 project — estimated 30% reduction in emissions from 2007 by 2030. Project includes improving city forest cover (erosion concern), reworking of electrical grid and building codes for energy efficiency, replacing all aging water pipes with focus on durability, and mandates on increased minimum allowable fuel efficiencies for cars.
Toronto (Canada)	Energy efficiency/renewable/emissions reduction	Infrastructure upgrading for durability, updating building codes for energy efficiency, green roof promotion, large number of wind power generators added, both on land and over water. Emissions reduction targets of 6% by 2012, 30% by 2020, and 80% by 2050 from 1990 levels.
Munich (Germany)	Energy efficiency/renewables/financial innovation/emissions reduction	Infrastructure and building code upgrades (similar to NYC and Toronto), wind power generators added, weather-based derivatives designed to manage wind power financial risks of variable winds; −10% every five years emissions reduction goal. Goal of 50% from 1990 levels by 2030.
London (UK)	Renewables/energy efficiency/emissions reduction	Major infrastructure and building code upgrades for energy efficiency, various wind and solar projects; rough goal of lowest per person carbon footprint in the world.
Shanghai (China)	Energy efficiency/emissions reduction/green industry promotion	80 billion Yuan for tree and foliage planting and water infrastructure upgrading, revamped tax structure to encourage green industry, plan for removal of 65% of vehicle traffic in the city.
Sydney (Australia)	Renewables/energy efficiency/emissions reduction	50% of 1990 emissions to be reduced by 2030. 80% of public employees use mass transit/bike/walk, attainable via city planning. Energy efficiency and water infrastructure upgrades, building code revamped for energy efficiency and carbon-neutral goal.

One such project, for example, is the eco-friendly train project in Mumbai, where the aim is that long-term infrastructure viability will be maintained and government expenses will be reduced by partnering with business to reduce train energy usage by over 30%. Such projects take the place of pure public sphere efforts with the objective of greater cost efficiency for government and higher profit for business from the government. This does, however, come with a greater degree of risk in terms of a project's success or failure, particularly when the project relies on unproven technological innovations to mitigate carbon emissions.

In some cases, CDM funding builds on existing locally owned private-sector initiatives such as the previously mentioned Karnataka Renewable Energy Project.[30] While such projects reflect an incentive to further local development goals (regardless of whether those goals are intrinsically eco-friendly or not), the underlying incentives (driven by CDM) still shape the projects so that they are "greener" than what would likely occur otherwise. However, the requirement of "additionality" in CDM-funded projects is hard to verify in practice.

There are also large-scale public–private partnerships, where the financial input of CDM and similar incentive mechanisms is either less significant or does not apply. In the current global economy, when large businesses partner with governments at a national or regional level, funding for large-scale experimental projects becomes possible. In the United Arab Emirates, construction is more or less complete for the world's first zero-carbon city, Masdar (while underway, construction was still just as carbon-intensive). This is notable for several reasons. First and foremost, the UAE is a country largely dependent on production and sale of fossil fuels (mostly oil) and this project represents a change from the status quo. Second, the scale of investment, which is roughly around US$ 22 billion, makes it one of the most expensive green projects in the world. Third, and finally, a key priority is profitability, in the hope that this will signal to others that similar projects can be profitable in other areas of the world as well.[31] The embryonic city, which lies near Abu Dhabi, has infrastructure designed to encourage energy saving and estimates are that it will use 75% less power

---

[30]Ravikiran Power Projects Private Ltd, Monitoring Report: 7.5 MW Grid-Connected Biomass Power Project (UNFCCC Ref. No. 0971), Version: Ravikiran/001, dated 4 September 2008 ('Monitoring Report'), p. 8. Available at: http://cdm.unfccc.int/UserManagement/FileStorage/13KBH5NLQM60FOWXY9PZ8J47TCISAD. Accessed 31 March 2009.

[31]This is an example of the demonstration effect, a point that we will come back to later.

than a conventional city of the same size, and all energy that is used will be generated using renewables.[32] That said, its price tag does not leave much hope for outright copy-cat cities elsewhere, but several of the city's (now proven) concepts can be used for retrofitting existing cities.

Business involvement in emissions mitigation also partly reflects the perceived profitability of going "green". For example, in Dubai, a company called Dynamic Architecture[33] is working on redefining skyscraper construction in terms of efficiency and also in terms of self-sustainability, suggesting new building methods as well as making skyscrapers into wind-power generating plants, able to power themselves and several city blocks at a fraction of the cost and construction time of a more traditional skyscraper. Another example is Interface Carpets, a carpet manufacturer. Carpet-making is oil- and carbon-intensive and CEO Ray Anderson led efforts to reduce carbon emissions in their processes by 82% over 12 years in absolute tonnage, while at the same time doubling profits.[34] Approximately, this is the reduction goal for the whole world set out for the long term under the UNFCCC negotiations to keep warming at 2°C. Thus, a case study of this company is a good example of how to reach that goal. Perhaps even more significant, it stands as a signal that the stated international goal is reachable even for fossil-fuel-intensive industries — and at a profit as well.[35]

Similar businesses are growing on a global scale and a large subsection of them, mostly from developed countries, attend the annual "Clean Equity"[36] conference in Monaco, where green industry leaders mingle to share ideas and network with each other. Here gather companies developing greener cars, better batteries, better solar cells, consultancies offering services on how to green your business, concept businesses for launching new geothermal, wind and solar energy ideas, companies selling green gimmicks[37] and several other types of green companies.

Oil companies have also embraced the statement that going green is profitable. This is embodied in the US Carbon Action Partnership

---

[32] http://www.nytimes.com/2010/09/26/arts/design/26masdar.html?src=mv.

[33] http://www.dynamicarchitecture.net/home.html.

[34] Incidentally, this earned him the nickname "the greenest CEO in the World" for a time.

[35] Mr. Anderson's speech on this at a recent TED conference may be found at http://www.youtube.com/watch?v=iP9QF_lBOyA.

[36] http://www.cleanequitymonaco.com/.

[37] Honda's suggestion of opening up more car options as driving gets greener may qualify as such a gimmick. http://earth2tech.com/2009/03/02/upcoming-honda-insight-turns-eco-friendly-driving-into-game/.

(USCAP)[38]; a large group of oil companies, mining companies and other heavy emitters who are essentially calling for regulation to be placed over them in terms of carbon emissions. USCAP calls for significant and early action by the oil industry and calls for the US (home to all head offices of the members) to take an early and significant stance on reducing carbon emissions. Climate change mitigation will almost inevitably fundamentally alter the way these companies do business and thus USCAPs purpose is to allow its members say in the process so as to minimize interruption to the global energy supply and to minimize insolvency risks for its members.

2.6. Unilateral measures by individuals

Individual actions are also having a significant impact on climate change mitigation. Recycling is increasingly becoming common across the globe. In many developing countries, recycling is a source of livelihood for the urban poor.[39] Compact fluorescent bulbs are also becoming more commonplace every day, with light emitting diode (LED) technology, which is even more efficient, progressing apace. Ultimately, the goal is to make households as energy-efficient and carbon-free as possible. For the dedicated, this may involve purchasing for energy efficiency, while installing home-based solar or wind power systems. If individuals have the will, funds and supporting legislation, this behavior can become common around the world. Individuals also influence higher levels of governance, businesses and whole groups of other individuals. In simpler terms, these individuals attempt to shift culture more toward the "carbon-free" mentality. Some who have put notable effort into this include significant political figures such as Al Gore and Arnold Schwarzenegger of the US, Nicholas Stern of the UK, and Chancellor Angela Merkel of Germany. Some celebrities and other well-known people, with varying degrees of effectiveness, have also advocated climate change action and left a mark, albeit a smaller one. These include David Suzuki, Sir Paul McCartney, Jimmy Buffet, Celine Dion, Keanu Reeves, Alanis Morrissette, and countless others, a large number of them well known internationally.

Of other individuals, completely unknown before the climate change issue arose, there are many who have had impact. Perhaps one of the most effective in the lead up to the 2009 Copenhagen meeting of the COP was

---

[38]http://www.us-cap.org/, some members include Shell, Chrysler, DuPont, Dow Chemical, GM, Ford and GE.
[39]http://www.guardian.co.uk/environment/2007/mar/04/india.recycling.

Greg Craven. Using YouTube as his initial medium, this small town physics and chemistry teacher created, first an ominous initial statement on climate change entitled "The most terrifying video you'll ever see" which generated several million hits, followed by a carefully planned and thought out seven-hour long series of videos entitled "How it all Ends" that expands on the initial message, responds to critiques, and discusses and explains the science of climate change for the average person in a way that cuts through all the media sensationalism and confusion. His argument for action on climate change was so compelling that several international news stations from around the world became interested and he was invited to give a speech at the American Geophysical Union at the end of 2010. His stated intent was to make his message "go viral" via as many media formats as possible and change mainstream culture in regards to views on emissions and climate change in general. These examples illustrate the point that individuals can, and do, influence large groups of people via existing social networks and, through them, seek to alter the mainstream culture enough to influence higher levels of authority and government.

3. The Rationale for Unilateral Measures

In the preceding section, we documented a sample of unilateral measures at both national and at sub-national levels. In this section, we discuss the rationale for these unilateral measures and their potential implications for the global climate change process going forward.

A number of the examples in the preceding section reflect the short-term self-interest[40] of nations/regions/institutions (henceforth, "entities") to undertake unilateral measures to attain some local objective that also happens to result in lower emissions. In other words, emissions reduction serves as the rationale needed to undertake a local objective that needed doing anyway. Nevertheless, the full range of unilateral measures being undertaken cannot seemingly be solely explained by this sort of reasoning, especially when considering initiatives that generate little or no direct private benefit, such as the prevalence of city-level emissions reduction targets.

Another potential explanation is in terms of collective identity. Certain forms of collective identity can be self-enforcing in that, conditional on other

---

[40]Examples include adaptation to the local impacts of climate change, ensuring energy security, halting the process of desertification and local development needs.

individuals accepting the same collective identity, it is in the self-interest of any one individual not to deviate, a point emphasized by Olson (1971) in his work on collective action. To the extent to which "going green" is viewed as an essential part (or natural extension) of the collective identity in a given entity, individuals in that entity will undertake unilateral measures to cut emissions. One would be hard-pressed to name a country that displays this attribute to their national collective identity, but this does not rule out sub-groups within a country or cross-national groups from possessing a "green" attribute to their collective identity.

A different, but potentially complimentary, rationalization of unilateral initiatives lies in "rule utilitarianism" (Harsanyi, 1977) where individuals belonging to a particular group, act to conform to a specific rule, given that all other individuals in the same group also conform to the relevant rule. Unilateral measures in such a group can be rationalized if each individual in that group finds it is optimal to cut emissions given that all individuals in that group conform to the rule of cutting emissions. The strength of this rationale in terms of explaining unilateralism lies in the costs involved. There will be some marginal cost cut-off point that limits the number of entities that can be part of such a group. Where exactly that would be would depend on the resources of the potential group and the nature of the measure(s) to be taken. Hence, the lower the cost (and/or greater the profit) involved in a given group rule, the larger the base for participation becomes.[41]

There are also arguments that unilateral measures can make sense in terms of the demonstration effects involved. By undertaking unilateral measures, certain entities not only demonstrate the feasibility of collective action and their awareness of the potential threats to other entities but also lower the cost of cutting emissions for all other entities as well.[42] Therefore, even if it is not in the direct short-term interests of certain entities to cut emissions, by anticipating that such activities will generate a similar response from others, such entities will undertake unilateral measures. The general point is that, as one country cuts its emissions, the (marginal) cost of cutting emissions for other countries may fall as well, thus making emission cuts more worthwhile in these latter countries. This type of

---

[41] This is also the type of rationalization climate change negotiations under the UNFCCC were seeking, by virtue of the fact that they are based upon UN consensus voting.

[42] A similar point has been made in a model of farsighted network formation in Dutta *et al.* (2005).

reasoning is typically behind highly experimental (and hence often costly) climate initiatives, such as the construction of carbon-neutral cities from scratch, and is a particularly popular approach.

For instance, it can be argued that the initial commitment to cut 50% of CFCs in the Montreal Protocol was critical to its success, as it lowered the costs of making even bigger reductions by providing a real incentive for the development of substitutes to chlorofluorocarbons (CFCs) (Benedick, 1998). The only real difference between this and the scenario described above is one of scale, so the Montreal Protocol may be taken as a precedent for the potential of such a mechanism.

Also, in an influential contribution, Pacala and Socolow (2004) have argued that implementing a series of "stabilization wedges"[43] will place the world, approximately, on a path to stabilizing CO_2 levels. If a highly industrialized nation (or an entity within it) implements some of these wedges within its borders, other nations (and entities within it) can learn from its experience and use the innovations (be they policy-based or technological) stimulated by such an attempt. For example, if a city introduces a raft of measures to induce more use of public transport, and some of these measures are successful, other cities elsewhere in the world can learn from its experience and implement similar measures. At a national level, reducing the cost of generating electricity by wind/solar power potentially benefits many countries and not just the country in which the innovation takes place. Such unilateral commitments induce innovation in technologies that lower the cost of switching to low-carbon economic activities by creating a market for such innovations. The argument is thus

---

[43]These are, by 2054, (i) double vehicle fuel efficiency, (ii) reduce the use of vehicles by half, (iii) reduce all building and appliance emissions by 25%, (iv) double the efficiency in obtaining energy from coal, (v) replace 1,500 GW of coal based energy with natural gas, (vi) introduce carbon capture and storage to power plants totalling 800 GW coal or 1,600 GW gas, (vii) use carbon capture and storage (CCS) at 500 MtC/year coal based H_2 power plants (or half that if gas is used), (viii) use CCS at coal-to-synfuel production plants of total capacity of 30 million barrels per day (assuming CCS is 50% efficient — i.e. 50% waste carbon is fed back into the system), (ix) replace 700 MW of coal power with nuclear, (x) replace 2,000 GW of coal power with 2 million 1 MW (peak) wind turbines, (xi) replace 2,000 GW of coal power with photovoltaic technology, (xii) Add 4 million 1 MW (peak) wind turbines for production of H_2 based vehicle fuel, (xiii) increase ethanol production by a factor of 100 for vehicle fuels, (xiv) halt tropical deforestation, plant 2 times as many new trees (300 Mha worth of land), and finally, (xv) practice conservation tillage on all farmland globally 10 times as much as currently practiced. For further information on Socolow wedges refer to http://carbonsequestration.us/papers-presentations/htm/Pacala-Socolow-ScienceMag-Aug2004.pdf.

that there are significant positive transnational externalities involved in any unilateral initiative.[44]

In the Organisation for Economic Co-operation and Development (OECD), Europe and large-population, rapidly growing developing countries over 50% of industrial emissions are accounted for by three to four industries (power generation foremost), and hence attempts to cut emissions and/or the adoption of open technology standards in these key sectors will be seen to have a significant potential impact on overall emissions within these countries. Switching to low-carbon activities requires technologies that relate primarily energy, infrastructure, transport and industry (Human Development Report, 2008) and clearly effective innovation in these technologies in one nation or region will generate positive transnational externalities.

It follows from this that, even if a majority of entities in a nation do not find it in their self-interest to cut emissions, a minority of entities might. Thus, even if a given country is not willing to commit to an emissions-mitigation process, a positive fraction of entities within each nation might be willing to cut emissions and thereby reduce the costs involved in crafting a future multilateral agreement.

3.1. *The meaning of unilateral initiatives*

Examining possible motives for unilateralism tells us little of the effectiveness or impact of those measures, nor whether announced plans are actually feasible or not. One needs to assess the breadth and scope of existing unilateralism in terms of lasting effects and, ultimately, whether the phenomenon of unilateralism will have a tendency to grow or diminish as time goes on.

Such lasting effects can be divided into a few broad categories: the direct effects of climate-related initiatives (for example, GHG reduction and adaptive infrastructure overhauls), other ancillary environmental effects, political effects, motivational effects, and cost/technological effects.

The current goal is to have as much direct positive effect on GHG reduction or direct adaptive measures as possible. By and large, the commitments entered into the Copenhagen Accord fall into this category. Due to a general lack of detail on how these goals will be met, however, it is difficult to analyze exactly their impact on emissions and adaptation

---

[44]The scope of such positive externalities may, however, be limited by issues of technology transfer and absorptive capacity across locales in the face of binding political and cultural constraints.

measures. This lack of detail is telling and is indicative of only minimal (or possibly null or negative) effects on emissions out to 2020 or so, given the amount of time needed to sort those plans out. Certainly such targets could be met without planning via the use of carbon credits, but this does little for emissions on a global scale and ultimately only has a redistribution effect on global wealth.

Of those goals in the Accord that have full plans for how targets will be reached, many are contingent on the international community providing funding to see the plans through to the end, making them less significant in terms of studying unilateralism. Of those that are well fleshed out and are fully independent, a general characteristic is that they are by smaller developing countries, both in terms of geographic size and economically. The logic is perhaps that, while these countries are still economically developed enough to import "green" technologies and implement them easily, at the same time they are not so developed so as to suffer from "technological lock-in" as most western countries do. Such countries include Macedonia and Tunisia, for instance (see Annex 1). But, given the lack of global influence these smaller developing countries have on a global scale, we cannot see the Copenhagen Accord rising to prominence as an effective method of propagating unilateralism unless that influence is greatly leveraged by other entities.

Ancillary environmental effects usually occur as a side effect of GHG reduction efforts, insofar as local pollutants are affected alongside GHGs. Their general impact, be it positive or negative, is on human health and the local biospheres. Widespread measures such as energy-saving programs and air scrubbers for industrial smoke stacks reduce overall pollution levels and are not limited to reducing/capturing just carbon, but also all the other waste related to energy production and industry. From a climate change perspective, this aids in preserving existing carbon sinks, although there are significant health benefits as well. The reducing emissions from deforestation and forest degradation (REDD) and other reforestation programs also fall into this category, save that REDD has this as a primary purpose, rather than an ancillary effect.

Negative ancillary effects are not as common, but are notable for their large impact, as they historically accompany larger projects. This was the case in a number of insufficiently planned hydro-electric power projects such as the Three Gorges Dam in China which has caused deforestation and raised concerns about erosion and landslides which could lead to flooding downriver, including the city of Shanghai, given the fact that the dam sits on a seismic fault. Also, there is the Belo Monte Dam now in construction in the Brazilian rainforest which will dam a river flowing into the forest and is forecasted to greatly disturb the Amazon Rainforest by flooding $668\,km^2$ of forest (and rotting the trees) and depriving water from reaching other areas, which will contribute to drought conditions.

Unilateral actions influence equal or higher levels of government in terms of the direction of policy. Typically, this influence can be summed up as a series of demonstration effects, with one entity displaying the feasibility of a given course of action to another entity. To use a major player in the international climate change negotiation as an example, China's recent high activity on climate change had, just before Durban, moved the country out of the group of "boulder" countries holding back a follow-on treaty following the first Stage of Kyoto.[45] China had also previously been demonstrably floundering on how to create a low-carbon city, and had then taken note of efforts to create low- and zero-carbon cities abroad and incorporated some of those ideas into low-carbon city building with the aid of experts. The first such city to incorporate these new ideas was Shenyang.[46]

China is picked as an example above primarily since the one-party ruling system gives it a rapid response time relative to other major players in the climate change negotiations in terms of response to the unilateral actions of others and allows it to implement dramatic and striking changes (those that will have significant impact on the international community's perception) more quickly.

Implementability may thus be defined as the ability of various plans to achieve the goals set out, given resource constraints. This is not defined to include political will or other such motivational aspects, which should be treated separately. For simplicity, we assume that as long as political will toward a goal is an issue, the goal cannot really be defined as "unilateral". The implementability question for the various goals set out previously is whether any of these are overly ambitious given the time and resources available.

4. Global Learning, the Role of Technology and IP, and the Road to a Low Carbon Paradigm

4.1. *The task of the Accords*

The task of the Copenhagen Accord is to cause a global convergence to a low emissions regime by effectively building on the positive externalities

---

[45]http://www.reuters.com/article/2011/11/16/us-un-climate-china-idUSTRE7AF1JU20 111116.
[46]http://www.chinadialogue.net/article/show/single/en/3916.

inherent in the unilateral initiatives under its banner. It is evident from Sec. 2 that the variety of different unilateral initiatives reflects a heterogeneity of interests, beliefs, motivation at the level of countries, regions, and groups. Some unilateral initiatives are driven by purely political ends for the purposes of the negotiation (bargaining chips, concessions in other international arenas), and others by perceptions of self-interest (adaptation to local impacts of climate change, ensuring energy security, halting the process of desertification, local development needs) while others are more globally preventive in nature (general GHG reduction accords, etc.). Nations (or groups within nations) might also undertake unilateral initiatives primarily for signalling collective identity to the international (national) community, in which case concepts of rule utilitarianism and demonstration effects come into play.

In theory, although low emissions may not emerge as the outcome of majority voting at a national level (at least in large countries due to heterogeneity of beliefs, culture, and/or opinions), unilateral measures may exist at various sub-national levels. Moreover, sub-national groups are more likely to have the autonomy to commit resources to unilateral measures in decentralized political systems that empower individuals and communities. An open question, therefore, is whether sub-national groups, such as provinces, states, or territories, which can exercise such autonomy in otherwise non-participating nations, should be allowed to include their commitments in the Copenhagen Accord as this process moves forward.

As the fraction of individuals unilaterally cutting emissions in a global strongly connected network of countries evolves over time, learning the costs of cutting emissions can result in the adoption of such activities globally and in our companion theory paper (Chatterji *et al.*, 2013) we establish that this will indeed happen under certain assumptions. Policy interventions that strengthen positive spillovers across national boundaries will increase the rate at which there is global convergence to a low-emissions regime, and even if these cannot be influenced on a national level for whatever reason, it may still be possible to alter policy at a sub-national level in some instances.

4.2. *Technology and the global IP regime*

Central to the debate is the idea of a global learning process, in which technology, innovation, and IP rights relevant to the climate change problem, could all feature. Thus, in the context of post-Copenhagen negotiations, a change in the way technology transfer works on a global scale similar to that proposed under paragraph 11 of the Copenhagen Accords could be key (Stern, 2007).

This proposal, which was presented by the G77 and China in Copenhagen (UNFCCC, 2008), sets out a fast-track process for the diffusion of relevant technologies to either high-emissions areas or those places where adaptation is already becoming a critical concern. As set out currently, this to be governed by an Technology Executive Committee (TEC) which will operate under the authority of the COP and operate using a new fund called the Multilateral Climate Technology Fund, largely financed by Annex II countries but supplemented by Annex I contributions, with the incentive being that contributions to the Fund would count toward a country's Bali Roadmap responsibilities.[47] The non-administrative, functional branch dealing with the actual technologies is called the Climate Technology Center & Network (CTC&N). The proposal also seeks to accelerate the rate at which research and development on such technologies is conducted and to finance it through venture capital and aid in rapid commercialization and diffusion whereupon, presumably, a portion of the funds devoted to the innovation would be recovered back into the multilateral pool. There is an inherent selection bias in this, since the Executive Body is selecting the innovations to go forward to commercialization, but this might be possibly minimized by the makeup of this group and the oversight of COP. Originally, this Technology Network was set to become operational some time in 2012; however, this was delayed, partially due to the advent of the second Phase of Kyoto and partially due to the fact that the CTC&N only received an organizational home at COP 18 in the form of a UNEP-led consortium.[48] Subsequently, the CTC&N had its first Board meeting in May 2013, beginning the task of assessing the technological needs of various countries.[49]

While the basic framework of this proposal is clear, there is little discussion so far of verifiability aside from the fact that the Executive Body would examine each case. A key issue that may arise is one that previously arose with the CDM under the Kyoto Protocol, that is the issue of how to ensure "additionality". In practice, this has been hard to verify. For example, firms would delay adoption of cost-effective low carbon technologies to benefit

---

[47] A key advantage of this is that the amount of funding provided is not dependent on the price of carbon, allowing the flow of funds to be much more stable than otherwise.
[48] http://www.unep.org/newscentre/default.aspx?DocumentID=2700&ArticleID=9353.
[49] For further information, the CTC&N homepage may be found here: http://www.unep.org/climatechange/ctcn/.

from CDM or use CDM to adopt technologies that they would have funded from capital markets or internal funds in any case (Olsen, 2007; Wara and Victor, 2008). And so, missing in this proposal thus far is the issue of what sort of conditions should be attached to these payments to ensure "additionality"/value added. In the case of carbon mitigation technologies, these conditions could be in the same terms as are commonly being made by nation states. That is, in terms of time-bound carbon emission or carbon intensity targets, and this could be particularly useful in key sectors such as energy, infrastructure, transport, and heavy industry.

Also, a conspicuously missing element of the proposal is how, exactly, it would interact with the current existing IP rights regime. What could be involved is a new global IP regime characterized by governments in countries developing publicly funded new technology that involves users in other countries at the development stage, paying a part (or whole) of the royalties paid by users in other countries for privately funded technology, joint ventures between relevant actors (either in the private and/or public sector) across national boundaries, and lowering the cost of local use (and adaptation) of proprietary technologies by designing an appropriate international licensing system. In other words, there would be a change from the status quo of the current international institutional architecture.

In order to qualify for funding in the proposed global IP regime, countries would have to adopt specific commitments, i.e. specific time-bound quantity targets like initially lowering carbon intensity followed by emission cuts, the adoption of low carbon technology (carbon capture and storage, solar and wind energy, etc.) in important sectors such as energy, infrastructure, transport, and industry. The funding of individual projects within a qualifying country could be decentralized so that royalties paid by users for privately funded technology originating elsewhere are refunded and the cost of local use (and adaptation) of such proprietary technologies subsidized. A portion of the funding could be reserved for research and development. Decisions on funding individual projects would be taken in the context of an overall carbon reduction plan for the country as a whole. Institutional design to ensure timely funding flows, monitoring, and evaluation would be essential to the successful operation of such a global innovation and technology transfer fund.

The details of such a scheme will be critical in determining the effectiveness of this proposal as, at present, innovations of the type needed particularly in the key sectors mentioned above typically have to go through years, and sometimes decades, of testing and red tape before they can become commercially available. If this generally remains the case under the proposed Technology Mechanism, then its effectiveness toward mitigating carbon and other emissions in a timely manner will be questionable, and to a lesser extent, this is also true of technologies related more toward adaptation. This process of testing and red tape, along with issues of adaptive capacity in countries that technologies diffuse to, is one of the main issues that raised the need for a fast-track diffusion process in the first place.

While not included in the proposal as it stands, the strength of the links (positive spillovers) between countries in this process would also be important. For example, the US and the EU would be especially important because of their central role in the world economy and their generation of innovation and technology transfer. Others such as China and India would be important because of the size of their populations and potential for emissions mitigation. For example, existing "clean coal" power plants and carbon capture technologies can be developed and further refined in the US and EU with a subsequent transfer to China under the mechanism proposed where it would have a significant impact on cutting emissions. Other links may reflect structural similarities, land use patterns, existing patterns of carbon consumption, etc. Such a structure, if included in the current proposal, would aid in the efficient distribution of funds by allowing them to be distributed according to characteristics such as the degree of spillover by type of technology and by targeting countries that have the greatest potential to generate spillover effects.[50] Such a policy regime would also involve platforms where information relating to unilateral initiatives can be exchanged and is likely to involve subsidized monitoring.

Identifying, quantifying and strengthening such spillovers will be key to the success of the proposed mechanism and could feasibly fit into the mandate of the Strategic Planning Committee within the proposed Executive Body on Technology. This will be essential, as encouraging the type of technologies needed in generating positive spillovers on these across countries is likely to be costly and trade-offs may become necessary.

In general, measures that reduce emissions inertia within a country and measures that strengthen the positive spillover effects across countries are both likely to be costly. With resource constraints, there is likely

---

[50]This would be due to specific characteristics such as size, influence, technological, and innovation capabilities, the degree of similarity with other national economies such as location, patterns of land and energy use, dominance of key sectors, neighborhood effects, etc.

to be a trade-off between the two such as subsidizing measures that improve the energy efficiency of domestic households or subsidizing low carbon technologies that reduce emissions in the energy generation. The latter may have a higher potential to generate spillovers across countries while the former will have a bigger impact on reducing inertia within a country.

But, despite these complications, the proposal has the potential, if the spillovers we mention above can be created in sufficient strength, to speed the convergence to a global low carbon regime significantly, particularly if the largest global actors in the climate change area indicate a willingness to become involved.

The process described here may take time to play out so that the emission cuts required to stabilize global temperatures may not be delivered quickly. We envisage a process of technology diffusion that involves chains of innovations with new inventions based on other low carbon technologies. Such a process may require roughly 5–10 years to play out for each innovation, or more if the innovations become controversial. Some of these new technologies may not be compatible with high-carbon technologies and entire factories may need to be retooled (thus raising the adoption costs of the new technologies). Although innovation and subsequent transfer of new technologies is essential, emissions reduction may be achieved by ensuring the spread and adoption of existing low-carbon technologies within and across countries. For example, households and firms within high-income countries could be persuaded to insulate their houses or install solar panels by a combination of subsidies (or low-cost loans), and by the extension of carbon markets to individual households and small firms/businesses. As already argued, subsidized technology transfer across countries (for example, the transfer of existing cleaner and more efficient power generation from coal to China and/or the greater use of carbon capture technologies in power generation globally) would require a new global IP regime.

The speed of convergence to a global low carbon regime would increase if entities in a given country choose to cut emissions even when it is not in their immediate short-run interest to do so, anticipating that such an action would induce an earlier switch by entities in all other countries. Individual economic actors in countries that (i) create the largest spillover effects, either directly or indirectly, on global learning, (ii) are pivotal (i.e. without whom global learning will be delayed substantially), and (iii) are willing to bear the costs of being one of the first to switch to low emission activities, are more likely to act in anticipation of inducing an earlier switch to low emission activities by other countries. Moreover, such behavior will be influenced by the strength of the spillover in learning across countries.

If such cross-country spillovers occur on the level this proposal would need in order to be considered a success, an almost inevitable question arises of what this would do to trade flows. If this mechanism is to be a central feature of global climate change adaptation and mitigation efforts, the implication is for a further rise in globalization and, to a limited extent, some integration between the trade and climate change spheres. This would have a number of benefits, not the least of which is giving the private sector incentive to be active on the climate change issue through the proliferation of innovations necessary for a global low carbon paradigm.

It also suggests an eventual enforcement mechanism in the form of trade sanctions or increased protectionism (or even the threat of such) against free riders or those who refuse to participate. Bundling trade and climate change negotiations together could ensure broader participation and compliance in climate change negotiations because the flow of immediate benefits associated with emission cuts (the benefits of lower trade barriers) could alter incentives for countries to participate in global negotiations. However, a necessary condition for such bundling to work is that the *threat* of increased protectionism by low-carbon nations be renegotiation proof, a condition (i.e. increased protectionist tendencies) more likely to met by nations already undertaking unilateral initiatives as demonstrated by recent talks on carbon-based border adjustments to address issues of leakage.

Finally, note that to achieve the goal of ensuring that the pace of innovation in low-carbon technologies is rapid, such a policy would have to be supplemented by other measures. If there is uncertainty over commitments to emission targets and carbon prices fluctuate over time, or they are too low or if too many economic activities are excluded from emissions trading, there may be little or no impact on behavior of firms and households. This may discourage innovation (costly investment in the production of new ideas) that lowers the relative cost of low-carbon activities in the first place.

5. Concluding Remarks

In this chapter, we discuss both the size and extent of the unilateral commitments to reduce carbon emissions that are being taken in countries around the world and their potential for inclusion in the evolving UNFCCC process. If multilateral commitments are to be largely met through unilateral processes (particularly ones already underway or planned), then commitments taken on by negotiators involve little additional cost. More broadly, the question is whether unilateral measures can act as an effective engine for reduction in carbon emissions and achieve the goal of limiting temperature rise to 2°C by 2050. Ultimately, this will depend on unilateral measures' relative effectiveness, their number, and their ability to create the synergies necessary to reduce the cost for other economies globally to follow suit and switch to low carbon. If these synergies exist, under this view the Copenhagen Accord process going forward should attempt to build on both national and subnational efforts to promote the development and spread of effective unilateral action and encourage implementation of policy that strengthens the spillovers of such actions across nations, which is key to the social learning process we have previously described above. Key to this process will be changes to the effective international intellectual property rights regime of the sort described in paragraph 11 of the Accord. A less restrictive regime is critical for allowing spillovers across nations to take place on a timescale, according to the current science, that would be meaningful for dealing with climate change. Thus, contrary to the popular view of the Copenhagen Accord being empty and a papered over agreement, the Accord has the potential to become a solid foundation for an effective post-Kyoto, post-2020 global climate change regime. Whether that potential will be realized remains to be seen.[51]

References

Benedick, R.E. (1998). *Ozone Diplomacy: New Directions in Safeguarding the Planet*. Cambridge, MA: Harvard University Press.

Barrett, S. (1994). Self-enforcing international environmental agreements. *Oxford Economic Papers*, 878–894.

Chatterji, S., Ghosal, S., Whalley, J. & Walsh, S. (2013). *Unilateral Emissions Mitigation, Spillovers, and Global Learning*, Glasgow Economics Working Paper no. 213-23, University of Glasgow, http://www.gla.ac.uk/media/media_296226_en.pdf. Accessed 14 November 2013.

China (2010). 12th Five-Year Plan of the People's Republic of China (2011–2015), trans. Delegation of the European Union to China. Available at: http://www.

---

[51] Developments at Doha mentioned *inter alia* at http://elgarblog.wordpress.com/2012/12/14/the-doha-deadlock-intellectual-property-and-climate-change-by-matthew-rimmer/, and also, http://www.unep.org/newscentre/default.aspx?DocumentID=2700&ArticleID=9353.

britishchamber.cn/content/chinas-twelfth-five-year-plan-2011-2015-full-english-version. Accessed 24 March 2013.

Coase, R.H. (1960). The problem of social cost. *The Journal of Law and Economics*, **3**, 1–44.

Dutta, B., Ghosal, S. & Ray, D. (2005). Farsighted network formation. *Journal of Economic Theory*, **122**, 143–164, 2005.

Gupta, S., Tirpak, D.A., Burger, N., Gupta, J., Höhne, N., Boncheva, A.I., Kanoan, G.M., Kolstad, C., Kruger, J.A., Michaelowa, A., Murase, S., Pershing, J., Saijo, T. & Sari, A. (2007). Policies, Instruments and Co-operative Arrangements. In *Climate Change 2007: Mitigation. Contribution of Working Group III to the Fourth Assessment Report of the Intergovernmental Panel on Climate Change*, B. Metz, O.R. Davidson, P.R. Bosch, R. Dave and L.A. Meyer (eds.), Cambridge, United Kingdom and New York, USA: Cambridge University Press.

Harsanyi, J.C. (1977). Rule utilitarianism and decision theory. *Erkenntnis*, **11**, 25–53.

Human Development Report (2008). *Fighting Climate Change-Human Solidarity in a Divided World*. UNDP: Palgrave Macmillan.

IPCC (2007). Climate Change 2007: The Physical Science Basis. In *Contribution of Working Group I to the Fourth Assessment Report of the Intergovernmental Panel on Climate Change*, S. Solomon, D. Qin, M. Manning, Z. Chen, M. Marquis, K.B. Averyt, M. Tignor and H.L. Miller (eds.), Cambridge, United Kingdom and New York, USA: Cambridge University Press.

Olson, M. (1971). *The Logic of Collective Action: Public Goods and the Theory of Groups*, 2nd Ed. Harvard University Press.

Olsen, K.H. (2007). The clean development mechanism's contribution. *Climatic Change*, **84**, 59–73.

Pacala, S. & Socolow, R. (2004). Stabilization wedges: Solving the climate problem for the next 50 years with current technologies. *Science*, **305**, 968–972.

Shapley, L.S. & Shubik, M. (1969). On the core of a system with externalities. *American Economic Review*, **59**, 678–684.

Starret, D.A. (1973). Externalities and the core. *Econometrica*, **41**, 179–183.

Stern, N.H. (2007). *The Stern Review of the Economics of Climate Change*. Cambridge: Cambridge University Press.

UNFCCC (1997). *"Kyoto Protocol"*, *United Nations Framework Convention on Climate Change*. Bonn, Germany.

UNFCCC (2008). Proposal by the G77 & China for A Technology Mechanism under the UNFCCC.

Wara, M.W. & Victor, D.G. (2008). *A Realistic Policy of International Carbon Offsets*, Stanford University Program on Energy and Sustainable Development, Working Paper #74.

Annex 1. Copenhagen Accord Commitments[52]

Annex 1 parties[a]	Commitment	Base year
Australia	25% reduction on base year 2000 levels by 2020 contingent on an agreement to stabilize levels of greenhouse gases in the atmosphere at 450 ppm CO_2-eq or lower. Reduction of 5% below 2000 levels by 2020 unconditionally, and by up to 15% by 2020 if there is a global agreement which falls short of the 25% reduction goal and under which major developing economies commit to substantially restrain emissions and advanced economies take on commitments comparable to Australia's.	2000
Belarus	5–10% reduction, which is premised on the presence of and access of Belarus to the Kyoto flexible mechanisms, intensification of technology transfer, capacity building and experience enhancement for Belarus taking into consideration the special conditions of the Parties included in Annex I undergoing the process of transition to a market economy, clarity in the use of new land use, land-use change and forestry (LULUCF) rules and modalities.	1990
Canada	17%, to be aligned with the final economy-wide emissions target of the US in enacted legislation.	2005
Croatia	Temporary target of −5% for Croatia. Upon the accession of Croatia to the EU, the Croatian target shall be replaced by arrangement in line with and part of the EU mitigation effort. No specified date given for achieving this target.	1990
EU (and all member states)	20% emissions reduction goal by 2020. As part of a global and comprehensive agreement for the period beyond 2012, the EU reiterates its conditional offer to move to a 30% reduction by 2020 compared to 1990 levels, provided that other developed countries commit themselves to comparable emission reductions and that developing countries contribute adequately according to their responsibilities and respective capabilities.	1990
Iceland	30% reduction, in a joint effort with the EU, as part of a global and comprehensive agreement for the period beyond 2012, provided that other developed countries commit themselves to comparable emissions reductions and that developing countries contribute adequately according to their responsibilities and respective capabilities. Target date for achieving this goal unspecified and could be set within post-2012 climate change regime negotiations.	1990

(Continued)

[52]Note that the information in this table is based solely off of country submissions to the Copenhagen Accord and hence information on actions and/or timelines may not always be complete, depending upon what details were provided in specific country submissions.

Annex 1. *(Continued)*

Annex 1 parties[a]	Commitment	Base year
Japan	25% reduction, which is premised on the establishment of a fair and effective international framework in which all major economies participate and on agreement by those economies on ambitious targets. Again, target date for achieving this goal unspecified but could be set within post-2012 climate change regime negotiations.	1990
Kazakhstan	15% target. No specified date given for achieving this target.	1992
Liechtenstien	Liechtenstein commits itself to reduce GHG emissions 20% below 1990 levels by 2020. If other developed countries agree to comparable reductions and emerging economies contribute according to their respective capabilities and responsibilities within a framework of a binding agreement, Liechtenstein is prepared to raise its target up to 30%.	1990
Monaco	30% reduction by 2020. — To achieve this reduction of Monaco intends to use the flexibility mechanisms established by the Kyoto Protocol and in particular the Clean Development Mechanism. — Goal to be carbon neutral in 2050, hence Monaco may exceed this 2020 target.	1990
New Zealand	Target between 10 and 20% below 1990 GHG levels by 2020, conditional on a global agreement that limits warming to 2°C and involves all developed countries in a meaningful way. Also, there should be an effective set of rules for LULUCF and there is an open, broad and efficient international carbon market.	1990
Norway	Assuming a global agreement to stabilize GHGs arises, 40% reduction by 2020. 30% by the same year otherwise.	1990
Russian Federation	15–25% with year for achieving goal unspecified. actual level of GHG emission reductions will depend on: — Ability of Russia's forestry sector to contribute to reductions; — the commitment of other major emitters to substantial GHG cuts.	1990
Switzerland	30% reduction by 2020 compared to the 1990 levels, provided that other developed countries commit themselves to comparable targets and that developing countries contribute adequately according to their responsibilities and respective capabilities. 20% otherwise.	1990

(Continued)

Annex 1. (*Continued*)

Annex 1 parties[a]	Commitment	Base year
Ukraine	20% by an unspecified date. Conditional on: — developed countries taking part in the Accord significantly; — keeping Ukraine's status as a developing country for the purposes of climate change agreements; — keeping the existing flexible mechanisms of the Kyoto Protocol; — keeping 1990 as the single base year for calculating Parties commitments; — To globally utilize Kyoto Protocol standards for calculation of quantified emissions reductions. (*Note*: the 1990 base year condition has already been violated, as can be seen elsewhere within this table)	1990
USA	In the range of 17%, in conformity with (at the time of the Copenhagen meeting of the COP,) anticipated US energy and climate legislation, recognizing that the final target will be reported to the Secretariat in light of enacted legislation.[b] The path set forth in this legislation would entail a 30% reduction in 2025 and a 42% reduction in 2030, in line with the goal to reduce emissions 83% by 2050. However, as of the time of writing, this legislation, The Waxman-Markey Bill, has been voted down, making USA reductions uncertain.[b]	2005

[a]Kazakhstan is a Party included in Annex I for the purposes of the Kyoto Protocol in accordance with Article 1, paragraph 7, of the Protocol, but Kazakhstan is not a Party included in Annex I for the purposes of the Convention.
[b]Currently, not all EU Member States are Annex I Parties.

Non-Annex 1 parties[a]	Commitment	Base year/ goal year
Afghanistan	Preparation of an Initial National Communication (INC), which will include specific national mitigation strategies and activities appropriate for the national context; Also to complete a national GHG inventory.	n/a
Antigua and Barbuda	Requesting "fast track" financing to pursue a green development path in 2015–2020; if financial and technical support forthcoming from international community, reduce emissions by 25% from 1990 base by 2020; will also craft national adaption plans.	1990/2020

(*Continued*)

Annex 1. (*Continued*)

Non-Annex 1 parties[a]	Commitment	Base year/ goal year
Armenia	Implementing a national program on energy saving and renewable energy (2007); expansion of natural gas and electric in transport; decrease methane emissions; reforestation initiative.	n/a
Benin	Initiative to reduce vehicle gas consumption; reforestation program; methane reduction program; no details specified.	n/a
Bhutan	Vows to retain carbon-neutral status indefinitely; adaptation plans dependant on international support and currently unspecified.	n/a
Botswana	Policies yet to be determined. Deforestation, energy efficiency, clean coal, and altering building codes mentioned as goals.	n/a
Brazil	Reduction in Amazon and "cerrado" deforestation; restoration of farm and grazing lands; energy efficiency and biofuel program; increased hydro and alternate energy production; create sustainable coal harvesting from forest; all goals to be achieved by 2020 for estimated 36.1–38.9% emissions reduction — base date unspecified.	unspecified/ 2020
Cameroon	Participation in REDD+; requests $30 million for 2010–2012 for adaption efforts.	n/a
Central African Republic	Increase forest cover by 25% by 2050; promote sustainable forestry; engage in REDD-related activities; promote sustainable agriculture; promote biogas use; energy-efficiency program targeted at urban areas; build low carbon towns/cities; build 35 MW of hydro-electric power by 2030; build 4,000 MW of wind power; vehicle emissions control program; build satellite imaging system and creation of a national observatory of the environment.	2010/2030 and 2050
Chad	Promotion of renewables- solar, biogas; rural and urban energy-efficiency programs; forestry protection and plan a way to implement a REDD+ strategy; emission reduction for agriculture planned; implementing more emissions friendly vehicle fuels (biogas).	n/a
Chile	20% CO_2 reduction from BAU scenario from 2007 out to 2020; international support required and focus will be on energy efficiency, renewables and LULUCF.	2007/2020
China	40–45% reduction in CO_2/GDP from 2005 to 2020; increase renewables to 15% of energy base by 2020; forest coverage increase by 40 million hectares and forest stock volume by 1.3 billion m^3 by 2020.	2005/2020

(*Continued*)

Annex 1. (*Continued*)

Non-Annex 1 parties[a]	Commitment	Base year/ goal year
Colombia	77% of energy base to be renewable by 2020; stabilize Amazon forest depletion to zero by 2020; increase biofuel production to the point where it accounts for 20% of liquid fuel by 2020; using flexible reduction mechanisms, estimated reductions of 17.4 tonnes of CO_2 annually are expected; inclusion of REDD principles in national policy-protected areas.	unspecified/ 2020
Congo	Creation of emission controls on residential and businesses; participation in REDD; creation of national environment monitoring agency; promote clean energy and efficiency; anti-erosion and more sustainable farming plans to be made; cultural programs aimed at efficiency.	n/a
Costa Rica	Tentative policy plan to attempt carbon neutrality by 2021; national carbon assessment underway; added cost of ~1% annual GDP estimated so Costa Rica requests financial aid to implement plans.	unspecified/ 2021
Côte d'Ivoire	Plan to develop decentralized renewables-based electric grid; unspecified energy-efficiency plans; plan for sustainable forestry and anti-soil erosion; create environmental monitoring system; create a plan for climate related disaster management.	n/a
Ethiopia	Over 5,000 MW hydro-electric to be added by 2015 and ~750 MW wind power by 2013; some smaller geothermal projects; biofuel and ethanol project underway out to 2015; extensive off-grid renewables installation by 2015; public transit using renewables planned; 0.7 million km^2 of lands protected and/or planned for restoration; agriculture planned for increased soil carbon retention; waste projects to reduce methane emissions; not dependent on foreign aid; plans very specific.	2010/2015
Eritrea	Non-specific plans on technology diffusion, energy conservation/efficiency, deforestation, sustainable resource use, disaster management and rebuilding; all of this to be transparent and findings shared nationally and abroad.	n/a
Gabon	Large forestry initiative to protect, restore and manage roughly 12 m hectares, with 4 million of that as strictly protected as biodiversity preserves; early planning on basic hydro-electric and solar for energy sector/industry/residential and associated public education on efficiency.	n/a

(*Continued*)

Annex 1. (*Continued*)

Non-Annex 1 parties[a]	Commitment	Base year/ goal year
Georgia	Develop a low carbon growth plan and low carbon strategy, particularly using renewables. However, Georgia is a state in conflict and any plans are to take this into account.	n/a
Ghana	Renewables plan including grid expansion, hydro and natural gas; update infrastructure to reduce en-route losses by 31%; efficient end-use appliances, machinery, etc.; promote cleaner transport practices and zero fugitive emissions; promote sustainable, minimal till farming; participation in REDD++ and promoting local afforestation initiatives; build waste water treatment plants.	n/a
India	25% reduction from 2005 base by 2020.	2005/2020
Indonesia	26% reduction by 2020 through land and forestry management, energy efficiency, renewables and waste management. Base date unclear.	unspecified/ 2020
Israel	20% reduction by 2020 from the BAU scenario; attained through a 10% share of renewables in national energy and 20% efficiency improvement in energy use. Green building and transport plans also in development. Base year unclear.	unspecified/ 2020
Jordan	Creating and optimizing transport infrastructure to reduce emissions; energy-efficiency program; grassland and oasis/wetland protection and growing nature reserves; waste management improvements; removed taxes on low carbon/energy saving technologies; building renewable power and retrofitting existing power plants and refineries for low emissions; halting deforestation; making use of livestock generated methane in farming; reworking military equipment to meet emissions standards.	n/a
Madagascar	Plans to decentralize grid and include a variety of renewables, with focus on hydro-electric; energy-efficiency program and low energy light bulb program; forest and biodiversity preservation plans covering 9,000 ha; participation in REDD+; promoting "green" fuel production (solids and liquids); less carbon-intensive farming; promoting less polluting ways of travel and use of biofuels.	n/a
Maldives	Achieve carbon neutrality by 2020.	(n/a)/2020
Marshall Islands	40% carbon reduction from 2009 by 2020, subject to sufficient international support.	2009/2020

(*Continued*)

Annex 1. (*Continued*)

Non-Annex 1 parties[a]	Commitment	Base year/ goal year
Mauritania	Increase forest cover from 3.2% in 2009 to 9% by 2050 and promote sustainable forestry; promote urban and rural energy efficiency, particularly through improved public transit and efficient light bulbs; utilize biomass and improve home stove efficiency; reduce emissions from coal energy; develop 800 MW/h capacity of solar by 2020; research other renewables.	2009/2020 and 2050
Mexico	Reduction of 51 million tonnes CO_2/year by 2012 from BAU scenario; reduce emissions by 30% from BAU by 2020.	unspecified/ 2012 and 2020
Mongolia	Hydro power projects underway (23 MW implemented with 220 in planning stages); Being examined: portable solar and wind power for nomadic tribes, coal washing to create higher grade coal, coal briquetting heating boiler upgrades for efficiency/retrofitting them into small thermal power plants, upgrading residential stoves and furnaces and implementing use of electricity for heating, insulation upgrading and efficient light bulb use, retooling industrial equipment/processes for efficiency and esp. the cement industry, livestock limitations and participation in REDD.	n/a
Morocco	Install 100 3MW micro-hydro plants by 2030 and a larger 40 MW plant by 2013; 2,000 MW of solar by 2020, including some solar-thermal; 1,000 MW by 2012 and 5,000 MW by 2030 of wind power; retrofit existing power plants for efficiency and low carbon; 20% of national power natural gas based by 2020; two nuclear plants (2 × 1,000 MW); lighting optimization; public education; low carbon labelling program for appliances; improvements to carbon measurement systems; various public transport projects; install systems to recover energy from industrial processes at four sites; promote clean energy with industry through the "Centre de developpement des Energies Renouvelables" [sic]; methane capture and re-use; reduce farming output; reforest 50,000 ha/yr until 1 million is reached — eta 2030; lighting, energy efficiency, and other low carbon urban planning projects.	2009/multiple (estimated reduction from each project and completion dates given)
Papua New Guinea	50% reduction by 2030 and carbon neutral by 2050; $80–90 million in green investments per annum planned.	unspecified/ 2030 and 2050

(*Continued*)

Annex 1. (*Continued*)

Non-Annex 1 parties[a]	Commitment	Base year/ goal year
Peru	Net zero deforestation by 2021; 33% renewable energy on the grid by 2020; design a system to address the mismanagement of solid waste.	(n/a)/2020 and 2021
Republic of Korea	30% reduction from BAU by 2020, base date unspecified.	unspecified/2020
Republic of Moldova	25% reduction from base 1990 year by 2020.	1990/2020
San Marino	Specific targets unspecified: promotion and development of renewables; emissions mitigation; update infrastructure for efficiency and, for energy, nearness to use site; rural and industrial energy-efficiency promotion, with informational campaigns; direct measures such as interventions for energy saving and the use of renewable energy sources.	n/a
Sierra Leone	Establish a National Secretariat for Climate Change (NSCC); altering national institutions to better allow them to facilitate mitigation and adaptation issues; establish 12 protected biodiversity sites by 2015; sustainable management of forests and catchment areas and restoration of Western region habitats; support for national forestry assessment; achieve 3.4 million ha forest coverage by 2015 — largely through policy and regulations; setting air/water/soil pollution standards, with regular monitoring of conditions; sustainable conservation farming; development of an Integrated Natural Resources and Environmental Management programme; development of clean and alternate energy sources, such as renewables, biomass and retooling incinerators for energy generation; enforced vehicle maintenance and promotion of mass transit.	unspecified/2015 for some items (timeline unclear for others)
Singapore	16% below BAU by 2020, contingent on a global agreement, although agreement not needed to start toward this goal.	unspecified/2020
South Africa	34% below BAU by 2020 and 42% by 2025, contingent on international support.	unspecified/ 2020 and 2025
Tajikistan	Build an inventory of GHG emissions; support energy-efficient technologies in new constructions; general support for adaptation and mitigation measures, tech transfer and capacity building; development of low carbon growth via renewables.	n/a

(*Continued*)

Annex 1. (*Continued*)

Non-Annex 1 parties[a]	Commitment	Base year/ goal year
Former Yugoslav Republic of Macedonia	New hydro, thermal, natural gas, and wind plants; infrastructural and behavioral energy-efficiency measures; replacement of coal to reduce GHGs; plant and infrastructure upgrades for efficiency, and liquid fuel transport in particular; building codes updated for efficiency; waste biomass reused for energy generation; retooling of thermal plants and introduction of solar for heating in public buildings; education on efficiency and energy measurement devices for public; modernization of vehicle fleets and use of alternate fuel types; traffic regulation and electrification of transport; landfill methane recapture; control of nitrous oxide; improved waste management systems; sustainable farming and farmer support; CDM training to enhance number of opportunities for projects, particularly in agriculture (further details in submission).	n/a
Togo	Increase forest cover from 7% in 2005 to 30% in 2050; improve forestry sustainability; reduce GHG emissions; improve both urban and rural energy efficiency including fuel substitutions and updated appliances/equipment; utilize biomass in energy production and reduce coal based emissions; promotion of renewables — solar, wind, biogas, biomass.	2005/2050
Tunisia	Various wind, solar and biomass energy projects underway, for electric and liquid fuel both as end products; use of biogas in industry and residential areas; use of natural gas for transport; development and expansion of public transit and central infrastructure planning for major cities aimed toward efficiency, centered around special economic zones; construction of solar powered homes; efficiency promotion programmes for industry; recovery of gases during petro production; reduce industrial emissions of phosphates and nitrous oxide; increase forest cover from 12.8% in 2009 to 16% in 2020; increase in protected forests from 17% to 20% by 2024; sustainable agriculture practices to be implemented, aimed at preserving water and fighting desertification; national strategy to be drafted for current to 2050 time horizon.	2009/2020 and 2024

[a]Some Parties have noted the need for international support when describing their actions.

Chapter 9

Compliance Mechanisms in Global Climate Regimes: Kyoto and Post-Kyoto*

Sean Walsh

University of Western Ontario

and

John Whalley

University of Western Ontario,
The Centre for International Governance Innovation

We discuss compliance mechanisms in global climate regimes focusing on both the Kyoto Protocol arrangements and what might follow post-Kyoto. Much of the literature on compliance more generally focuses on severity of penalties and mechanisms for determining compliance in terms of the interpretation of agreements. In Kyoto, elaborate procedures exist but are largely for the resolution of disputes over procedural issues in measurement of emissions, so that penalties are not centrally discussed. Weak enforcement seems to be the result and the challenge post-Kyoto will be to strengthen these mechanisms.

1. Introduction

From its initial set up in Rio in 1997, the Kyoto Protocol (UNFCCC, 1998) was simultaneously viewed both as a landmark achievement in international treaty making and also inadequate to the task, especially in its enforcement provisions. But the Protocol was hailed as a great achievement in bringing together a large number of participants in the negotiation (even though not all took on formal carbon limitation), achieving significant depth in its commitments and establishing an arbitration and dispute settlement procedure as part of the treaty (Oberthür and Lefeber, 2010). The Protocol is inadequate to the task as far as the primary issue of excessive carbon

---

*We are grateful to the Ontario Research Fund and to the Centre for International Governance Innovation for financial support.

emissions are concerned. While there are reduction targets, they do not provide for sufficient depth of cuts over a long enough period covering key countries to reach the goal of halting temperature rise at a global 2°C increase from 1990 levels. And the attempts in the recent and still ongoing UNFCCC process to establish a globally cooperative regime adequate to this purpose have also encountered difficulties; first in Copenhagen in 2009, in Durban in late 2011, and in Doha in 2012. Here we discuss enforcement and compliance in both the Kyoto Protocol and whatever global regime may follow in its place past the now agreed upon Phase 2 of the Protocol out to 2020, whether that involves a Phase 3 of Kyoto or a more independent approach more in line with the Copenhagen Accord with the extent of global standards involved only relating to reporting of actions taken.

Superficially, there appears to be much to like about Kyoto and its enforcement mechanisms. There are seemingly exhaustive and fast track dispute settlement and arbitration systems set out in the treaty. However, in practice, these systems incorporate weak penalties and have thus far not aided compliance with Kyoto commitments. Countries have threatened to fail in meeting their Phase 1 Kyoto Protocol commitments (notably Canada, who has now withdrawn from Kyoto entirely) and the treaty-based mechanisms able to reverse this seem few. With this structure as the potential platform for a post-Kyoto compliance mechanism, the question is where could we go from here in terms of compliance mechanisms keeping in mind that the post-stage 2 Kyoto regime could either build on the previous stages and build in complexity, or turn in an entirely different direction, perhaps based off of the Copenhagen Accord.

In this chapter we, firstly, discuss alternate approaches to climate agreement compliance approaches, including entering agreed terms into domestic law; enforcement via escrow account mechanisms (the nature of the account and whether in the US funds or some other type of currency are discussed), with those in non-compliance forfeiting their share of the account to those in compliance; using trade as a retaliatory mechanism, either justified under the World Trade Organization (WTO, 1947, General Agreement on Tariffs and Trade (GATT) Article XX) or otherwise; opting for a more passive enforcement system such as the creation of a climate regulatory rating system; or, lastly, retreating from the goal of limiting warming to 2°C and falling back on the de facto enforcement regime of weakened country credibility should they not meet their treaty commitments. The question with this last option is how much loss of credibility there would be relative to more standard agreements that could spill over into other international meetings/negotiations in failing to meet a climate change-related agreement.

Next we document arrangements regarding compliance mechanisms in the Kyoto Protocol and evaluate the limited experience with them thus far. We then discuss some approaches to strengthened compliance that could be used in a post-2020 regime. Developing countries have thus far refused to allow the Protocol to be discarded[1] and hence it is likely that it will be the basis for any future agreement, at least in part. We discuss alternative approaches to an enforcement regime of any treaty to follow Kyoto post-2020, based on the premise that the current regime has thus far done little to encourage compliance and/or involvement of the world's major emitters. Finally, we examine the options for enforcement in the Copenhagen Accord (UNFCCC, 2009b).

2. General Considerations with Enforcement Mechanisms in Climate Change Agreements

Prior to the Kyoto Protocol, negotiations engaged in discussion of environmental agreements paid little attention to enforcement mechanisms for those agreements.[2] Negotiators came largely from environmental ministries where there was little prior involvement in treaty making. It was assumed that the broad acceptance of the importance of environmental protection would carry the day, and any transgressors would be shamed into compliance through political mechanisms including media coverage, which for political masters would affect their probability of re-election. Formalized treaty-based arrangements regarding compliance did not enter the picture, and were thought not needed. Only with climate change, with large-scale participation by countries under UN auspices did the situation change and the need for compliance arrangements became accepted as paramount.

The effectiveness of enforcement regimes in international treaties rests ultimately on the size and enforceability of penalties. This has long been accepted in game theoretic literature from which the so-called "Folk Theorem" (see Rubinstein, 1979) has evolved; that any allocation that is feasible is supportable by a structure of trigger strategies (penalties which

---

[1]The principal reason for this is that the Protocol embodies the UNFCCC concept of common yet differentiated responsibilities between developed and developing nations for climate change which they wish to protect.

[2]The 1987 Montreal Protocol was a notable exception.

depend on specific actions) if the trigger strategies are permitted to embody draconian enough penalties. Barrett (1994) has in turn suggested that if the enforcement arrangements in Kyoto are so weak that enforcement becomes infeasible, that a better way to proceed on international arrangements on climate may be to begin with smaller more focused treaties (such as the Montréal Protocol) which are designed and proven to be enforceable. Legal scholars, however, generally assume that political considerations as to what is acceptable will always limit the scope of enforcement in practice, and appeal to such notions as the punishment fitting the crime.

This being the case, we can consider a range of more specific penalty arrangements, each stronger than those contained in Kyoto, but limited nonetheless. These include commitments backed by funds deposited in an escrow account with funds of noncompliant participants returned to those who comply, having terms of treaties fully entered into domestic law so that transgressors can be sued, trade sanctions against non-compliant parties, and monitoring and regulating mechanisms.

2.1. *Trade penalties for environmental agreements*

A common starting point for negotiators regarding enforcement is to ask what can be learned from the experience of the WTO on trade. A large part of the global experience in treaty enforcement is enshrined in the WTO and its previous incarnation as the GATT. However, the principles employed in this arena do not easily apply to the environmental sphere. For example, one common practice in trade is to impose greater penalties on an offending country relative to the damage caused by an infraction in a claimant country, but outside of trade penalties, which would run the risk of violating Most Favored Nation (MFN) status, there is little an environmental treaty can impose. Such a treaty is generally restricted to penalties regarding restrictions on participation in carbon markets and increased carbon reduction goals relative to the initial agreement, which the Kyoto agreement already has and, presumably, are both things readily and easily ignored by a country not seriously considering limiting its emissions.

WTO dispute settlement evolved over time from 1947 with accumulation of experience with panel procedures, and the sharp tightening in the effectiveness of enforcement following the 1994 Uruguay Round. Disputes center on the interpretation of provisions of agreements, not confronting issues of measurement as in the emissions case for climate change.

Nonetheless, there is a provision in the WTO charter that covers environmentally based trade restrictions — Article 20, but it has never been tested on any extensive scale and the limits of that provision (in terms of what are valid environmental grounds for protectionist measures) have been determined through dispute settlement on a case-by case-basis in the past. In other words, there exists the possibility that attempting to utilize Article 20 of the WTO charter to cover all climate change-related penalties could simply open a new UNFCCC-style discussion in the WTO over the interpretation and use of the article in regards to climate change. But with the WTO discussion more likely (and able) to consider the possibility of WTO reform, possibly by expanding upon Article 20, and generally developing climate-trade linkage to deal with the climate change issue, it would be a breakthrough for the rest of the negotiations to end up with a workable basis of trade-related penalties for an enforcement mechanism to work with. The political sticking point to starting that conversation would be that the climate change discussion would no longer be officially entirely under UN auspices, and some countries could take exception to that (namely, those without WTO membership, or those who lose a significant number of allies/negotiating leverage in moving the venue to the WTO).

Linking climate and trade in such a way would not simply be a matter of politics though — there are also technical issues to work out. For example, one common WTO penalty-strengthening structure sometimes proposed is an N-1 retaliation scheme; in which all other WTO parties commit to retaliate against a member found through dispute settlement to be in violation. In the trade case, it would work by having all other members impose a trade restriction on the offending party. The climate analog is for a country not upholding its climate commitments to see the carbon-emission restrictions lightened by all other parties, which is counterproductive and not effective as a deterrent to individual country violation. Similarly, having the offending party locked out of all carbon markets means that party simply continues business as usual without counting the environmental costs — a similarly toothless measure and one that provides a poor example to other parties in an emissions-reducing arrangement. Thus, linking trade and climate change regimes in such a way would require creative thinking.

Strengthening penalties for a climate change regime's enforcement mechanism is a theme that is repeatedly raised to craft more effective enforcement. As mentioned, the current Bretton-Woods-based structure for global cooperation was not built with trans-national environmental matters in mind and the trade penalties under this system are generally ill-suited for enforcement of a climate change mitigation treaty, as demonstrated by the Kyoto Protocol. Thus, moving forward past Kyoto, regardless of what the post-Kyoto climate deal entails, we should recognize that the Bretton-Woods framework has little to offer in terms of "teeth" to make an environmental treaty enforceable as long as climate remains outside its sphere.

This is also the case for proposals to link trade measures to non-participation in multilateral emissions-reduction agreements through carbon-based border tax adjustments based on the carbon content of traded goods. These violate the MFN provisions of WTO, generate resentment of developing countries and fall shy of their emissions-reducing objectives.

2.2. *Incorporation into domestic law*

Another approach to enforcement of climate change arrangements does not involve the Bretton-Woods system for enforcement (but may also be the most politically difficult to get implemented). It is to incorporate fully any commitments into national law, hence making them enforceable via civil litigation in national court systems. This could also help clarify the interpretation of the common but differentiated responsibilities principle in UNFCCC but also risks multiple interpretations arising in each national court (and what issues fall under environmental law could vary by country). Punishment severity and even the type of laws used for dictating when and how that punishment for non-compliance comes to pass may vary widely. To counter this divergence somewhat and at least allow for comparison, it might also be possible to develop a standard global measurement system as the basis for court decisions, although countries such as the UK who already have climate change-based legislation in place (in the form of the 2008 Climate Change Act) may complicate this process.

The idea of entering commitments into domestic law could also be relevant for the Copenhagen Accord, which for now rests on ill-defined national verification with little by way of penalties, as this Accord, *de facto*, is the post-Kyoto multilateral regime should no other successor regime arise. The Accord, if negotiators were to make commitments binding through domestic legal enforcement, could also incorporate enforcement and penalties.

2.3. *Escrow account*

Another possibility is to create a global escrow account to which all countries commit funds. Issues would also arise as to the location, size, and management of the funds; and how the managers of the fund are to make determinations of compliance. The structure of such a fund would be that when one party to the negotiation violates the terms of their commitments, their portion of the escrow account funds is in some way distributed (evenly or unevenly based on some criteria) to the remaining parties who are in compliance. If excess funds from some party in non-compliance were redistributed unevenly, this could easily be made to reflect the common but differentiated responsibilities principle in UNFCCC. A disadvantage is that it encourages a beggar-thy-neighbor approach in the sense that any given party has a temptation to work, actively or passively, against the carbon-mitigation efforts of all other parties for financial gain. However, seen in a more positive light, one could also say this "disadvantage" encourages a race to the bottom in terms of emissions.

2.4. *Agency rankings*

Another approach to enforcement that could be used is ongoing judgement of performance on mitigation and adaptation to climate change via an officially established international agency. This could operate akin to credit rating agencies such as Moody's or Standard and Poor's and could help with enforcement (or common but differentiated responsibilities for that matter) especially in decisions regarding the disbursement of any funds created for dealing with climate change. Theoretically, this could also be a guide as to which countries pay into such funds as well as how much. How to rate a country, and on what criteria, are the key components of this, as well as who exactly would be doing the rating. We have several successful rating agencies, even if they are not climate change-based, that could potentially lend support and credibility. And as an additional benefit, this would entail creating a sense of competitiveness among countries, aiding in the achievement of whatever goal the post-Kyoto regime sets out.

3. Enforcement Mechanisms in the Kyoto Protocol

Negotiations on the Kyoto Protocol ended in 1997 at COP 3 and the final document was then opened for signing. However, the Protocol as negotiated was lacking in detail, especially in the area of enforcement and compliance. The subsequent negotiations to "flesh out" the Protocol finished four years later at COP 7 in 2001 in Marrakesh; a follow-on negotiation which aimed, among other things, to define the compliance regime.

3.1. Origin and structure

The Kyoto Protocol's compliance mechanism is part of the Marrakesh Accord agreed in 2001 (UNFCCC, 2001), an amendment to the original Kyoto Protocol document. In the compliance area, the focus is on specific articles in the original Kyoto Protocol agreement. These include Article 3, paragraph 1, which covers the setting of emissions targets for 2008–2012, Article 5, paragraphs 1 and 2, which deal with the creation of national inventory systems of greenhouse gas (GHGs) compatible with IPCC methods/best practices (and are thus comparable to each other), and Article 7, paragraphs 1 and 4 on continually reviewing and updating the process, and other ancillary provisions.[3] In Phase 2 of the Kyoto Protocol, Article 3 has been subsequently updated to show new targets for 2020, which are, save for a few exceptions, (for now, prior to inter-party agreements shifting the burdens between them) a uniform 80% of base 2,000 emissions plus some modifications[4] from Stage 1 performance. It has also been updated to allow burden sharing agreements for emissions reduction between parties. Articles 5 and 7 have remained much the same and were not part of the Doha Amendment made at COP 18 (UNFCCC, 2012).

The core of the compliance system lies in a Kyoto "Compliance Committee", which reports directly to the UN. This has two branches, facilitative and enforcement, as well as a plenary body drawn from branch members. The Committee comprises 20 people (10 per branch) and, across its mandates, draws on members in roughly equal measure from Annex 1 and non-Annex 1 countries, with terms lasting either two or four years depending on the position (longer term for senior positions). Of critical importance is the general mix of competencies within each branch, because of the complexities of implementation of Kyoto Protocol measures. This is one of the considerations in addition to Annex 1/non-Annex 1 that is reflected in decisions on how to divide up Committee members among the branches, and if there is a lack of expertise, branches are allowed to call upon outside experts for consultation at need. The need for two branches is largely reflective of how unprepared the UNFCCC saw the world

---

[3]These remaining provisions have mostly to do with privileges associated with staying in compliance, the most significant of which is the ability to participate in global carbon-trading markets.

[4]See, in particular, Article 3, paragraph 7 bis modification to the Kyoto Protocol, found in Article 1F of the Doha Amendment.

was for implementing GHG-reducing measures and is also reflective of the differing treatment that can be expected between Annex 1 and non-Annex 1 countries, with the enforcement branch having little to do with non-Annex 1 countries under the Protocol's terms (Ulfstein and Werksman, 2005).

The facilitative branch is largely concerned with aiding individual countries in the implementation of Kyoto Protocol commitments, mindful of the common but differentiated responsibilities principle in the UNFCCC and particularly the avoidance of adverse effects on developing country parties (Kyoto Acc. Article 3, Paragraph 14). If and when a ruling of non-compliance is passed forward from the enforcement branch, it is the task of the facilitative branch to provide aid and put forth suggestions to the non-compliant country/party to allow them to come into compliance. In practice, the largest task of the facilitative branch has been to standardize and codify GHG-emissions measurement systems and the national accounts data used to monitor emissions.

The enforcement branch requirements regarding the competencies of members relative to the facilitative branch differs. They also deal less with developing countries and focus mainly on Annex 1 country plans and assessments of whether they will meet their goals set out for emissions reduction in the Kyoto text. Other compliance issues involve procedural matters such as not properly setting up a national inventory system for keeping track of emissions or not submitting emissions data annually, as required, to the general Conference of Parties (COP) assembly of the UNFCCC. The enforcement branch is also the entity to be called on to settle disputes over data and its accuracy,[5] although it can, at need, call for assistance from the facilitative branch. Most compliance activity to date has not warranted the involvement of the enforcement branch, as the deadline for emissions reductions is 2012. However, now that we are past this date, the enforcement branch will embark on a three-year process[6] of determining levels of compliance with the emissions-reduction targets and other matters such as the creation and standardization of a system of national accounts for emissions, and subsequent penalties for non-compliance. The most significant of these penalties can include shutting

---

[5]These can arise between countries or, most commonly, between the expert review teams and the country in question over data and reporting requirements under the Protocol.

[6]This three-year period assumes there will be appeals to at least one verdict reached and reflects this. The process could be shorter if there are no appeals or issues.

out a party from international carbon-trading markets and a 1.3 times increase in the level of emissions reduction required in Phase 2 of the Protocol.

3.2. *The handling of complaints*

The process by which complaints, or more formally, "questions of implementation", are dealt with begins with a submission of a complaint to the Compliance Committee chair or Secretariat by a signatory to the Protocol. Those who can raise questions of implementation are limited to the parties to the Protocol and, save when a party files such a submission on itself, first requires some credible and reasonably well-documented proof of misconduct to be presented. Once submitted, the nature of the issue involving implementation determines which branch (facilitative or enforcement) it is passed to by the Committee, a decision to be made within seven days. Most complaints are initially given to the enforcement branch, as Annex 1 countries are still trying to cope with the inexact measurement of their emissions in a reasonably standardized and comparable manner. To date, all complaints made deal with breaches of procedure, although now post-2012, we may see complaints dealing with the breaking of commitments.

This stands in contrast to the WTO process where there have been no complaints raised by a party against themselves. There is always a party being explicitly harmed at the base of the complaint, necessitating the WTO mediate between the two parties. If no resolution can be reached, punishments can be imposed by the infringed member acting against the infringing party. In Kyoto, if harm has been done, it is to "the World" (including those regions not in Kyoto). Hence the Compliance Committee, at least on matters of procedure, has thus far spoken in its capacity as "the World" rather than as a collective body of members and both issued complaints and passed judgements.

The processing of questions of implementation raised by parties can then follow either a normal or expedited track depending on the time sensitivity of the issue and the inclinations of the parties involved. The normal procedure takes 35 weeks after allocation to a particular branch, and the expedited procedure 16 weeks. A preliminary examination of the issue explores whether the submission and issue presented (if not submitted by the offending party itself) meets the requirements of being Protocol-based and is sufficiently backed by supporting data. The parties in question (as well as the public) are then notified at the end of three weeks (two in expedited cases) whether the question of implementation will be pursued or not under Kyoto compliance mechanisms. The Secretariat is to ensure that all parties are kept abreast of proceedings, although only the branch members and perhaps a team of hired experts can be a part of the deliberations as to whether the issue is to be pursued or not.

Assuming an issue is pursued, the infringing party, the party that submitted the complaint, the team of expert reviewers designated under Protocol Article 8, the COP as a body, and the other branch of the Committee are then invited to submit information for a hearing on the issue. The time allowed for submissions and requests is 10 weeks (four in expedited cases). The submitting party and branch involved can choose to withhold information submitted from the public until a final decision is rendered. The deliberations in the hearing take four weeks (two expedited cases) and at the end, the branch of the Committee overseeing the proceedings renders a preliminary verdict. From this time on, parties are allowed a further 10 weeks (four expedited) to submit further information to either reinforce or try to mitigate or cancel the preliminary ruling. After this, the branch, possibly with the aid of experts and the other branch, will disseminate the information and render a final decision after another four weeks (two in expedited cases). At this point, all information on the case is in the public domain to ensure transparency. The party that the decision is about may decide to appeal the decision, but only if it feels it has been denied due process and can successfully argue its assertion to the COP, which renders decisions on appeals among its other tasks in overseeing the Committee.

If the final ruling is against the party in question, and one of the articles mentioned at the start of this section has been ruled to have been violated by them, each branch then, immediately after an appeal window of 45 days, imposes the "consequences" of such a ruling that fall under their respective jurisdictions. And the term "consequences" is in quotations because this is where the Kyoto Protocol enforcement mechanism weakens. In the name of such consequences, the facilitative branch can only impose facilitative consequences on the party in question if the ruling goes against them. The penalty is for the facilitative branch to provide advice, financial and technical assistance, and assist in the creation of a plan to bring the party back into compliance (if the enforcement branch requires one).

The enforcement branch can, at its discretion, also impose consequences depending on the severity of the infraction. The first is a declaration of non-compliance. The second is to require the infringing party to create a report on the nature and causes of the infraction and the creation of a plan to deal with it, complete with timetables, midterm goals and progress reports. The third is the suspension of the party's ability to participate in global carbon-trading markets.

If the ruling is that a party's emissions have exceeded their set limit agreed under Kyoto (as opposed to not complying with a given Protocol procedure), then other options become available to the enforcement branch as well. The first is a penalty to take place in Phase 2 of Kyoto which involves whatever new limitation is agreed, with an extra burden to eliminate the surplus emissions from the initial commitment period of 2008–2012, plus an additional 30% of that excess amount. The second is a suspension of all ability to make carbon transfers, not just within an emissions trading system (ETS). Finally, the enforcement branch can order a report to be drafted by the infringing party specifically on what caused the failure to reduce emissions and a plan to meet the new target set out for the party's second commitment period (whatever that ends up being).

This is the sum total of all measures that can be taken against an offending party to the Kyoto Protocol and it is easy to see why some find it lacking in force. However, at the same time, it is hailed by some as the most successful attempt formally to lock in and police the international community to date on any issue, not just emissions commitments and climate change.

3.3. Experiences to date with questions of implementation[7]

To date there have been eight instances of questions of implementation posed under the Kyoto compliance process[8] that required the intervention of the enforcement branch. All of these complaints have been resolved as of the time of writing. These are the cases against Greece, Canada, Croatia, Lithuania, Romania, Ukraine, Slovakia, and Bulgaria.[9] And although

---

[7]For more details concerning specific questions of implementation, refer to the UNFCCC main site: http://unfccc.int/kyoto_protocol/compliance/questions_of_implementation/items/5451.php.

[8]There have also been many smaller complaints filed, all by the G77, against various countries regarding a failure to keep the Protocol secretariat informed as to when late reports will be submitted. In other words, these complaints are about maintaining transparency.

[9]To date, all procedural complaints against countries (which is the only type submitted thus far) have been initiated by the Kyoto Protocol enforcement mechanism itself (i.e. the

these countries likely did not meet their required Kyoto carbon-emission limitations (save for cases like Canada where the country exited Kyoto entirely), that is not a question open to enforcement procedures as of yet (at least not in the public record) as the First Kyoto commitment period has only just ended. All of the existing questions of implementation and complaints are based on alleged violations of procedure. Canada, for instance, allegedly failed to set up a national registry for carbon accounting in the time allotted to do so and a complaint was issued by the compliance committee after this came to light in Canada's submitted report. During the initial phases of the investigation, Canada set one up and it was deemed sufficient despite several flaws being noted and the complaint was dropped shortly after the initial hearing.

Greece had similar issues with national accounting, first noted in their December 2007 report to the Kyoto Protocol secretariat, but they had less activity in progress to rectify the situation, and so the claims against them were not dropped and the complaint advanced through the system with a finding against Greece. Greece was judged in non-compliance, was ordered to submit a plan to bring them back into compliance and was restricted from participating in global carbon markets or acquiring clean development mechanism (CDM) credits until such a plan was successfully implemented.

Croatia's situation was more complex and involved questions over their accounting method and issues of time frame and geography. It involved confusion over precisely what information they were responsible for collecting. Several special rules in the UNFCCC charter concerning economies in transition were involved, but ultimately the committee ruled against Croatia since the Kyoto Protocol does not provide leeway to use these special rules in this case. Ultimately, Croatia was ruled as violating procedures, and carbon-trading privileges were suspended.

Lithuania is undertaking a prolonged overhaul of their emissions measurement systems, which caused questions to be raised by the Compliance Committee, who initiated a complaint. The overhaul is focused on not allowing measurement of emissions to meet UNFCCC minimum data quality standards, despite several previous recommendations by the Committee to facilitate compliance during the overhaul. Lithuania's new system is in place as of July 2011 but this was discounted for the end of 2011 reporting period as insufficient. The ruling was non-compliance

---

compliance committee), using a country's submitted reports to the Protocol's secretariat regarding progress on their commitments as the basis for initiating a complaint.

pending a full report on the new system and if it meets minimum reporting requirements, with a consequence of suspended participation in Kyoto carbon-trading mechanisms.

Bulgaria's case, once again, concerns the use of national accounts. The finding was that their system did not provide sufficiently transparent or accurate emissions data and involved a staff judged not to have the proper competencies or resources to manage a carbon accounting system. The ruling was of non-compliance, with a strong suggestion to use experts to aid them in setting up the system properly.

The three most recent questions of implementation were filed against Romania, Ukraine, and Slovakia, all of which ended in a non-compliance ruling. Romania's case initially only involved an alleged failure to put land use, land-use change and forestry (LULUCF) in its national carbon accounting. Initial investigations by the enforcement committee have seemingly since revealed several weaknesses in their method for measuring emissions in all sectors in Romania, leading to inaccurate figures. Romania has acknowledged that it is trying to improve emissions measurement and that solutions to these problems are still at an early stage. In response, the enforcement branch has ordered a full review of their national system, so as to be able to assess the "completeness, accuracy and transparency" of their system. In the mean time, carbon-trading privileges were suspended. Later, the final ruling upheld these findings and Romania was declared in non-compliance.

Ukraine's situation is very similar to Romania's — a general weakness in carbon accounting, and in addition, an issue of consistency of measurement across years. Again, the ruling was non-compliance until this is fixed.

Slovakia's situation revolves around thier 2011 emissions report where the expert review team took issue with some accounting calculations in the report and recommended solutions. The question of implementation arose when Slovakia disagreed with the expert review team's recommendations. Absent these recommended fixes, Slovakia's accounting was deemed insufficient and was ruled in non-compliance until this was resolved.

3.4. *Withdrawal from the Protocol*

In response to a question of implementation, or indeed any other events, it is possible for a party to withdraw from the Kyoto Protocol, although such an action takes a year to implement. In Durban, both Canada and Japan indicated their intention to withdraw and have now done so. The exit provision of the Protocol is in Article 27, which states that after the Protocol takes effect for a party, three years after that date, they can begin the process of withdrawing from it. The process, while involving only a written document to the UN Secretary General (the Depositary), requires a full year of notice before withdrawal can take place. Several European Union (EU) countries (principally Spain, Italy, and Austria) also seem likely not to be in compliance with their Kyoto emissions reduction commitments. A key difference relative to the cases of Canada and Japan however is that EU countries are under the overall blanket of the EU, which has its own reduction goals. These are likely to be met as a whole and hence individual EU country shortfalls are of lesser importance and, to some degree, these were expected and hence prepared for by the overarching EU commitment.

4. Lessons for the Post-Kyoto Regime

What are the lessons to be learned from the Kyoto Protocol experience with compliance as we work toward the next climate regime for the post-2020 period? The first would seem to be that, in large part, the impending failure of a potentially significant number of countries to comply with their Kyoto commitments and carry them forward into Kyoto's Stage 2 commitment period seemingly lies to some degree in the minimalist penalties associated with non-compliance. A strengthened penalty system with significant impact and costs imposed on violators would seem helpful for any post-2020 treaty arrangement seeking to achieve its objectives of significant emissions reductions. The second would seem to be that, while the Kyoto penalty structure is weak, the mechanisms designed to process complaints and arbitrate disputes seem to be holding together, although this may simply reflect a structure in which the compliance mechanism has yet to confront any serious issues and potential conflicts.

Those Kyoto Protocol participants that are in line with their (non-trivial) emissions reduction targets have in large part done so with at least some aid from carbon credits purchased by them from carbon-reducing projects in developing countries. In 2010, for instance, carbon credits accounted for 7% of all EU reductions,[10] a figure that has risen each year as local initiatives to reduce carbon emissions relatively cheaply become

---

[10]http://www.icis.com/heren/articles/2011/05/03/9456514/un-carbon-credits-account-for-7-of-2010-compliance.html.

fewer. One important issue for a more inclusive Kyoto follow-on climate change treaty is how countries would perform when several developing countries have their own reduction targets and are not as willing to sell credits to developed countries (and with higher carbon credit prices)? While including the developing countries in the next regime is a goal being sought to make it more effective, it also decreases the availability of cheap carbon credits, forcing more local carbon reduction initiatives from those who earlier bought carbon credits under the Kyoto Protocol. The increased difficulty for current buyers of carbon credits would seemingly require stricter enforcement with stronger sanctions behind them than the current Protocol if even more countries are not to fail to meet their targets once negotiated. This is particularly the case since the next regime would need to be more ambitious in its reduction targets if it is to meet a goal of a 2° limit for warming by 2050.

Stricter penalties in a post-Kyoto regime, however, require some creative thinking since, unlike with lower national levels of governance, there is no international court system that can enforce international agreements. The enforcement of any successor treaty to Kyoto is likely to also be largely a matter of political process rather than law, with credit ratings, interest rates and capital inflows being the most likely tangible items affected by the outcome. Historically, for international treaties this has been sufficient to achieve compliance, and most successful international treaties to date are effectively self-enforced,[11] but with various international bodies (with proven enforcement mechanisms) acting as a ruling council as a back-up should serious conflict arise. Multiple international institutions serve this function for the Montreal Protocol as needed (including the WTO when trade in ozone-depleting substances needed to be restricted) (see UNEP, 2007 and Sarma 2005), as the UN International Court of Justice does for the Law of the Sea, for example (see UN, 1982, Part XV). In these treaties, this structure facilitates compliance and provides increased legitimacy.

But this does not seem to apply to the case of the Kyoto Protocol, as the internal incentives to stay in compliance as opposed to deviating are weak and the Protocol's enforcement is not linked in similar fashion to any established international institution to give penalties extra weight

---

[11]The exception to this is the GATT and later the WTO, which has evolved a rule system to keep countries in line based on trade retaliation for actions outside these rules, rather than the more politically based consequences already mentioned.

or credibility. Hence, a number of countries are likely to fail in meeting their Kyoto targets. And the reasoning of these countries seems to be that the short-term economic costs of action outweigh the likelihood and severity of sanctions for country-specific climatic inaction. Thus we again seemingly reach the conclusion that stronger penalties are needed if a post-Kyoto treaty is to succeed.

A further central issue is whether or not Kyoto remains the platform on which any future post-2020 treaty will be based. Developing countries, in particular, are striving to keep the Kyoto Protocol so as to keep developed countries to their Kyoto commitments. But, global negotiations to broker the second Phase of Kyoto under the UNFCCC have followed a very rocky path. Following Kyoto, there have been several key COP meetings, including those at Bali, Copenhagen, Cancun, Durban, and Doha. In Bali (2009) (UNFCCC, 2007), a Roadmap was built for a follow-on treaty to Kyoto that included four pillars of needed actions: mitigation, adaptation, technological development, and finance and investment. These were agreed to provide the framework on which to build a new treaty. However, developing–developed country disputes centrally involving the UNFCCC-charter-enshrined principle of common but differentiated responsibilities (CBDR) caused plans to fall apart in Copenhagen two years later, and the Copenhagen Accord (UNFCCC, 2009a) was drafted at the last minute as a stopgap agreement in which countries may voluntarily enter unilaterally into non-binding climate change-related responsibilities.

The aftermath of this was seen in Cancun a year later in 2010 (UNFCCC, 2010) where the UNFCCC negotiation process was questioned as to its value, given limited results, and was only narrowly saved by the significant progress being made on Reducing Emissions from Deforestation and Forest Degradation (REDD) and the design of the technology network and associated fund for climate technologies/diffusion being included as part of the Copenhagen Accord. More encouragingly, and unlike Kyoto, at the interim meeting in Bangkok between Cancun and the COP 17 in Durban, there was an expressed desire to negotiate targets and an enforcement mechanism together, rather than targets first and enforcement later, as happened with the Kyoto Protocol. This has yet to bear any fruit however, with the advent of the second Phase of the Protocol.

In the Durban meeting, with the original Kyoto treaty coming into its final year and some countries beginning to drop out of the treaty, the feasibility of using it as a basis for a future, post-2012 treaty was lessened. And the Copenhagen Accord is not currently well structured to become a global treaty in the same sense that the Kyoto Protocol was either, as it depends heavily on unilateralism. Hence, in absence of any clear path to take, negotiators decided to use Durban to take stock of where things stand. This ultimately meant that enforcement was not a large topic of discussion, but one notable idea was informally embraced — that, unlike what happened in Kyoto, any future treaty should have targets and enforcement negotiated as a single package, rather than separately. We discuss the outcome of Durban in greater detail in a later section.

In Doha for COP 18, this talk of new enforcement measures was largely set aside, with the goal turning to preventing Kyoto from expiring with nothing to take its place. In that sense, a second Kyoto Phase was the easiest course to take.

With the Kyoto process seemingly lacking in its ability to achieve overall emissions reductions, since global emissions are still rising, any future enforcement mechanisms should be flexible enough to respond to any deal that follows Kyoto. A new arrangement could, for instance, consist of multiple regional deals, or even national targets, rather than one overarching global arrangement depending on what is seen as more effective (and agreeable).

This uncertainty presents a dilemma for enforcement as far as measurement issues are concerned. On the one hand, Kyoto-type enforcement is based on common principles of accounting and practice, and regional deals would most likely not have common measurement across countries. There is thus a strong possibility that giving up on a global deal could hinder the ability to measure global emissions accurately and hence hinder the ability of compliance mechanisms to hold countries to account for their emissions actions (or lack thereof). On the other hand, meaningful emission reduction schemes may be more likely to succeed when nations (or sub-national entities) are allowed to design their own plans to lower emissions, unrestricted by a global agreement, i.e. from the bottom-up. However, we maintain that even then it is critical to have some form of global agreement to standardize measurement so as not to derail enforcement efforts, whether those efforts are international, national, or otherwise, as enforcement mechanisms will all need precise measurements of emissions to reach determinations of compliance/non-compliance regardless of jurisdictional size. Whether or not the Kyoto Protocol is preserved in some meaningful form going forward, it has provided a standard for measurement of emissions and if future agreements are to be enforceable, that measurement system, at minimum, should not be abandoned.

4.1. *The need for an enforcement system*

The need for an enforcement regime itself may also be challenged in the process of negotiation. As already mentioned, the general record of international treaties on enforcement is exceptional, with no major compliance issues but also with few terms spelled out as to what happens if a party does not comply in most cases. This is because it is implicitly understood that the major loss by countries out of compliance is credibility, both in its commitments to the treaty and for other existing and future agreements, essentially creating a situation where a party would be, to some degree, cut off from the global system if they were to renege on an agreement. If an agreement is exceedingly burdensome to a party, the statutes for legitimately withdrawing from a treaty set out by the 1969 Vienna Convention (UN, 1969) would apply. Countries that cannot abide by the treaty initially do not join.

In the climate change case, firstly, there is considerable pressure for as many countries as possible to join,[12] and secondly, with carbon commitments as deep as bearable (some believe that the 2° target is unreachable already), and, lastly, climate considerations still largely disconnected from the rest of the international treaty system. The first two points differentiate a climate treaty from other international treaties in that typically there is either a large group committing to shallow action, or a smaller more dedicated group committing to deeper action (Barrett, 1994). Climate change prevention treaties on a global scale, by necessity, must aim to be all-inclusive and also seek to achieve deep reductions. Thus, unlike other international treaties, an enforcement system is necessary to achieve compliance. The third point, however, limits the penalties that any enforcement system can use to be similar to what is in the Kyoto Protocol and reduces the impact of any loss of credibility from failure to comply within the global system.

4.2. *Emissions reduction without an effective enforcement mechanism*

Particularly damaging in terms of concluding climate change negotiations successfully is to fail to consider the situation where an agreeable

---

[12]While the majority of emissions are being produced by a minority of countries, the inclusion of smaller emitters is still desired so that adaptation efforts and the deployment of green technology can be coordinated, as well as the coordination of carbon-mitigation measurement across the world. Also, the minority of heavy-emitting countries (principally the G20) has been disinclined thus far to act outside of the UN process and forge bi- or multi-lateral agreements on climate.

enforcement mechanism is not forthcoming. In this case, it would perhaps be better to choose one of two second-best options that can work without one. These are the two more common forms of international treaties that have proven successful — that of strong action by a dedicated minority, or weaker action by the majority. Inherently, these options give up on the goal of holding warming to a 2° increase from 1990, but would still be better than doing nothing. The dedicated minority that could affect substantive change in this case is, roughly, the G20 — the larger emitters — while the weak action by many countries would be characterized by giving up most actions against mitigation and focusing more on adaptation, to prepare for the climatic changes to come.

4.3. *Climate enforcement in 2011: Bangkok and Durban*

In discussions going into Durban, enforcement was at the same time fairly low key compared with other issues but equally central to many of them. Discussions in Bangkok in April 2011, just previous to Durban, hinted at new directions towards enforcement several times but did not deal with the issue centrally. Nonetheless, these two meetings hold more interest than the recent 2012 COP 18 in Doha in terms of enforcement issues, as it was not yet clear that a second Kyoto Phase would occur (with the enforcement regime in Phase 1 carried forward) and more possibilities were discussed relative to COP 18.

In Bangkok, the US made mention of enshrining carbon commitments in domestic law, but this was in reference to unilateral commitments and not more global treaty-based commitments. Thus, this option is, at least, seemingly on the table, although it was not centrally discussed later in Durban. Somewhat related is the possibility that global enforcement will be little discussed going forward, as Japan, Canada, and the US continued to hold to the stance in Bangkok and Durban that a second global treaty in the same vein as Kyoto is not acceptable (IISD, 2011a). With this, a second treaty, such as the now negotiated Kyoto Phase 2, will be hard pressed to be effective, as without US (and Chinese) involvement a large portion of global emissions will be unaccounted for.[13]

Also referenced several times in Bangkok were the "pre-conditions" for countries that would allow for their inclusion in a second global climate

---

[13] As of 2007, the US accounts for 19% of global emissions, while China accounts for 21.3%, for a joint total of roughly 41% (World Bank, 2011).

treaty, an umbrella term that differs in meaning[14] for each country, but for many (notably the Annex 1 countries and the larger developing countries) includes both enforcement issues and resolution of Kyoto Protocol commitment shortfalls. This covers not only Annex 1 country commitments, but also globally comparable measurement systems for each country's emissions. If this is an issue, and if Kyoto commitments need resolving once and for all before we can move forward to a new regime, then serious discussion cannot take place until compliance has been determined or not and the Kyoto enforcement mechanism fully plays out, meaning 2012 at earliest and 2015 at latest, leaving a second Kyoto Phase as the only acceptable regime for the interim that does not leave a gap between regimes.

This is seemingly the scenario beginning to be played out in Durban, with negotiators giving up on a new treaty relatively early during the meeting. They instead focused more on forming committees and special panels to take stock of what has been done and what needs to be done still, in the hopes of generating some meaningful conclusions that will allow the negotiations to proceed further in COP 18 in Doha, in Qatar. Despite the Kyoto Protocol still being active, this gave the meeting the feel of an inter-regime debate. With the Protocol about to conclude at the end of 2012, and since abruptly abandoning Kyoto mechanisms all together would be highly disruptive at this point, countries were, at their discretion, to pick whether to involve themselves in the Copenhagen Accord or in a second round of the Kyoto Protocol (with the only significant difference being a new set of emissions targets) or both or neither going forward. This decision was essentially one of maintaining the status quo while the committees and panels collect and analyze data and no significant improvements were made to either the Accord or the Protocol. Compliance, other than perpetuating the old Kyoto compliance regime under Second Phase, did not make any significant progress in Durban over what was discussed in Bangkok (IISD, 2011b).

The imprecise nature of the scientific evidence and our inability to measure emissions accurately despite the systems set up to do so may also explain in part why Durban ended as it did, as this issue continues to be a major factor in determining the validity of actions and determining what has and has not been done. Estimates in Bangkok ranged from a prediction that Kyoto Protocol principles are enough to keep the world

---

[14]Indeed, some of the discussion in Bangkok was of a schedule for defining some of what these pre-conditions were.

under 2° of warming on one hand, and on the other that we are facing an annual gap of 5–9 gigatonnes of CO_2 equivalent between pledges made and where we need to be to stay under 2° warming (IISD, 2011a). This uncertainty undermines most overt attempts at enforcement (and in the context of this paper, especially those suggested involving the WTO), with calls for observing standard MRV[15] practices in any initiative being the extent of action in both Bangkok and Durban. For most potential global enforcement regimes to work effectively, this uncertainty over measurement needs to be resolved.

A great deal of discussion in Bangkok focused on the new Technology Mechanism and Network, and with this there is potential for a technological escrow account that could facilitate an N-1 enforcement regime. The effectiveness of that would depend on the nature of the technology considered within the Network — primarily how reliant it is on skilled workers rather than just information (how effectively technology could be held back) — and how useful the network might prove to be as a resource generally. However, as of the end of Durban, the mechanism was not being predicted to begin operation until 2012 at the earliest (IISD, 2011b), so discussion of utilizing it for enforcement purposes would have to wait until there is some dependency on the Network so its loss would be an effective deterrent, such as for a post-2020 regime.

More encouraging, and almost generally accepted throughout both meetings was the idea that targets are only as strong as the rules that back them, and that targets and governing rules for any new regime should be decided and negotiated as distinct interlinked packages, rather than negotiate targets first with the enforcement rules to be decided later, as happened in Kyoto. A new negotiating paradigm thus seems to be emerging, and this could incorporate some of the suggestions for enforcement mentioned above, particularly if a global network under Kyoto for measuring emissions emerges and there is improved quality emission measurement.

Also critical is whether these scenarios will differ from Kyoto significantly enough to entice countries such as the US, Canada, and Japan, who have stated that they will not join a Kyoto successor treaty, into joining a global agreement. There was some related discussion in Durban in the Ad Hoc Working Group on Long-Term Cooperative Action on this issue, with

---

[15]MRV = Measure, Report, Verify.

a conclusion reached that specific country contexts must be considered in any new regime in terms of emissions and adaption targets and matters of compliance (IISD, 2011b).[16] This runs counter to the mostly binary Annex 1–non-Annex 1 approach of the Kyoto Protocol and the implied increased flexibility could aid in getting broad agreement for a new treaty. Thus, there could be some interesting and progressive discussion ahead for a post-2020 regime, but whether this will be shorter-term or in some future discussion several years distant near the end of Kyoto Phase 2 depends on when the ideas behind different rule-target scenarios (and the results of each scenario) can be fleshed out and whether the current ability to measure emissions is sufficient to implement them.

5. Concluding Remarks

In this chapter, we have summarized the enforcement mechanism in the Kyoto Protocol and its history to date and discussed possible post-Kyoto approaches to enforcement. The general consensus seems to be that while the Protocol's enforcement system is relatively well-designed, penalties for non-compliance are weak and constrained by the current international architecture, which was not designed to handle large physical spillovers of externalities between countries. This has limited the Protocol's effectiveness. We then move on to discuss whether new conceptual frameworks might be used to strengthen enforcement in a post-Kyoto regime. The precise form such a regime may take is still a matter of discussion even with Durban as a setback and it may or may not even be global in nature. This limits our suggestions to framework ideas, rather than concrete plans.

The alternate frameworks we discuss include, first, entering all measures agreed into domestic law on a treaty-wide scale, an approach that has been previously suggested by the US but otherwise has not been discussed.[17] Second, we discuss enforcing a global treaty through the use of an escrow account, with joint contributions of funds, technology, etc., and parties out of compliance forfeiting their share to those in compliance. This was not discussed in Bangkok or Durban, but remains an option and could utilize either funds, the new technology mechanism and network using US dollars or some other currency to function. Third, we discuss linkage to trade as a

---

[16] Also see Section I of the COP decision (FCCC/AWGLCA/2011/L.4) for original text.

[17] Note that this does not preclude countries from entering measures into law unilaterally, as in the case of the UK.

way to enforce climate treaties and utilizing WTO style conflict resolution as issues arise; perhaps using an expanded article 20 of the WTO charter as its basis. Fourth, we discuss a more passive enforcement system involving rating agencies on countries' environmental performance that could also be used as a guide to determine the distribution of existing funds. The greatest difficulty remains in getting accurate and consistent measurement of emissions.

And finally, we could fall back on a weaker second-best agreement that does fall more comfortably within the existing international architecture and is more tractable, acknowledging that actions in such an agreement may not be deep enough to achieve the stated goal of a 2° limit on warming, and preparing accordingly. This final option gives up on both the Kyoto Protocol in its current form and a successor treaty with similar goals and starts down a new negotiating track. However, this needs to be discussed given the deadlock in the negotiation following the Durban meeting in December 2011 in terms of post-Kyoto arrangements and given the relative lack of potential effectiveness in Phase 2 of Kyoto given the exit of key emitters from the agreement.

The discussion in Bangkok in the run up to Durban presented an intriguing new negotiation framework, with a growing insistence on negotiating targets, their enforcement (presumably Kyoto-style to be used as a jumping-off point) and penalties for non-compliance all as a single package. This is in clear contrast to what happened when negotiating targets and enforcement were discussed in the Kyoto Protocol negotiations. This could induce creative combinations of targets and penalties that could include the suggestions above, as it implies a trade-off between the level of commitments and the stringency of penalties imposed for non-compliance.

References

Barrett, S. (1994). Self-enforcing environmental agreements. *Oxford Economic Papers*, **46**, Oxford University Press, 878–894.

Barrett, S. (2008). Climate treaties and the imperative of enforcement. *Oxford Review of Economic Policy*, **24**(2), 239–258.

IISD (2011a). Summary of the Bangkok Climate Talks: 3–8 April 2011, *Earth Negotiations Bulletin*. Available at: www.iisd.ca/climate/ccwg14/. Accessed 2 March 2013.

IISD (2011b). Summary of the Durban climate change conference: 28 November– 11 December 2011, *Earth Negotiations Bulletin*. Available at: www.iisd.ca/ download/pdf/enb12534e.pdf. (further Durban coverage available at www. iisd.ca/climate/cop17/). Accessed 2 March 2013.

Oberthür, S. & Lefeber, R. (2010). Holding countries to account: The Kyoto Protocol's compliance mechanism revisited after four years of experience. *Climate Law*, **1**, IOS Press, 133–156.

Rubinstein, A. (1979). Equilibrium in supergames with the overtaking criterion. *Journal of Economic Theory*, **21**, 1–9.

Sarma, K.M. (2005). Compliance with the Montreal Protocol. In *Making Law Work: Environmental Compliance and Sustainable Development*, D. Zaelke *et al.* (eds.), Vol. 1, Chapter 3. London (UK): Cameron May.

Ulfstein, G. & Werksman, J. (2005). The Kyoto compliance system: Towards hard enforcement. In *Implementing the Climate Regime: International Compliance* O.S. Stokke *et al.* (eds.), London: Earthscan.

UN (1969). Vienna Convention on the Law of Treaties. Available at: http://un treaty.un.org/ilc/texts/instruments/english/conventions/1_1_1969.pdf. Accessed 2 March 2013.

UN (1982). United Nations Convention on the Law of the Sea. Available at: http://www.un.org/depts/los/convention_agreements/texts/unclos/ UNCLOS-TOC.htm. Accessed 2 March 2013.

UNEP (2007). Compliance Mechanisms under selected Multilateral Environmental Agreements. Available at: http://www.unep.org/DEC/docs/Compliance mechanisms under selected MEAs.pdf. Accessed 2 March 2013.

UNFCCC (1998). "Kyoto Protocol to the United Nations Framework Convention on Climate Change. Available at: http://unfccc.int/resource/docs/convkp/ kpeng.pdf. Accessed 15 April 2011.

UNFCCC (2001). Implementation of the Buenos Aires Plan of Action: Adoption of the Decisions Giving Effect to the Bonn Agreements: Procedures and Mechanisms Relating to Compliance Under the Kyoto Protocol, (FCCC/CP/ 2001/L.21). Adopted by the Conference of the Parties (COP) at their 7th meeting in Marrakesh. Available at: http://unfccc.int/resource/docs/ cop7/l21.pdf. Accessed 23 March 2011.

UNFCCC (2007). Report of the Conference of Parties on its thirteenth session, held in Bali from 3 to 15 December 2007, Part Two: Action taken by the Conference of Parties at its thirteenth session. Available at: http://unfccc. int/resource/docs/2007/cop13/eng/06a01.pdf. Accessed 15 April 2011.

UNFCCC (2009a). Report of the Conference of the Parties on its fifteenth session, held in Copenhagen from 7 to 19 December 2009. Addendum. Part Two: Action taken by the Conference of the Parties at its fifteenth session. Available at: http://unfccc.int/resource/docs/2009/cop15/eng/11a01.pdf. Accessed 15 April 2011.

UNFCCC (2009b). Copenhagen Accord. Available at: http://unfccc.int/resource/ docs/2009/cop15/eng/l07.pdf. Accessed 15 April 2011.

UNFCCC (2010). Report of the Conference of Parties on its sixteenth session, held in Cancun from 29 November to 10 December 2010, Part Two: Action taken by the Conference of Parties at its sixteenth session. Available at: http://unfccc.int/resource/docs/2010/cop16/eng/07a01.pdf. Accessed 15 April 2011.

UNFCCC (2012). Doha amendment to the Kyoto Protocol to the United Nations Framework Convention on Climate Change. Available at: http://unfccc. int/files/kyoto_protocol/application/pdf/kp_doha_amendment_english.pdf. Accessed 24 October 2013.

World Bank (2011). World Development Indicators Database. Available at: http://databank.worldbank.org/ddp/home.do. Accessed August 2011.

WTO (1947). General Agreement on Tariffs and Trade: Article XX. Available at: http://www.wto.org/english/docs_e/legal_e/gatt47_02_e.htm. Accessed 2 March 2013.

Index

Printed in the United States
By Bookmasters